1987

*The Country Blues*

BOOKS BY SAMUEL B. CHARTERS:

*Jazz: New Orleans, 1885–1957*
*The Country Blues*

# The Country Blues

*SAMUEL B. CHARTERS*

*With a new introduction by the author*

*A DACAPO PAPERBACK*

Library of Congress Cataloging in Publication Data

Charters, Samuel Barclay.
The country blues.

( A Da Capo paperback )
Reprint of the ed. published by Rinehart, New York.
1. Country music—United States—History and criticism. 2. Blues (Songs, etc.)—United States—History
and criticism. I. Title.
[ML3556.C475C7 1975b]      784      75-14122
ISBN 0-306-80014-4

This Da Capo Press edition of *The Country Blues* is a reproduction
of the first edition, incorporating some author's corrections,
published in New York in 1959. It includes a new introduction prepared
for this edition and is reprinted with the permission of the author.

Acknowledgment is made for permission to quote from the following: *Big Bill
Blues* by Big Bill Broonzy Copyright © 1936 by MCA Music, A Division of MCA,
Inc. Copyright renewed; *How Long, How Long Blues* by Leroy Carr Copyright ©
1929 by MCA Music, A Division of MCA, Inc. Copyright renewed; *I'm Gonna
Move to the Outskirts of Town* by William Weldon Copyright © 1942 by MCA
Music , A Division of MCA, Inc. Copyright renewed.

First paperback printing August, 1975
Second paperback printing February, 1977

ISBN: 0-306-80014-4

Published by Da Capo Press, Inc.
A Subsidiary of Plenum Publishing Corporation
227 West 17th Street, New York, N.Y. 10011

Manufactured in the United States of America

*for* **Moses Asch**

I don't really know whether your work could be called "creative" in an artistic sense, but the continued effort you have made to document the music of the world's peoples seems to me to include a creative concept that has given us a new awareness of both the music around us and the life that has produced it. Is this "Art"? I think so—in the fullest sense of the word.

# *Preface to the 1975 Edition*

It's always difficult to go back to something you wrote
years before. For one thing you certainly wouldn't use
the words and phrases you used then, and there are
always opinions you've forgotten you once held. And
with a book like this, written when research in the field
was only beginning, there is the final embarrassment of
errors of fact. But I find that these things don't bother
me that much when I look at *The Country Blues* again.
Since I wrote it when I did and the way I did for particular reasons, and given the period of American life
that it came out of I would probably, going back to those
years, write much the same kind of book.

When I look back to the 1950's now (the book was
published in the fall of 1959) I find I have no great nostalgia for the period. I don't think it was a great moment
in American life—not that anyone else seems to think so
either, but there's been a wave of nostalgia for the arti-
facts of the '50's. It wasn't a period of apathy, a period

in which nothing happened, as it's sometimes described. I don't think of Americans as apathetic people. They have, rather, a clear conception of what they expect of society and what they believe to be their own role in it. If their voices weren't audible in the '50's it was because the American system was giving them what they wanted. It was a period of relative prosperity, stable prices, and—once past the disastrous first year of the Korean War—the containment policy against the Soviet Union seemed to be working. Europe was recovering, there was considerable technical innovation in many fields, and there seemed to be a more or less effective policy against what the American people considered "internal subversion." American society is a society that does reject any strong pulls away from its own general consensus except in periods of crisis, and once McCarthy had provided a few scapegoats for failures of American policy in the 1940's he was pushed aside and the emotions he had aroused were expected to dissipate, if only on the surface. So the calm of the '50's was an illusion, it only reflected a point in time when much of the society felt that the system, as they conceived it, was working.

But for many of us what was happening was frightening. There were serious problems in the society: inequities, imbalances, and—to use a word that isn't heard so much now—injustices, but there was no effort being made to deal with them. The effort, instead, was to ignore them, and there was considerable hostility toward anyone who insisted on pointing them out. The national consensus, which certainly is at the heart of American life, was stifling any effort to break through to a clearer comprehension of America's problems. But how could we break through it? How do you do something to deflect the course of a society that you feel has lost its sense of direction? This was a problem that some people were beginning to face in the 1950's, and when I think of these years it's this that still stays with me, the sense I had of people scattered across the country trying to find a different ethic, a different response to the American environment. It was a kind of nervous ferment that was to come boiling out in the 1960's. What we were trying to do, many of us, was find a way to turn our disillusionment into political terms. We were trying to turn what we did with our lives into a political act, and what I did, in part, was write this book.

I say "in part" because everything I was doing during this period was part of this same effort. *The Country Blues* was, for me, another tract in a series of tracts I'd been turning out since the early '50's. The books, articles, and the field recording I'd been doing were my own private revolution. In simple terms I was trying to effect a change in the American consciousness by presenting an alternative consciousness. I felt that much of what was stifling America was its racism, and what it desperately needed was to be forced to see that the hypocrisy of its racial attitudes was warping the nation's outlook on nearly every other major problem it was facing. And I also felt that the black culture itself was a necessary element in the society. The white culture had developed this same kind of defensive hypocrisy toward so many elements in its life, from sexuality to personal mores. In the black expression I found a directness, an openness, and an immediacy I didn't find in the white. The texts of the blues were strong and honest, using language in a way the white culture hadn't used it for hundreds of years. The searching complexities of jazz were more representative of the city life I found around me than the artificialities of white popular music. I found that the awareness of the real sources of power in the society, the consciousness of social inequalities, and the direct expression of sexuality in the black culture was so much closer to the American reality that I felt I somehow had to make people conscious of what these other voices were saying. At the same time I believed that if I could make people hear the voices of black Americans they might begin to see them as human beings, and not as stereotypes.

How did this affect the books I wrote? I decided early in the '50's that I wouldn't accomplish anything by directly attacking what I felt had to be changed. I was still wary after the McCarthy period, and also this would have involved an extension of a kind of personal egotism that I don't have. I could have shouted, and I could have criticized—but instead I tried to present an alternative. If my books from this time seem romantic it's because I tried to make them romantic. I was trying to describe black music and black culture in a way that would immediately involve a certain kind of younger, middle-class white American. They were the ones most ready to listen, and they were the ones, also, who could finally force some kind of change. The books were written as tracts for them, and the field recordings were a first step to get them across the line to where they could begin to listen for themselves. When I look back at what I wrote during this period it often seems a little insistent to me, the romanticism a little strident, but I was trying to get people to listen, and this seemed to be the most direct way to get through.

With *The Country Blues* I was also facing another and more immediate problem. I had been doing research in New Orleans since the early '50's about the origins of New Orleans jazz, and after seven years' work had finished the biographical dictionary of black musicians in New Orleans from 1885 to 1957 that was published in 1958 as *Jazz: New Orleans*. I realized, during the years of interviewing and research that went into the book, that the older men who had created the modern black culture were dying, and since they had been forced to grow up in a largely illiterate society there were almost no written records of what they had done or how they'd done it. At the same time as I was doing research in New Orleans I'd begun doing work with the bluesmen, but there were too many of them and, unlike the New Orleans musicians, they were scattered all over the South. There was some research going on, but it was small in scope, and most of the work was of an ethno-musicological nature. There was almost no historical work being done with particular individuals—it was general and social. When *Jazz: New Orleans* was published I began working intensively in the South, trying to find and record older blues artists, but I realized I couldn't do the job myself, and that there wasn't a lot of time left to do it. I shouldn't have written *The Country Blues* when I did; since I really didn't know enough, but I felt it couldn't afford to wait.

So *The Country Blues* was two things. It was a romanticization of certain aspects of black life in an effort to force the white society to reconsider some of its racial attitudes, and on the other hand it was a cry for help. I wanted hundreds of people to go out and interview the surviving blues artists. I wanted people to record them and document their lives, their environment, and their music—not only so that their story would be preserved but also so they'd get a little money and a little recognition in their last years. So there was another kind of romanticism in the book. I was trying to make the journey to find the artists as glamorous as possible, by describing the roadsides, and the farms, and the shacks, and the musicians themselves. What I was doing wasn't academic, and it wasn't scholarly, but it was effective. I left the United States for more than a year soon after it was published, and when I returned there were already people out in the South doing the necessary work. Certainly I wasn't the first to go into the South—Alan Lomax had been there years before me—but I had tried to turn the direction of the research away from his kind of cultural musicology, and away from the kind of sociological analysis of blues texts that was typified by Paul Oliver's first book, which came out the next year. At least part of what I'd attempted to do in *The Country Blues* had been successful.

I went on with the work for a few more years, partly because I had the sense of a job half-finished, and also because I wanted to be sure that the original concept was still getting through. But in 1963 I wrote *The Poetry of the Blues,* which was very clearly political in its implications, and also was quite successful, and in 1964 I was involved in the blues workshop at the Newport Folk Festival. Every major blues rediscovery, with the exception of Son House, was there, including Skip James,

Robert Wilkins, Mississippi John Hurt, Sleepy John
Estes, and Robert Pete Williams. At the same time I was
meeting the younger researchers who had taken up the
work in the South. I felt then that I could stop. My own
personal involvement was with my own poetry and with
other creative work that I was doing at the same time. I
continued with the multi-volumed study, *The Bluesmen,*
but other work, for the first time, took precedence.

I felt also that I could stop because I had never been
interested simply in a mass of information about old
bluesmen, as important as that was. From the beginning
I had been interested in the larger concept of opening
the consciousness of the white American to a fuller comprehension of the possibility for new expression and self-
understanding through an involvement with the black
culture. When I began to meet young performers in the
early '60's who were extending their own creative boundaries through the blues I felt even more that what I'd
been trying to do had been successful, and it was time
to move on to something else. This doesn't mean I was
interested in the hundreds of performers who more or
less were imitating black singers. It was the handful of
creative performers who had found something in the
blues to focus or strengthen their own concepts that I
found exciting. When I returned from another trip outside the United States in 1966—this time to India and
Japan—I became involved in the San Francisco music
scene, and spent most of the next four years working
with the group Country Joe and the Fish. Their fusion
of blues and folk materials and political satire seemed to
point to a new music, a kind of music that I'd hoped
would come out of all of this. For a moment, in the '60's

it seemed possible that we might break through to the larger aims we'd had in the sloughs of the '50's.

It was, however, only a brief moment. Vietnam forced a kind of change in attitude toward some aspects of American foreign policy, and the black revolution forced some change in the worst aspects of legal discrimination, but the changes didn't have any larger effect. The mistake all of us made was to think that the United States, beneath the surface, was ready to change. Instead there seemed to be a determined effort to return to something like the '50's, when the society was functioning, and there was no serious challenge to a complex web of attitudes and policies that were forcing the country further and further into what seemed to be a blind alley. The whole issue became confused over side issues like narcotics and sexual expression, and the artistic energy that had been released with the fusion of all these musical styles finally was channeled into the same kind of commercial exploitation that the musicians had first tried to reject. For me, personally, there was one demonstration too many, and one billboard too many telling me I should love it or leave it. I left in the late spring of 1970, returned for a short period later in the year to finish up some work I'd begun earlier, and in 1971 moved to Sweden.

Perhaps this makes it clear why *The Country Blues* is the book it is, and it should also be clear why it's being reprinted without an effort to correct the factual errors. The book, in its way, is an artifact of the 1950's. I have tried to do the work of correcting errors in *The Bluesmen,* and already its first volume needs extensive revision to include newer research. *The Country Blues,* instead, comes from a different time, and it still represents what I was trying to do then. Only one paragraph has been deleted from the original, a short description of the Chicago blues scene that wasn't fair either to the artist, Muddy Waters, or the scene itself. I'm still not sure how it made its way into the final manuscript.

One thing that I wanted particularly to leave unchanged about the book is its emphasis. Even though I was trying to interest a young middle-class white audience in the blues I tried to give them a somewhat balanced picture of the blues by structuring the book around commercial blues marketing. In other words I tried to keep the emphasis, as much as possible, where the black audience would have placed it. So I didn't give much space to artists like Skip James or Charley Patton, who became cult figures with young white guitar players. Instead, I was concerned with artists like Lonnie Johnson, who were spectacularly successful with their own black audience. This effort to involve the white intellectual in the larger patterns of black life wasn't particularly successful. Instead of accepting black culture they tended to select certain artists out of it—artists who, generally, came closest to a·white concept of what a blues artist should be. I don't want to suggest that I reject this attitude completely. We use another culture just as we use the past, as raw material to build our own present. The art museums, after all, are filled with magnificent examples of African sculpture, taken out of context and presented as art objects, but without dimming their beauty or their importance as human expression. But I would like to leave this emphasis in *The Country Blues* unchanged, since it's also of value. In *The Blues-*

*men* the concern is more with the artists who have directly affected the white audience.

As I said, looking back at *The Country Blues* fifteen years later I'm not disturbed by it, despite sections of it that I'd never write the same way again. Perhaps it represents a personal nostalgia for some of the things I felt in the 1950's. Certainly a belief that something could be accomplished was in its pages, and there was somehow a kind of naive belief that if America could be made to face its problems it would begin the effort to solve them. If, as a political act, what I did lacked reality, at least it had a kind of simple honesty about it. It's hard to believe that I might ever think in so simple terms again, even though I still believe we somehow have to keep making these gestures. Despite their futility they're often the only gestures we have a chance to make.

—Samuel Charters
Saltsjo Boo
Sweden, 1975

# Introduction to the 1959 Edition

It is difficult writing the first extended study of any subject, and it has been especially difficult writing a first study of early blues singers and their recordings. The problem of organizing the material into a coherent pattern was almost overwhelming. There has been, too, an over-riding sense of responsibility toward the material. A close friend, Frederic Ramsey, Jr., faced the same problem when he edited the first historical study of Jazz, "Jazzmen," in the late 1930's. We have both been disturbed to note that further work in the field has tended to simply follow the lines which he and the other contributors to "Jazzmen" had developed, despite some serious omissions and errors of emphasis. To avoid this I have tried to discuss every major blues artist as fully as I was able.

It has seemed to me artificial to discuss the music on any other level than that of its relationship with its own audience. This has resulted in an extensive study of the marketing and sales of blues records in order to achieve as high a degree of objectivity as possible. It would be relatively simple to select groups of recordings and develop a thesis on either a musical or a sociological basis, but the truth has been that the blues audience is capricious and not in the least concerned with musical or sociological concepts. Two singers, Rabbit Brown and Robert Johnson, have been discussed at length, despite their minor roles in the story of the blues. Brown was discussed in a contemporary review and some further comment seemed important, and the music of Robert Johnson was of considerable interest to the study of blues styles.

A further difficulty of a first study is that there will be considerable error. Seven years went into my first study, *Jazz: New Orleans, 1885–1957,* but within a few months of its publication I had found enough fresh material to rewrite the work completely. I sincerely hope that this study of the blues will lead to intensive research in the South by many individuals who will pick up the work at this point. I have been working in the South for a number of years, but the area to be covered and the number of important singers has made it difficult to cover the entire field.

Many of the fine group of research specialists with whom I am associated on the staff of *Record Research* magazine have been of considerable assistance in clearing up some of my confusions on the technical aspects of the recordings. Walter C. Allen was able to give me valuable information on the early years of the Paramount Record Company and John Steiner had an important knowledge and first-hand experience with the company's race recording policies. Dan Mahoney discussed with me details of the Columbia 14000 series, and both Bob Colton and Len Kunstadt, editors of *Record Research*, have been of considerable assistance. Mr. Robert Gilmore, of Southern Music Company, discussed with me the recording activities in which he participated in the South in the late 1920's. Frederic Ramsey, Jr. allowed me to use information he had obtained in a series of interviews with engineers of the Columbia and Victor Companies. My grateful acknowledgment is made to all of these men.

I would have been unable to hear many of the rare blues recordings without blues collectors Pete Whalen, Pete Kaufman and Ben Kaplan. They have played hours of music for me and a further acknowledgment is due them.

In the trips through the South I have been made welcome by a number of wonderful people, and I would like to thank Mr. and Mrs. Charles Fish and Charles McNett, Jr., of New Orleans; Julian Lee Rayford, of Mobile, Alabama; Mr. and Mrs. Russell Cassidy and Trebor Tichenor, of St. Louis, and Mr. and Mrs. John Steiner, of Chicago, for their generous hospitality.

A final acknowledgment is due to my wife, Ann Charters, who has taken time from her own research to discuss the manuscript at various stages of its development.

*S. B. Charters*
May, 1959

# Contents

Preface to the 1975 Edition     vii

Introduction to the 1959 Edition     xvii

1   A Music ". . . Extraordinarily Wild and Unaccountable."     19

2   "That Gives Me the Blues to go Back to Dallas."     32

3   The Crazy Blues     43

4   Blind Lemon     57

5   "You Don't See Into These Blues Like Me"     73

6   ". . . The Noisiest Damn Place in the World."     86

7   Dr. Stokey, Dr. Benson, Dr. C. E. Hangerson     100

8   The Memphis Jug Bands     107

9   "Goin' to Kansas City"     131

10   Leroy Carr     138

| | | |
|---|---|---|
| 11 | The 14000's | 148 |
| 12 | Blind Willie | 156 |
| 13 | "Big Bill Broomsley" | 166 |
| 14 | "I Got the Bluebird Beat" | 182 |
| 15 | 49, 51, 61 | 195 |
| 16 | Robert Johnson | 207 |
| 17 | "Hey, Mama, Hey, Pretty Girl." | 212 |
| 18 | Brownie McGhee | 221 |
| 19 | "The Mommies and Daddies from Coast to Coast" | 232 |
| 20 | Muddy Waters | 245 |
| 21 | Lightnin' | 254 |
| | Appendix    Recorded Blues Backgrounds | 269 |
| | The Blues Recordings | 274 |
| | Index | 279 |

*The Country Blues*

In a poor, shabby room in the colored section of Houston, a thin, worn man sat holding a guitar, playing a little on the strings, looking out of the window. It was a dull winter day, a heavy wind swirling the dust across the yard. There was a railroad behind the houses, and a few children were playing on the rails, shivering in their thin coats.

"There's a song my cousin learned when he was out on the farm." He was talking partly to me and partly to a friend of his, sitting in the shadows behind him. "Smokey Hogg got a little of it, but there hasn't been nobody done it right." Then he began singing:

"You ought to been on the Brazos in 1910,
Bud Russell drove pretty women like he done ugly
  men. . . ."

He was singing one of the most famous work songs of the Texas penitentiary farms, "Ain't No More Cane

on This Brazos." His eyes were closed, he was singing
quietly:

> "My mama called me, I answered, 'Mam?'
> She said, 'Son, you tired of working?'
> I said, 'Mama, I sure am.' "

He sat a moment, thinking of the hot, dusty sum-
mers on the flat cotton lands along the Brazos River,
thinking of the convict gangs singing as they worked,
the guards circling them slowly, a shotgun across the
saddle.

> "You ought to been on the Brazos in 1904,
> You could find a dead man on every turnin' row. . . ."

He shook his head; then he began to sing parts of the
song again, playing his guitar a little. He stopped to
drink some gin out of a bottle under the chair. He
drank nearly a half pint of raw gin, using the metal cap
of the bottle for a glass. His friend looked over and
smiled, "He's getting it now." The singer went over
two or three runs on the guitar; then he nodded and
began singing:

> "Uumh, big Brazos, here I come,
> Uumh, big Brazos, here I come.
> It' hard doing time for another man when there ain't
>     a thing poor Lightnin' done.
>
> You ought to been on the Brazos in 1910,
> Bud Russell drove pretty women just like he done
>     ugly men.
> Uumh, big Brazos, oh lord yes, here I come.
> Figure on doing time for someone else, when there
>     ain't a thing poor Lightnin' done.

My mama called me, I answered, 'Mam?'
She said, 'Son, you tired of working?'
I said, 'Mama, I sure am.'
My Pappa called me, I answered, 'Sir?'
'If you're tired of workin' what the hell you going to
     stay here for?'

I couldn't . . . uumh . . .
I just couldn't help myself.
You know a man can't help but feel bad, when he's
     doing time for someone else."

The man was named "Lightnin'" Hopkins, from outside of Centerville, Texas. "Ain't No More Cane on This Brazos" was a song he had heard when he was a young man, working in the fields. His own song was a reshaping and reworking of the old work song into something intensely personal and expressive. He had changed it into a blues.

# 1

## A Music "... Extraordinarily Wild and Unaccountable"

The blues, as a distinctive musical form, is probably not much older than the years just before the first World War, but the style and emotions of the blues have been a part of the music of the Negro in America for over 150 years. A blues is a personal song, with intensely personal emotional characteristics. The blues became the emotional outlet for Negro singers in every part of the South, and as the rich confusion of music from the fields began to fall into loose patterns, the blues became a part of the fabric of Negro life itself.

The frightened, miserable creatures that the slave ships landed in Southern water-front cities brought with them the rich musical traditions of Africa, and they tried to carry their music with them into their crowded, filthy slave cabins. They sang in the long hot afternoons in the fields and they sang in the lonely quiet of evening.

**19**

The practice of separating the slaves so that there were no tribal groups on any single plantation weakened their musical traditions, and the desperate need of the slaves to cross somehow the barriers that separated them from anything beyond their wretched existence forced them to learn whatever they could of the music they heard around them. They learned the music of the hymns, singing the lines after the itinerant preachers at religious services, and they picked up little songs and airs from the overseers, who whistled or sang to themselves as they rode through the fields. The plantations were scattered and isolated, most of them poor and dirty, with an impoverished social life, but there were occasional dancing parties or evening musicals. The dance tunes, even some of the dance steps, were quickly imitated by the slaves. Travelers in the South in the years before the Civil War described in journals and letters their first startled glimpse of the intent black audience that hurried to every activity at the plantation house.

An English actress and singer, Fanny Kemble, lived with her husband and children on a plantation on the Georgia Coast in the winter of 1838–1839 and her journal, published in 1863, contained mentions of the slave music. A neighbor was being rowed back to his plantation on a nearby island by a crew of slaves, and she described the scene as the boat pulled away:

> Mr. M— sat in the middle of a perfect chaos of such freight; and as the boat pushed off, and the steersmen took her into the stream, the men at the oars set up a chorus, which they continued to chant in unison

with each other, and in time with their stroke, till the voices were heard no more from the distance. I believe I have mentioned to you before the peculiar characteristics of this veritable Negro minstrelsy—how they all sing in unison, having never, it appears, attempted or heard anything like part singing. Their voices seem oftener tenor than any other quality, and the tune and time they keep something quite wonderful; such truth of intonation and accent would make almost any music agreeable. That which I have heard these people sing is often plaintive and pretty, but almost always has some resemblance to tunes with which they must have become acquainted through the instrumentality of white men; their overseers or masters whistling Scotch or Irish airs, of which they have reproduced these *rifacciamenti* . . . the tune with which Mr. M—'s rowers started him off down the Altahama, as I stood on the steps to see him off, was a very distinct descendant of "Coming Through The Rye . . .[1]

Most of the singing that she heard was a crude imitation of European singing, but she sensed that there was something more to it than just imitation:

I have heard that many of the masters and overseers prohibit melancholy tunes or words, and encourage nothing but cheerful music and senseless words, deprecating the effect of sadder strains upon the slaves, whose peculiar musical sensibility might be expected to make them especially excitable by any songs of a plaintive character, and having reference to their particular hardships.[2]

[1] Kemble, Frances Anne, *Journal of a Residence on a Georgia Plantation in 1838–1839*, New York, Harper & Bros., 1864.
[2] Ibid.

As she stayed on into the winter she heard more and more singing that she was completely at a loss to understand:

> My daily voyages up and down the river have introduced me to a great variety of new, musical performances of our boatmen, who invariably, when the rowing is not too hard, moving up or down with the tide, accompany the stroke of their oars with the sound of their voices. I told you formerly that I thought I could trace distinctly some popular national melody with which I was familiar in almost all of their songs; but I have been quite at a loss to discover any such foundation for many that I have heard lately, and which appeared to me extraordinarily wild and unaccountable. The way in which the chorus strikes in with the burden, between each phrase of the melody chanted by a single voice, is very curious and effective, especially with the rhythm of the rowlocks for accompaniment.[3]

The first collections of slave songs in the 1860's show that Fanny Kemble had been an accurate listener to the music around her. She loathed slavery and pitied the poor, half-civilized Negroes to such an extent that her neighbors found her unpleasant and dangerous, but she was a professional singer, and she was able to listen to the singing and the raucous instrumental music, mostly banjo playing, with some detachment. These collections of songs show that most of the music was related to some European source, but that the singing style and musical approach were only dimly related to European music, and that there was a small group

[3] Ibid.

of songs that survived the prohibitions on lyrics about the hardships of their daily life. She herself heard one that interested her enough that she remembered the simple words:

"Oh, my massa told me, there's no grass in Georgia."

It was the cry of a slave who had been sold away from one of the more northern states, Carolina or Virginia, and had found the labor in the rice and cotton lands of Georgia harsher than the labor in the tobacco fields. She had heard the first cry of the blues.

The editors of the collection, *Negro Slave Songs of the United States,* published in 1867, found, as Kemble had, that most of the music they had collected was derivative, but the closer they came to the working slave the closer they came to the "extraordinarily wild and unaccountable" music that Kemble had heard. They described one short song as "A very good specimen, so far as notes can give, of the strange barbaric songs that one hears upon the western steamboats." The melody seems to have been completely beyond their abilities to transcribe, but it sounds like a minor-keyed, wailing song of the West African tribes. The words are less difficult to trace:

"Gwine to Alabamy, oh
For to see my Mammy, oh.

"She went from ole Virginny
And I'm her pickaninny."

They were similar to many popular minstrel songs.
    In writing an introduction to the collection, one of

the editors, William Allen, felt that they had gotten a somewhat distorted picture of slave music. The music had been collected at a mission school at Port Royal, Georgia, and Allen felt that the circumstances had made it difficult to get the songs of the fields or cabins:

> I never fairly heard a secular song among the Port Royal freedmen, and never saw a musical instrument among them. The last violin, owned by a "worldly man", disappeared from Coffin's Point 'de year gun shoot at Bay Pint' [the first bombardment of the Civil War in November, 1861]. In other parts of the south "fiddle songs," "devil songs," "corn songs," "jig tunes" and what not, are common; all the world knows the banjo and the "Jim Crow" songs of thirty years ago. We have succeeded in obtaining only a few songs of this character. Our intercourse with the colored people has been chiefly through the work of the Freedmen's Commission, which deals with the serious and earnest side of the Negro character. . . . There are very few [songs] which are of an intrinsically barbaric character, and where this character does appear, it is chiefly in short passages, intermingled with others of a different character. . . . It is very likely that if we found it possible to get at more of their secular music we should have to come to another conclusion as to the proportion of the barbaric element.[4]

The only songs they heard were the same rowing songs that Kemble had heard twenty years before, some slow and relaxed, others strong and fast ". . . when the load was heavy or the tide was against us." They

[4] Allen, William Francis, *Negro Slave Songs of the United States,* New York, A. Simpson & Co., 1867.

caught the refrain of one corn song, ". . . shock along, John," and the wild lyrics of another, "Round the Corn, Sally":

> Five can't ketch me and ten can't hold me
>    Ho, round the corn, Sally!

but the strong current of "barbaric" work songs eluded them.

The editors of *Negro Slave Songs* were among the first serious collectors of the music of the Southern slaves, but stage personalities had been performing slave songs and dances, with great success, for years. The "Ethiopian airs" of the early minstrel stage were often a closer imitation of slave music than many people realized. The love songs, melancholy and touching, were thinly disguised melodies from the European music-hall stage, but the jig tunes and walk-arounds often have a strong resemblance to the minor-keyed, wailing songs that Kemble and Allen heard. When the first minstrel shows were performed in the 1840's, many of the performers were young men from the Southern countryside and the songs often honestly described slave life:

> "They take me out to 'tater hill,
>    make me dance against my will.
> They make me dance on sharp edge stones,
>    while every nigger laughs and groans.
> Oh Rob Ridley, oh, oh, Rob Ridley, oh.

> "Long heel wooley head choke to death
>    with butter,
> Master catch the nigger drunk, loafing
>    in the gutter.

Put him on the treadin' mill to make
him work the harder.
The crows are talking French to the
turkey buzzard's father.

"As I went up to Lynchburg Town,
I broke my yoke on the coaling ground;
I drove from there to Bolwing Spring
and tried to mend my yoke and ring.
Oh Jonny Boker, help this nigger.
Do, Jonny Boker, do." [5]

There was a famous collection of minstrel songs
by the Christy Minstrels in 1853, but most of these
were the more conventional songs and ballads, or the
early songs of Stephen Foster. In 1858, a member of
Buckley's Minstrels, a banjo player named Phil Rice,
published a small book titled *Phil Rice's Banjo Instructor*,

containing the most popular
BANJO SOLOS, DUETS, TRIOS AND SONGS
Performed by the
BUCKLEY'S, CHRISTY'S, BRYANT'S, CAMPBELL'S, WHITE'S
and other celebrated bands of minstrels.[6]

Rice's instructions were discouragingly difficult—
he used a set of symbols written above each note of
music which indicated whether the note was to be
struck, half struck, plucked, strummed, or stroked—but
for examples he used most of the best-known jigs and
fiddle tunes of the period. There were thinly disguised
Irish reels, hornpipes and English country dances, but

[5] Rice, Philip, *Phil Rice's Correct Method for the Banjo*, Boston,
O. Ditson & Co., 1858.
[6] Ibid.

there were others, with strange modal harmonies, and a sharply rhythmic dissonance, like "Ole Dan Tucker," "Ole Pee Dee," "Jonny Boker," "Green Corn," "Ole Grey Goose." Either they were slave songs or Rice was familiar enough with slave music to be able to arrange the melodies in a style similar to examples of slave music. One of his first exercises was the famous "Juba," the minstrel solo dance that was supposed to have been taken from the plantations. The dance steps have been lost, but the music is certainly right from the plantation. It is a monotonous West African dance melody that had been picked on gourd banjos by slaves for generations. Probably many of the ". . . fiddle songs, devil songs, corn songs, and jig tunes" that the editors of *Slave Songs of the United States* were unable to find in the South were being played with riotous enthusiasm every afternoon in dozens of theatres and "museums" in New York City.

The Civil War passed over the South, leaving chaos and destruction, and a frightening new life for the freed Negroes. They were uneducated and almost without any comprehension of the social patterns that would have helped them to survive the violence and turmoil of the years of Reconstruction. Some slaves had stayed on the plantations even after word of the Emancipation Proclamation had spread through the South, but for most of the slaves the faint breath of freedom was intoxicating. Their excitement was deeply troubling to Southerners who had tried to justify slavery to themselves by pretending that the slaves were happy with the system. Younger slaves were too delirious at the thought of freedom even to pretend that they wanted the South to win. One of the bitterest moments for the Confederacy came in the trenches at Petersburg, when Southern troops found themselves facing a battalion of freed Negroes, fighting for the Union. Some of the older people still tried to cling to their belief. Storekeepers in border states displayed posters with a tattered slave leaping into the air and shouting, "Dis Union Forever." The words were spaced so that the slave could be saying either "disunion" or "this union," depending on the customer's sympathies. The South would have avenged itself on the new "freedmen" even without the tragedy of the Congressional Reconstruction policies.

In an effort to force some order into the frightening civil chaos, the Southerners forced the Northern occupation troops to allow them to reimpose more and more restrictions on the rights of the new "freedmen." The climax came in 1876 when the new Republican President, Rutherford B. Hayes, after assurances from influential Southern leaders that they would guarantee the civil rights of the Negroes, removed the last of the Federal troops from the South. As the troops were withdrawn to Northern garrisons, the Negroes were forced into a servitude little better than slavery. The Southerners quickly overwhelmed any resistance, killing and beating hundreds of "freedmen." The fact that the Negroes were almost helpless, unarmed and completely disorganized spurred many of the Southerners on, and the country roads rang with the hoofbeats of the horses of the night riders, most of them members of a new secret order, the infamous Ku-Klux Klan.

With servitude and brutality still harsh realities,

the Negroes preserved the field cries and chants of the years of slavery. The work songs still expressed their frightened despair and self-pity or their strong pleasures. The clearly African singing of the fields and prison yards was still a part of the life of the South. Without overseers to force the musical outcry into "nonsense" songs, the music took on a new intensity. The great spirituals reached a more or less finished form in the years between 1870 and 1890, and the work songs became almost crude blues. A leader cried in a levee shout along the Mississippi in the 1890's:

> "Oh, rock me, Julie, rock me.
> Rock me slow and easy.
> Rock me like a baby."

The simple cry: "Oh, my massa told me, there's no grass in Georgia," had been only the first halting expression of a rich and vital music.

The work-song material that became part of the first blues was slight. It was so fragmentary that most of the men collecting songs and music in the South made no mention of "blues," which were still short, formless cries, unnoticed in the endless work chants. About 1904 a man in Auburn, Alabama, collected, in the work songs from the fields outside of town, most of the simple phrases that were the heart of the early blues.[7]

> Some folks say de fo' day blues ain't bad,
> But de fo' day blues am de wust I eber had.

[7] White, Newman I., *American Negro Folk Songs*, Cambridge, Harvard University Press, 1928.

The song was sung other places and there were lines:
"Some folks say de Memphis blues ain't bad," or "Some
folks say de St. Louis blues ain't bad." The blues never
stayed still.

>De four day blues ain't nuffin'
>But a woman wants a man.

>When a woman takes de blues
>She tucks her head and cries.
>But when a man catches the blues,
>He catches er freight and rides.

>If de blues was whiskey
>I'd stay drunk all de time.

>De blues ain't nothin'
>But a poor man's heart disease.

And there was one of the most simple and intense of
the early blues verses:

>I got de blues,
>But I'm too damn mean to cry.

Auburn is in poor farm country about twenty-five
miles northeast of Tuskegee Institute in central Alabama. Thin grass and sparse growths of pine cover the
low, rolling hills. The roads are cut into the red, sandy
clay, and they stream with water in the spring rains.
Unpainted board cabins are scattered along the streams
and valleys, wash hanging on the dirty porches, children playing in the littered yards. The people still work
in small fields, struggling to raise a scanty living out of
the poor soil. In the fields the older people still sing the

work songs of the slaves who toiled in the sun a hundred years ago; and across the fields at night, the yellow light from an oil lamp brightening a rain-streaked window, there is sometimes the lonely sound of the blues.

# 2

## "That Gives Me the Blues to Go Back to Dallas"

In the 1880's and 1890's, many Southern Negroes found a new way of life in Southern towns and cities. The South's desperate effort to build up the cotton-processing and steel industries brought people in from the farms in steadily increasing numbers. Most of the mill hands were poor whites from the mountain areas, but thousands of Negroes also found work in the new mill centers. They were jammed into filthy, ramshackle slums and tenements or given cheap, one-room company houses lined up along company roads, but there were jobs, and a feeling of being hidden in a crowd. They had been helpless in their isolated cabins.

Many of the cities with large Negro sections were port cities, like Norfolk, New Orleans, Memphis, Savannah, Mobile, or Charleston, and gangs of Negroes sweated to load and unload the hundreds of ships that carried the bulk of Southern freight. The pay was poor, but the jobs were casually organized, and a man who wanted a day's wages could usually find some little job.

The lonely field cries and work chants were almost forgotten in the crowded cities, but the singing style and the emotional directness survived. There was an insecure imitation of the music of the day, but as the strong tradition of country music mingled with the more conventional city music both musical styles began to change. The city music became more intense and expressive, and the country music began to use loose rhymes and more regular rhythms. The most important change in the country musical styles was the new use of the rough harmonic form that was the heart of the early blues.

There was no name for the early blues. When a New Orleans musician named Harrison Barnes came into the city from a plantation in 1907, there were piano players working in brothels in the colored tenderloin section, just across Canal Street from the white section, Storyville. The piano was in the saloon, the girls in darkened, dingy cribs off a hallway leading from the bar. In the afternoons, when there wasn't much business, the piano player left the door to the cribs open, and the girls, sitting by themselves in tattered robes, fixing their nails or hair, or just lying on the noisy bed looking out through the shutters, would call out to him to play the tunes they wanted. Harrison hummed one or two of the old tunes.

"They was slow tunes, unhappy. They was what they call blues now, only they called them ditties in them days."

The use of the word "blues" to describe a mood
or feeling is very old, going back to the sixteenth century.[1] In the nineteenth century it was a common expression in the United States, though there was some
confusion as to exactly what it meant to be "blue." In
1824, "in a fit of the blues" meant "a depression of
spirits." In 1853, a Boston newspaper, the *Yankee
Blade*, recommended a humorous novel ". . . to all
who are afflicted with the blues, or ennui . . ." In the
1850's, it meant boredom. By the 1880's it meant unhappiness: "Come to me when you have the blues."
The word was used occasionally in song titles, but as a
slang expression, without reference to any Negro musical style. By 1910, the term "blues" was heard everywhere, and there was an expectant moment while the
term and the music that was to be called "the blues"
became more and more popular. The first published
"blues" finally came out in March, 1912, and the rush
was on.

The late W. C. Handy, a colored bandleader from
Memphis, always called himself the "father of the
blues," and he certainly was one of the earliest and
most successful blues writers, but his first "blues" composition, "Memphis Blues," was not a blues at all, and it
was the third published piece in 1912 to be called a
"blues." The first was Hart Wand's "Dallas Blues,"
published in March; the second was Arthur Seals's
"Baby Seals' Blues," published in August; Handy finally
brought out his blues in September. Both Handy and
Arthur Seals were Negroes, but the music that they
titled "blues" is more or less derived from the standard

[1] *Oxford English Dictionary.*

popular musical styles of the "coon-song" and "cake-walk" type. It is ironic that the first published piece in the Negro "blues" idiom, "Dallas Blues," was by a white man, Hart Wand.

Hart was a young musician who lived with his family in Oklahoma City. His father had been one of the first men into the Indian Territory, and he had set up a tent drugstore in the new city. Hart worked for his father, and led a little dance orchestra that played for occasional society affairs in Oklahoma City or for dancing at the Indian reservations at Wynewood and Purcell. He played the violin, and he often practiced in the back room of his father's store. There was a little tune he'd made up to play with his orchestra; he doesn't remember hearing it anywhere, and he used to play it during the afternoons when he was practicing. There was a colored porter working for them, who had come into the territory from Dallas. He used to whistle the tune along with Hart's playing. One afternoon, as he stood listening, leaning on his broom, he said, "That gives me the blues to go back to Dallas."

The phrase stayed in Hart's mind, and he had a young pianist friend, Annabelle Robbins, arrange the tune for him. He published it himself in March, with the title printed in gold on dark blue paper, and he put it in five-and-ten-cent stores around town at ten cents a copy. The first printing was gone in a week. He had a second one done and started taking it to other towns near Oklahoma City. Orders began coming in from music stores in other cities. The second printing went almost as fast as the first. It was a sensation. He didn't even have time to copyright it until it was in the third edition. He finally sent a copy of the third edition to the copyright office and it was entered on September 12, 1912.

"Dallas Blues" is still popular, and the original arrangement itself is a fine melodic composition. There is only one strain and it is played twice, first as a simple blues melody with a simple bass line, then with considerable embellishment. Between the two arrangements almost every characteristic of later commercial blues writing was introduced. The melody is a simple twelve-bar blues, in three four-bar phrases, very similar to the later blues pattern; then there is a short phrase on the subdominant harmony—which Handy later used as the first line of the chorus of "Atlanta Blues"—and the last phrase of the first group is repeated. Twenty bars in all, it was easy to play and whistle, and within a few weeks it was a favorite the length of the Mississippi River. It had no words, and Hart didn't think of it as a song at first. He regarded "blues" as a new musical style, just as "ragtime" had been. There were words added in the 1920's, but they were the work of a professional Chicago lyricist.

The second published blues, "Baby Seals' Blues," came out in the summer, and it was published by its composer, a vaudeville comedian named Arthur "Baby" Seals. It was published in St. Louis, probably after Seals had played through the Southwest and heard "Dallas Blues." The cover advertised, "Featured by the KLASSY, KOONEY, KOMEDY PAIR, Seals and Fisher." It was a popular song rather than a real blues, as Wand's tune seems to be, but there was one verse which showed up later in different surroundings:

> Sing-em, sing-em
> Sing them blues,
> 'Cause they cert'ly sound good to me.
> I've been in love these last three weeks
> And it cert'ly is a misery.

Bessie Smith used just about these words and Seals' melody on a later recording called "Preachin' the Blues."

Finally, late in September, Handy rushed into print with a three-strain instrumental cakewalk that he called "Memphis Blues," and the "father of the blues" had entered the field.

Handy's attitude toward the music of his own race has been somewhat opportunistic. He has described how he decided that there was some value to the music of the country Negro:

> I hasten to confess that I took up with low folk forms hesitantly. . . . As a director of many respectable, conventional bands, it was not easy for me to concede that a simple slow-drag and repeat could be rhythm itself. . . . My own enlightenment came in Cleveland, Mississippi. I was leading the orchestra in a dance program when someone sent up an odd request. Would we play some of "our native music" the note asked. This baffled me. . . . A few moments later a second request came up. Would we object if a local colored band played a few dances? Object? That was funny. What hornblower would object to a time-out and a smoke—on pay? We eased out gratefully as the newcomers entered. They were led by a long-legged chocolate boy and their band consisted of just three

pieces, a battered guitar, a mandolin, and a worn-out bass.

The music they made was pretty well in keeping with their looks. They struck up one of those over-and-over strains that seemed to have no very clear beginning and certainly no ending at all. The strumming attained a disturbing monotony, but on and on it went. . . . A rain of silver dollars began to fall around the outlandish, stomping feet. The dancers went wild. Dollars, quarters, halves, the shower grew heavier and continued so long I strained my neck to get a better look. There before the boys lay more money than my nine musicians were being paid for the entire engagement. Then I saw the beauty of primitive music.[2]

At least Handy was honest about his motives. His usual story of the composition of "Memphis Blues" was that it was written for the 1909 mayoralty race in Memphis. William Talbot and E. H. Crump were the rival candidates and Crump had hired Handy's orchestra to play at the opening of his campaign. The rally was held in the afternoon at the corner of Main Street and Madison Street and Handy's band struck up the little piece he had written for the occasion. It was called "Mister Crump," and Handy described it as such a sensation that people danced and shouted around his band, asking him to play it again and again. He remembered people singing these words as they jumped and shouted:

> "Mr. Crump don' 'low no easy riders here.
> Mr. Crump don' 'low no easy riders here.

[2] Handy, William Christopher, *Father of the Blues*, New York, Macmillan & Co., 1941.

> I don't care what Mr. Crump don' 'low,
> Gonna barrel-house anyhow.
> Mr. Crump can go and catch himself some air."

It is at this point that Handy's story becomes confused. These words don't fit the melody that he published as "Mister Crump." They were usually sung to the melody called "Mamma Don' 'Low," and the words referred to Crump's supposed intention of driving prostitution out of the city. What Handy remembered hearing was a song that the opposition was singing about Crump! The shouting and confusion he noticed was probably a disturbance by the Talbot forces to try to harass the opening of Crump's campaign!

In the summer of 1912, Handy decided to publish his little orchestra piece, "Mister Crump." On the title page he used "Mister Crump" as a subtitle and "Memphis Blues" as the new title. He never said why he decided to call his composition a blues, which it certainly was not, but it was probably the excitement over "Dallas Blues" that caused him to rename "Mister Crump." In his later writing, Handy denied any knowledge of Wand's composition, but "Dallas Blues" sold well in Memphis as early as May and June, and it is difficult to believe that Handy, the most active orchestra and band director in Memphis, did not see the music. His scoring of "Memphis Blues" is very similar to Annabelle Robbins's arrangement and the fourth phrase of Wand's melody was used in the later Handy composition.

Like "Dallas Blues," Handy published "Memphis Blues" as an instrumental piece. It had no words. But unlike "Dallas Blues" it was a resounding failure. Handy was unable to sell the music. Discouraged by the lack of sales, he sold the plates and rights for fifty dollars and a thousand unsold copies for another fifty dollars. The Memphis music-store owner who bought it managed to talk the famous minstrel man "Honey Boy" Evans into using the piece in his New York engagement the next spring and engaged a professional lyricist, George A. Norton, to write some words for it. It was republished in New York in the spring of 1913 with a picture of Evans's band on the cover and a note saying that the piece had been featured by the "famous Handy Orchestra of Memphis." As a song, "Memphis Blues" was more successful than it had been as the old instrumental piece, but it still was not a sensation. It became more popular as other blues were published, and by 1915 and 1916 was very well known.

Handy later complained bitterly that he was cheated out of the rights to his song, but the man who bought the rights from him was acting in good faith and had as little idea as Handy did that the song would become so successful. Certainly a great deal of its success was due to "Honey Boy" Evans, who was at the height of his popularity when he introduced it.

In Memphis there was some question as to the actual composition of the final version of "Mister Crump," the version advertised as "Played by Handy's Orchestra." Older musicians said that it had been written by the orchestra's clarinet player, Paul Wyer. Handy himself described the day Wyer came into the orchestra. There was no music for him to play, but ". . . the young musician improvised a part better than if one had been written." In 1950, members of Wyer's family said that he was living in Buenos Aires and that Handy was in touch with him. An acquaintance of Handy's wrote to ask for Wyer's address, and the request was ignored. When it was made a second time, Handy abruptly broke off the correspondence.

It should be said in Handy's defense that he never pretended that his compositions were original. When he was interviewed by Dorothy Scarborough in 1925 in connection with her book *On the Trail of Negro Folk Songs*, she quoted him as saying that he had gotten his melodies from folk sources:

> Each one of my blues is based on some old Negro song of the South, some folk-song that I heard from my mammy when I was a child. Something that sticks in my mind, that I hum to myself when I'm not thinking about it. Some old song that is part of the memories of my childhood and my race. I can tell you the exact song I used as the basis for any one of my blues.[3]

Of Handy's seventy-some published compositions, the only successful ones were those using melodies he heard or remembered from his Memphis days.

In 1913, Handy and a friend started the Pace-Handy Music Company and published "Jogo Blues," a tune he'd gotten from a local piano player. In 1914, he added two strains to "Jogo," gave the second strain a tango beat—since, as he later explained, the tango was all the rage—called it "St. Louis Blues," and both Handy and the blues were on their way to fame and fortune.

Of the three men who had first published "blues" in 1912, only Handy became rich. Baby Seals continued

[3] Scarborough, Dorothy, *On the Trail of Negro Folk Songs*, Cambridge, Harvard University Press, 1925.

working on the vaudeville stage and was a popular entertainer for many years. He wrote songs occasionally,
and a few were published, but it had been only an accident of time that put his rather thin song into prominence, and he never advertised himself as a blues composer.

Hart Wand moved to New Orleans and went into
business, successfully manufacturing lettering devices
and rubber stamps. He is a respected and well-liked
member of the business community. "Dallas Blues" is
the only song he ever wrote, and he still thinks of it as
a sort of souvenir of his youth. Royalties have been paid
on it every three months for the last forty-seven years,
and if a visitor at his office asks about "Dallas Blues,"
everyone smiles and looks around to Hart who comes
to shake hands and introduce himself. While he talks,
there is usually someone who begins quietly humming
his song.

Handy stayed in Memphis for a few more years,
then in 1917 he went to New York City and expanded
his publishing activities. In New York he was to spend
much of his time working on the "father of the blues"
story, and for several years it seemed as though the
blues had followed him to Broadway.

# 3

## The Crazy Blues

Until Hart Wand, Baby Seals and W. C. Handy had published their blues songs in 1912, the blues were a confused and endlessly varied musical form. The blues were the personal expression of singers in every part of the South, and the forms and styles of each were distinctly his own. The blues songs brought the country blues into the popular entertainment world, where a young woman who wanted to make a hit with the latest number could learn the words and music of a "blues" from a piece of sheet music. The first blues songs were so popular that hundreds of songs, the "city" blues, were composed in the style of "Dallas Blues" or "Memphis Blues." The style was so popular that the country blues seemed almost forgotten, but the men who had been singing their blues on the streets of Southern cities or at little parties out in the country went on singing and developing their country-blues styles. Despite the popularity of the city blues, it was not long before the

**43**

country blues were being played and sung everywhere there was a young and excitable Negro audience.

When Handy got to New York, he was only one of a large group of song writers who were trying to make a fortune writing blues hits. There were the colored song writers Perry Bradford, Joe Jordan, James P. Johnson, Clarence Williams, Noble Sissle, Eubie Blake, Spencer Williams and Maceo Pinkard, and there were almost as many white song writers trying to turn out successful blues—Irving Berlin, Walter Donaldson, Roy Turk, Jack Yellen, Milt Ager, Ted Snyder, Gus Kahn and Arthur Von Tilzer. The blues they were writing were almost indistinguishable, but they had a raffish, colorful quality to them. There were more or less straight blues songs; "Alcoholic Blues," "Sugar Blues," "Snaky Blues," "Bunch of Blues," "Down Where They Play the Blues," "Crazy Blues," "Don't Care Blues"; occasional popular songs with a blues title like Jerome Kern's "Left All Alone Again Blues," and hundreds of humorous blues, "You Can Have Him, I Don't Want Him, Didn't Love Him Any How Blues," or "Broke and Busted Can't Be Trusted Blues." Along the boardwalk at Coney Island and in a dozen noisy cafés in the city there were new dance orchestras called "jass bands" playing, most of them featuring blues tunes. The bands were often responsible for their own blues. "Livery Stable Blues," "Yelpin' Hound Blues," "Bluin' the Blues," and "Satanic Blues." New York, Tin-pan Alley, and young people throughout the country were blues happy. It was as exciting and bewildering as the rag-time craze had been twenty years before.

Along Broadway there were dozens of singers who

were causing a sensation "moaning the blues." Most of them were white girls, cashing in on the popularity of the "miss-my-man" blues that Tin-pan Alley was grinding out. The great colored vaudevilian, Bert Williams, was singing and recording blues songs, but they were novelty songs like "I've Got The Sorry I Ain't Got It, You Could Have It If I had It Blues." The songs the girls were recording were pretty thin and artistically at least deserved most of the things that self-appointed moralists were saying about them:

> I've got those moany—groany—sax—O—phoney
> Sax—o—harmony blues . . .

> Hey listen to the saxophone,
> Hey listen to the trombone moan. . . .

> Oh home, home again blues. . . .

Bert Williams had the last word. On one of his most popular records he sang:

> "Ever'body's talkin' 'bout those doggone blues,
> But I'm happy. . . ."

Perry Bradford seemed to be the shrewdest and most determined of the colored blues writers, and he was responsible for opening up recording opportunities for colored singers. There was a beautiful young girl in Harlem named Mamie Smith whom Perry wanted to sing his songs. He walked the streets for months, going from record company to record company, trying to convince someone that there was a commercial opportunity in having a colored girl sing the blues. Finally, in the spring of 1920, he talked Ralph Peer, the recording director of a new company called OKeh Records, into letting Mamie record. Her first record—OK 4113, "That Thing Called Love" and "You Can't Keep A Good Man Down"—was released in July, with Mamie listed simply as "Mamie Smith, contralto." Within a few weeks the record was selling by the hundreds in every Harlem record shop and Peer rushed Mamie back into the recording studio. Her record of "Crazy Blues" and "It's Right Here for You," OK 4169, sold by the thousands. With "Crazy Blues," OKeh suddenly became a major record company, the colored blues singers suddenly became worth their weight in gold, and the whole area of records for a colored market was opened up.

In these first months of the blues' success it seemed as though the blues had lost their folk roots. Most of the singers were young girls who were vaudeville entertainers, and most of the blues were composed by the New York writers. Girls like Mamie Smith felt that they were bringing to ragged country singing a more artistic and sophisticated singing style, and many of the song writers felt that their use of the blues ideas in writing endless love songs had taken the "crudity" out of the blues. The accompaniments were usually a "red hot jazz band" or a "scintillating master of the keyboard." It was city music, "city blues," and the women singers, the slick blues songs and the stylish accompaniments seemed to have less and less relationship to the music still being sung in the South.

The audience that was buying blues records was to turn the record companies more and more to the blues of the rural South. The World War had brought thousands of Negroes into Northern cities to the shipyards and mills that were working with feverish haste to equip the new, hastily recruited army. Most of them were from the South, and they moved into Negro districts in the large cities, bringing with them their enthusiasm for music and singing. There was a rush into many Southern cities with industry or port facilities. Norfolk, Birmingham and Charleston were soon crowded with workers. Most of the new ones were young, anxious for excitement, and for the first time they had money to buy what they wanted. When they discovered that the record companies could be persuaded to bring out records by Negro performers, they began buying records by the thousands. OKeh finally started a separate numerical series, the 8000 series, for "race records," and they advertised, "Who first thought of getting out Race records for the Race? OKeh, that's right. Genuine Race artists make genuine blues for OKeh. . . ." Ralph Peer was trying to think of a catalog title for his new records, and rather than calling them "Negro" records, decided on "Race" records, and the name lasted.

As long as the companies were advertising almost exclusively in the North, their interest was in the young girls singing the city blues, and the records sold well to the young people in the cities, but their advertising soon began to reach a Southern audience. Large newspapers published for a colored audience had sprung up in most of the Northern cities. The largest of them, the Chicago *Defender* and the Pittsburg *Courier,* were distributed to every state in the South. In the farm areas, where people couldn't buy copies, they subscribed for them by mail or borrowed them from people in town. There were pages of news about Negro personalities, Negro athletics and entertainment, and pages of news about local social affairs. Almost every city had a reporter who sent the local news up to the paper and it was published in separate columns for every Southern state. The record companies selling the new race records were soon advertising in both the *Courier* and the *Defender* and in the first few months of advertising they were deluged with orders for records. It was these newspapers that took the companies out of the Northern cities and into the Southern countryside.

In 1922 and 1923, the recording companies were spending more and more money on advertising, and through record shops in Northern cities, they were advertising that any of their records could be purchased by mail. The mail-order businesses were much more important in country areas in the 1920's than they are today, and this mail-order business was very profitable. As the companies began to reach a larger and larger rural market, they realized that the most popular blues singers in the South were not the girls who were making the endless records of the city blues, but local singers, singing the country blues.

The country blues were generally sung by men accompanying themselves on the guitar, with a highly developed interplay between their singing and the guitar accompaniment. Their music was related to the city-blues styles in the arrangement of the lyrics and the harmonic patterns, but the singing styles and the rhythms were from the music of the fields and work gangs. The country blues were an intense individual expression of the deepest strains of Negro music in the South.

Paramount Records, in Chicago, was almost exclusively handling race artists and they were very concerned with the Southern market. They began to get requests for records by country-blues singers: so in July, 1924, they tried recording an old entertainer named Charlie Jackson, who sang and played a six-string guitar banjo. In August, 1924, they advertised:

Well Sir, Here He Is At Last!
Papa Charlie Jackson!
Singing his ORIGINAL LAWDY LAWDY BLUES
on Paramount Record 12219.
Buy It From Your Dealer Today!

Paramount was probably the least likely record company in the United States to be recording Papa Charlie Jackson. It was almost by accident that they had found themselves in the race-record business.

Paramount was owned by a furniture company, the Wisconsin Chair Company, in Grafton, Wisconsin, a small town between Chicago and Milwaukee. The company handled every kind of home furnishing, and about 1914 they became interested in selling phonographs. They discovered that people would buy phonographs if they could get records, so in 1917 the Wisconsin Chair Company went into the record business with a small subsidiary they called Paramount Records. Their first records were 9-inch or 9½-inch vertical-cut recordings of popular songs and dance music, but in the early 1920's the company began trying to sell their phonographs to the large Negro populations in Chicago and Detroit. In August, 1922, they began issuing a race-record series, the 12,000 series, to sell along with their phonographs. There was a phonograph for sale for eleven dollars in most of the stores on Chicago's south side, so the Wisconsin Chair Company did poorly with its phonograph sales, but their record company was immediately successful.

There was old recording equipment, some of it handmade, in their "New York laboratories" in Port Washington, Wisconsin, but most of the Paramount recording was done on a contract basis by a man named Orlando Marsh, who had a studio called the Marsh Laboratories at the corner of Jackson and Wabash, on the east side of the Loop in Chicago. The studio was on the second floor, over a music store. Marsh was a conscientious, imaginative recording engineer, but everything about the Paramount business operation was cheap, and the quality of the recordings was very poor. Marsh was one of the first men to build and use an electric-carbon microphone, but he used it very badly. Despite the inadequacies, his studio was used by three or four recording companies in the Chicago area. Gennett used him occasionally, and he recorded the famous King Oliver-Jelly Roll Morton duets for Autograph. His studio did all the test work and cut the wax masters, but the metal plating was done at the Paramount plant at Port Washington. There was something called the Paramount Studios on Wacker Drive, near the river, but Marsh seems to have done most of the recording.

A man named Supper, at Port Washington, was supervisor of recording, with J. Mayo Williams, in Chicago, handling the race series. Williams was a young colored booking agent who had been a popular football player in his college days, and had come to Chicago determined to become successful in the theatrical world. He rented office space and began booking colored talent, working as an agent for many of the younger singers. Paramount found him easy to work with and finally hired him to direct their race recording. He still worked as agent for many of the artists, and despite what he paid them as Paramount's recording director, as their agent he got his standard agent's price. He handled musical copyrights through a Paramount subsidiary, the Chicago Publishing Company, and made considerable money with some of the successful blues. He usually listed himself as a composer. Arthur Laibley and Arthur Satherly worked with Williams, and there was a young girl, Alethea Robinson, working as a general assistant. The recording directors did almost everything. They supervised recording, searched for new artists, did promotional work, even sold chairs. The Wisconsin Chair Company had very little respect for its race-record series. At Port Washington the colored artists had to use the freight elevator to get to the studios, and a secretary remembered one of the blind singers coming into the office on a windy winter day and asking for a handkerchief. One of the men threw him a dust cloth.

Despite the poor quality of their records and their attitude toward their singers, the company made money. Retailing for $.75 on the Paramount label and from

$.35 to $.59 on an even cheaper Broadway label, there were thousands sold. In 1924, they absorbed the Black Swan race series and issued race material from several other companies—Gennett, QRS, Banner, Regal, Arto and Emerson. A Chicago businessman named John Steiner, who has purchased the rights to the old Paramount material, has estimated that the factory was pressing as many as 100,000 records a month, almost exclusively for the colored market. It was a big business. A repressing, on a fast moving record, was 1,500 records, which Steiner thinks was the quantity that a single machine could press in a day's work. Workmen would begin heating the plates in the early morning; then press the records, keeping the machine hot, until after dark.

The first recordings by Papa Charlie Jackson sold well and Mayo Williams auditioned other blues singers from the South. In 1926, the company released records by Blind Lemon Jefferson, from Dallas, Texas, and Blind Blake, from Jacksonville, Florida. Paramount was soon selling thousands of records to the Southern audience. Papa Charlie continued to record for them for the next four years; though toward the end of his career he was used to cover hits by other singers. He was a tall, awkward man, unable to read or write. To record a new song he had to have someone sitting behind him whispering the words into his ear, just as many of the blind singers did. He made one magnificent band record in his Paramount days, "Salty Dog," with Freddie Keppard's Jazz Cardinals on Paramount 12399. As he starts to sing, Keppard booms out, "Sing it, Papa Charlie!" Then as the record ends, Charlie shouts, just in case anyone missed Keppard's announcement, "Papa Charlie done sung this song." Charlie still went out every season on the vaudeville circuit, singing his two big hits, "Salty Dog Blues," his second Paramount recording, Paramount 12236, and "Shake That Thing," Paramount 12281. The melody for "Shake That Thing" was used for several later blues songs, but "Salty Dog" was always associated with Papa Charlie:

> Funniest thing I ever saw in my life
> Uncle Bud came home and caught me kissing his wife.
> Salty Dog, oh, yes, you salty dog.

Arthur Blake, "Blind Blake," was a good guitar player and singer, and despite a rather nasal quality to his voice, his records were even more popular than Papa Charlie Jackson's. He played in a rhythmic dance style with considerable melodic inventiveness. His first record, "Early Morning Blues" and "West Coast Blues" on Paramount 12387, was advertised October 2, 1926, and it sold well. He recorded sixty-eight more blues for Paramount over the next four years. He was a heavy drinker, but his landlady, Mrs. Renett Pounds, at 4005 S. Parkway, tried to watch out for him as best she could. Two of his most popular records were trio versions of "Hot Potatoes" and "Southbound Rag" with the famed clarinet player, Johnny Dodds, and the excellent drummer, Jimmy Bertrand, who played xylophone and slide whistle. Blake's guitar playing filled out the trio with a strong, swinging beat. When the sales of his records began to drop in 1929 he got in touch with a friend, George Williams, who was managing the "Happy-Go-Lucky" show, and played with the show

until late 1930 or 1931, when he returned to Jacksonville.

A man named Fred Boerner, at Port Washington,
was doing an aggressive mail-order business for Paramount, selling a variety of things to Southern customers. His shelves were littered with dream books,
love potions and charms of all kinds. In December,
1927, he promoted the first collection of country blues,
*The Paramount Book of the Blues:*

> Ask your dealer or write us for the new 44 page Para-
> mount Book of the Blues. Attractively bound and
> decorated. Includes big Blues hits by such famous
> artists as Blind Lemon Jefferson, "Ma" Rainey, Blind
> Blake, Ida Cox, and others, with separate sections for
> songs of each. Pictures and autobiographies of the
> well known stars.
>
> Retail Price, 35 cents.

The company advertised in the race newspapers and
the popular singers got considerable mention, but there
was a tasteless style to the drawings, and singers like
Ma Rainey or Blind Lemon Jefferson were unpleasantly caricatured. There were photographs with some
of the ads, and occasionally there was genuine enthusiasm for an artist or a recording, but generally the
advertising was as cheap as the rest of the business.
Paramount ran a few promotions in the late 1920's.
There was the famous Ma Rainey "Mystery Record"
with Ma's picture on the label and an advertised fourteen thousand dollars in prizes for naming the song,
but Steiner hasn't been able to find any evidence that
any money was ever paid. There was another record
with Ma's picture, her "Dream Blues," and a birthday

record for Blind Lemon Jefferson in 1928. The company even tried a few records for special holidays. In 1925, they advertised a list of eighteen spiritual records for Easter, and for Christmas in 1927 they released a startling blues by Elzadie Robinson, "The Santa Claus Grave Blues," on Paramount 12573. Blind Lemon did the Christmas record the next year, "Christmas Eve Blues" and "Happy New Year Blues," on Paramount 12392, and Blind Blake did a "Lonesome Christmas Blues" on Paramount 12867 in 1929.

Mayo Williams left Paramount in March, 1927, to start a record company of his own, and after he left the Paramount blues lists became more and more confused. Blind Lemon, Blind Blake and Ma Rainey were still selling records, but the company was soon recording dull, obscene party blues. There were a few new singers like Charlie Patton, Sam Collins, or Son House, but they were too intensely personal to appeal to any kind of large audience. These singers, from Mississippi, sang some of the most moving blues on the Paramount lists, but as they were beginning to record the depression was beginning to throw its shadow across the South.

Paramount's entire attitude was so entirely opportunistic that, after the company stopped producing records, they made almost no effort to preserve the Negro music that had been recorded. A few of the records were issued on Champion label, but the rest of the catalog was simply discarded. When Steiner went to Port Washington to find out what he had acquired when he took over the company, he found that most of the masters had disappeared. He found priceless metal stampers, valuable even as scrap metal, used to repair leaky chicken coops on nearby farms. The masters that were left were often unmarked, in no order, and it was months before he even knew what he had. Paramount didn't seem to understand the music that was recorded for its race series, but Mayo Williams supervised the recording of some of the finest music recorded in the 1920's, and their policy of recording very cheaply and taking a chance on almost anything preserved early musical styles that might have been lost if Paramount had not been in Chicago. Almost every style of Southern singing was represented in their blues lists, and the singing of their most successful country blues singer, Blind Lemon Jefferson, was a magnificent display of the music of the early country blues. Lemon was fat, dirty, dissolute, but his singing was perhaps the most exciting country blues singing of the 1920's.

# 4

## Blind Lemon

The country around Alec Jefferson's farm is rolling
farmland, with thin, straggling brush in the creek bottoms. The plowed cotton fields sprawl on the soft
slopes, rich and wet with spring rains, stiff and dull in
the summer heat. Spruce, pine and scrub oak line the
edges of the fields, and their seedlings spring up around
the ruins of abandoned farm buildings. From a small
hill near Alec Jefferson's farmhouse at Couchman you
can see across the fields to the buildings of Mexia,
Texas, twelve miles to the southwest. The scattered
buildings of Wortham, Texas, stretch along the railroad
tracks five or six miles to the west. There are fields of
old oil rigs between the two towns, with gasoline en-
gines still working some of the old wells. The spindly
scaffoldings are rusted and weathered. The ground is
black with oil waste, but the only signs of oil money
in Wortham are three or four ugly church buildings,
built out of brick and designed to resemble funeral

parlors. Wortham's main street runs three blocks; from the Mexia road to the railroad tracks. Most of the buildings are one-story brick, with low, overhanging eaves of corrugated iron sheeting. There is one gaudy metal-front building from the 1880's, with low relief designs and scroll work stamped into the thin iron sheets. Wortham is a small market town, a crossroad in lonely country.

Early in the 1890's Alec Jefferson married a young widow named Classie Banks, who was living on a neighboring farm. Classie had two sons, Clarence and Izakiah, by her first husband, and she had seven children by Alec Jefferson, the oldest a girl named Francis. Their first son was named John Jefferson; the other girls were named Martha, Mary, C. B. and Gussie Mae. In the summer of 1897 there was another son, a small plump baby that they named Lemon. The other children did the best they could to take care of the new baby on the lonely farm. Lemon was born blind.

Lemon grew up with the other children, playing their games, running with them across the fields, sitting quietly while they tried to sneak up on rabbits. The rabbits skittered away from the children with a sudden rush that made them shriek with excitement. Lemon seemed to be able to follow them anywhere they went. When they would run across the fields and into the brush along Cedar Creek, south of the farm, he'd run after them, stand listening to them cross the footlogs over the stream, then slowly walk the footlogs after them. The neighbors thought he had a kind of gift, and they would sit in the Jeffersons' kitchen, watch him wrestle in the yard with the older boys, and talk with Classie about her son.

About 1907, the railroad was built through Wortham and the children used to sneak away from the farm to watch the trains. Lemon's brother, Johnny, tried to hang from a slow-moving freight and fell under the wheels. The older children ran screaming to the farm, but Johnny had been cut to pieces, and he was dead before Alec and Classie could get there.

When Lemon was fourteen, he was almost as fat as his mother and father and he was beginning to play the guitar and sing. A blind boy in the poor farm country in central Texas had to make some kind of living, and begging on the streets with a guitar was about the only way for one without any schooling. The neighbors showed him what they knew, but ". . . Lemon had a gift." The music seemed to be in his fingers. After he'd been playing for a few months, he began going into Wortham, to sit on a chair under the overhanging eaves of the feed store or the dry-goods store and playing for the people who came in town to shop. He sat there all afternoon, an earnest fat boy, wearing glasses over his eyes, singing into the darkness as the noise of people talking and laughing filled the street in front of him.

Before he was twenty, Lemon was singing for picnics and parties at farms scattered between Wortham and Mexia. He was one of the best-liked entertainers in his part of the county; so he decided to try singing in Dallas. In 1917 he said goodbye to his mother and father and took the train to Dallas. He was twenty years old.

The singing was harder in Dallas. No one knew him, and he had to make enough money to pay for his room and board. At the farm he had always had meals ready for him and a bed to sleep in. He sang night and day:

"I stood on the corner and almost bust my head,
 I stood on the corner; almost bust my head.
 I couldn't earn enough money to buy me a loaf of
   bread."

At first the singing wasn't enough. He wrestled for money in Dallas theatres. Since he was blind, he could be billed as a novelty wrestler. He weighed nearly 250 pounds, so he was never hurt, but it was a rough way to make a living. As soon as he started making a little money singing, he left the theatres. He worked engagements around Dallas, and sang for dances in the neighboring small towns. His cousin, Alec Jefferson, remembered Lemon's coming out to Waxahachie to sing for "country suppers" when Alec was in his teens.

Of course, my mother didn't let me go to them country suppers often. They was rough. Men was hustling women and selling bootleg and Lemon was singing for them all night. They didn't even do any proper kind of dancing, just stompin'.

They'd go down to the station and get him in the afternoon. He'd start singing about eight and go on until four in the morning. Sometimes he'd have another fellow with him, playing a mandolin or a guitar and singing along, but mostly it would be just him, sitting there playing and singing all night.

When Lemon was in Dallas, he spent most of his nights in the red-light district. He never let anyone lead him because he didn't want people to think he was blind, but he'd go into the brothels with other singers, and he'd let the other man collect the contributions. Lemon would feel his way to a chair against the wall and he'd sing and play until he had enough to get some liquor. He'd finish the night drunkenly fumbling with one of the girls, his guitar shoved under the chair so nobody would step on it. It was a raw, dirty life, but Lemon was successful at it. He got his own car and driver and when he'd come back to the farm for a visit, he'd let the driver go into town and give the girls rides. About 1922 or 1923 he married a girl named Roberta and they had a son two or three years later. He'd gotten so fat that, when he played, the guitar sat up on his stomach, the top of it just under his chin.

There was an intense musical atmosphere in the slums of north Dallas in the 'twenties, and Lemon learned from everybody he met. In his later records there were field songs, hymns, derivative city blues and vaudeville songs, all from the nights of listening to other singers. He would pick up a man's songs and his guitar style. There was a little of almost every style of blues guitar on the records. The Texas men sang in a high, crying voice, with the biting tone of the guitar whining behind them. All the loneliness and poverty of the dry, empty fields of central Texas was in their singing. When Lemon left the streets and brothels of Dallas, his blues training was finished.

Lemon traveled hundreds of miles in the middle

'twenties. Other singers remember seeing him as far east as Alabama, south along the Texas coast, even in Memphis. A preacher from Hearn, Texas, remembered Lemon on the streets during the cotton-picking season, a crowd around him while he sat on a stool, singing. He came during the weeks of picking, when there was money and crowds in town on Saturday afternoons. He'd play for suppers and dances on Friday night, get drunk, lose his money or spend it on a woman. Then he'd be out on Saturday, sweating off his hangover, trying to get the price of a meal and some liquor. He was already famous in his world, and people hung around him, listening. "He was about the best we had, him being a traveler, you know." He wore a broad-brimmed Stetson hat, stained with sweat, to keep the sun off his face, and when the sun went down, he usually had some sort of cloak to go around his shoulders. In September, picking season, the nights begin to get a little cold.

In and out of Dallas, living a chaotic life, he and his wife drifted apart. She came to Couchman a few times and stayed with Classie and Alec, but she hardly ever knew where Lemon was or who he was with. The neighbors remember her as a quiet, mousy woman, who hung back when she was with Lemon and his family.

Sometime in 1924 the record companies became interested in Lemon's singing. There is a story that the first recordings were done in the rug department of a Dallas department store, after a local music shop had arranged for the session, but Lemon's first records were made for the Paramount Company, and Paramount did all its recording in studios in the Chicago area. There may have been some tests done in Dallas, but the company sent for Lemon and recorded him in Chicago.

In the spring of 1925, he recorded "Beggin' Back" and "Old Rounder's Blues," but Mayo Williams was dissatisfied and didn't release the record until the summer of 1926. In February, 1926, he recorded Lemon a second time, and in April, Paramount advertised their first record by Blind Lemon Jefferson:

> Here's a real old-fashioned blues by a real old-fashioned blues singer—Blind Lemon Jefferson from Dallas. This "Booster Blues" and "Dry Southern Blues" on the reverse side are two of Blind Lemon's old-time tunes. With his singing he plays the guitar in real southern style.

On most of the advertisements they included some of the words:

I couldn't buy no ticket, I walked to the door,
My baby's left town, she ain't coming here no more.

and there was a picture of Lemon, wearing a suit, looking very respectable and earnest.

Lemon's first record was a success both for him and for Paramount. On the first of May, the next month, they were advertising a new record by ". . . that sterling old-time guitar strumming blues singer from Dallas. . . ." It was Paramount 12354, "Long Lonesome Blues" and "Got the Blues." There was a cartoon of Lemon acting out the words of the song, "I'm going to the river, going to carry my rocking chair." On the third of July they put an advertisement in the Chicago *De-*

*fender,* which simply said that everyone should watch the space next week for Lemon's new record. Next Saturday's paper advertised "Black Horse Blues":

> Go get my black horse and saddle up my gray mare,
> Going to get my good girl, she's in the world some-
> where.

Lemon's relationship with Mayo Williams and Paramount was far from pretty. He was paid very little, and seems to have gotten only token royalties from his many successful records. He stayed with Paramount because Williams pimped for him. Lemon, by this time, was a dirty, dissolute man, interested in very little besides women and liquor. At the end of a recording session, Williams would have a few dollars for him, a bottle and a prostitute.

OKeh tried to hire him away from Paramount in 1927, but after two sessions in March, doing "Black Snake Moan" and "Matchbox Blues" on OK 8455, he went back to the old arrangement.

When Williams left Paramount in 1927, there was a strain in the company's relations with Lemon. Laibley and Satherly, who had worked with Williams, were still with Paramount, but Lemon seems to have been partly the responsibility of the young girl with Paramount, Alethea Robinson, and she still remembers Lemon with a shudder of disgust.

As Lemon began to run out of the songs from the Texas farm country, he began singing more and more of the thin city blues, with their endless sexual double meanings and musical dullness. He even tried singing with piano accompaniment for three recordings in 1927.

The Louisiana cane fields, 1892.    *Photo from Mrs. M. K. Farrier*

# *The Southern Background*

Shacks on the outskirts of Gretna, Louisiana, 1892.
*Photo from Mrs. M. K. Farrier*

BLIND LEMON JEFFERSON.

*Photo from John Steiner*

WORTHAM
The young Lemon
Jefferson often
sang in front
of this store.
*Photo by
S. B. Charters*

# "One Kind Favor I Ask of You..."

A FIELD OUTSIDE OF WORTHAM, TEXAS
The stone marking Classie Jefferson's grave is in the foreground; the grave
of Lemon's sister beyond it. Lemon's grave is between theirs, unmarked.
*Photo by S. B. Charters*

AN OKEH ADVERTISEMENT,
MARCH, 1929—LONNIE JOHNSON
*Material from New York Public Library*

A PARAMOUNT ADVERTISEMENT,
DECEMBER, 1926—
BLIND LEMON JEFFERSON
Instructions for ordering by mail
included in the ad. *Material from
New York Public Library*

A pianist named George Perkins was hired to do the best he could with Lemon's grandly irregular singing. By playing very carefully and listening to Lemon with earnest concentration, he was able to do an adequate accompaniment, staying with Lemon almost all the way. He deserves some mention in any discussion of piano players of the 'twenties for doing as well as he did. At one point Lemon paused and shouted: "Whip that piano, Mister piano whipper," which he probably intended as a sweeping, if vague compliment.

There was a record for Lemon's birthday in 1928 as a Paramount promotion idea. His picture was used on the label with a streamer over his head reading, "Blind Lemon's Birthday Record." The *Defender* carried the advertisement on August fourth. The record, Paramount 12650, "Piney Woods Money Mama" and "Low Down Mojo Blues" was a poor one and sold very badly, despite Lemon's picture. Without Mayo Williams to supervise the recording, Paramount was losing direction in its blues lists. There was so much obscenity on many of the records that there would still be trouble reissuing a lot of them. Lemon had never sung without considerable sexual imagery, but he very seldom sang anything as bad as the Beale Street Sheiks and the Hokum Boys were recording for Paramount. Lemon began to lose some of his popularity. The cartoon ads began to caricature him more and more sharply, and there was less attention paid to his new songs. There was a small ad in the *Defender* on December 28, 1929, then an advertisement for the Paramount "Hometown Skiffle" record on February 22, 1930, saying that Lemon had recorded with Papa Charlie, Charlie Spand, Blind

Blake, Will Ezell and the others for another Paramount personality promotion. The advertisement was mistaken. In February, 1930, Lemon was dead.

Lemon's family had only confused accounts of his death. A memorial record, Paramount 12945, "Wasn't It Sad About Lemon," by Walter and Byrd, said that he died on the streets of Chicago, but that seemed to be the only detail they were certain of. Lemon was singing for parties around the southside, and he was recording nearly every month. He would stumble away from the parties drunk and he'd stand on a corner waiting for his driver to come pick him up. If he didn't have any money, he'd get to a streetcar stop and wait with his guitar in the wind and snow of the Chicago winters. There was a spell of bitter cold during the winter, and he recorded during the afternoon at the Paramount Chicago studios. The last title was "Empty House Blues." Lemon left the studio after dark, saying that he was going to sing at a house party, and walked into the driving snow. Sometime early the next morning he was found lying on the street, frozen, the snow drifted over his body. His guitar was lying beside him. Paramount said that he had dropped dead from a heart attack, and that he had frozen as he lay dead on the sidewalk. Some of his family heard that he left a party too drunk to find his way, and froze sitting in the gutter. Others said that he was waiting on the street for his car and driver, but they never found him. There is probably no way of ever knowing what happened to Lemon in the darkness of that winter night.

Paramount tried to do the best they could for him. They paid Will Ezell, an erratic pianist recording for them, to take Lemon's body to Dallas, and they saw to it that Ezell, who had intended to cheat them, stayed on the train to Dallas. Friends brought the body to a church in Wortham. It was still bitterly cold, but Classie and Alec came to the church with the rest of the family, and hundreds of neighbors followed the hearse after the ceremony. They buried him in a small country graveyard across the fields from Wortham.

In four years of recording, Lemon had sung seventy-nine blues for Paramount and two issued blues for OKeh. It was a beautifully moving and sensitive group of blues. Many of them were direct reworkings of old field cries and work songs. He shouted the melody in a long, free rhythmic pattern, and the guitar sang behind the voice in a subtle counterpoint. Many of the songs were from the Texas prisons:

Gettin' tired of sleepin' in the low down, lonesome cell.
Lord I wouldn't be here if it had not been for Nell.

Lay awake and just can't eat a bite.
She used to be my rider but she just won't treat me right.

I asked the government to knock some days off my time,
The way I'm treated I'm about to lose my mind.

I wrote to the Governor to please turn me loose,
Since I didn't get no answer I know it ain't no use.

Gettin' tired of sleepin' in that low down, lonesome cell,
Lord I wouldn't be here if it had not been for Nell.

I hate to turn over and find my rider gone, . . . Lordy
   how I moan.

Lord I wouldn't be here if it hadn't been for Nell,
I'm getting tired of sleeping in this low down, lonesome cell.

His attitude toward woman was a hard, bitter
shrug at their faithlessness:

Slippin' 'roun' the corner, runnin' up alleys, too,
I went slippin' 'roun' the corner, runnin' up alleys, too.
Watchin' my woman, tryin' to see what she goin' to do.

Sit down in the street one cold dark stormy night,
I sat down in the street, one dark and stormy night.
Tryin' to see if my good girl; she goin' make it home
   all right.

I believe she's found something that probably made
   her fall.
She must did found something and I believe made
   her fall.
I stood out in the cold all night and she didn't come
   home at all. . . .

Peach Orchard Mama, you swore nobody'd pick your
   fruit but me.
Peach Orchard Mama, you swore that no one'd pick
   your fruit but me.
I found three kid men shaking down your peaches
   free. . . .

One man bought your groceries, another joker paid
   your rent,
One man bought your groceries,
   another paid your rent.

While I was working your orchard and giving you
   every cent.

It was in his sexual imagery that Lemon was his
most poetic. The "black snake" image had been used in
the blues for years, but Lemon brought to it his own
intensity:

Hey—ain't got no mama now.
Hey—ain't got no mama now.
She told me late last night, you don't need no mama
   nohow.

Um—um, black snake crawling in my room.
Um—um, black snake crawling in my room.
Yes some pretty mama, better get this black snake
   soon.

Uum—what's the matter now.
Uum—what's the matter now.
Tell me what's the matter, baby, I don't like no black
   snake nohow.

Well, I wonder where this black snake's gone.
I wonder where this black snake's gone.
   Lord that black snake, mama, done run my mama
   home.

He sang every kind of song, even the country
hymns. People in Texas remember him singing a song
that they thought was ". . . the old horse that pawed in
the valley." Usually that was all they could remember.
"That's all that I can call of that song, 'old horse pawed
in the valley, old horse.'" There is a folk hymn from
central Texas, "The White Horse Pawin' in the Valley,"

and it is probably the same song. When Lightnin' Hopkins first saw Lemon in the summer of 1920, Lemon was singing at a picnic for the general association of the Baptist Church, and the Baptist Association would not have stood for "Black Snake Moan" or "Piney Woods Money Mama." He recorded one hymn, Paramount 12608, the simple "See That My Grave Is Kept Clean":

Well there's one kind favor I ask of you,
One kind favor I ask of you,
Lord, there's one kind favor I ask of you,
Please see that my grave is kept clean.

It's a long lane that got no end,
    (three times)
And it's a bad way that don' never change.

Lord, it's two white horses in a line,
    (three times)
Going take me to my buryin' ground.

Have you ever heard a coffin sound?
    (three times)
Then you know the poor boy's in the ground.

Dig my grave with a silver spade.
    (three times)
You may leave me down with a golden chain.

Have you ever heard a church bell toll?
    (three times)
Then you know that the poor boy's dead and gone.

At the words, "Have you ever heard a church bell toll?" he strikes the bass strings of the guitar in a slow, tolling of a death bell.

Around the farm at Couchman now there is a life-
less quiet. The road has fallen into ruin, and the buildings are deserted. Most of the fields have been turned
into pasture and scattered bunches of cattle graze in
the brush along Cedar Creek, where Lemon used to
play with his brothers and sisters. The girls have moved
to Plainview, a half brother has a cabin south of Street-
man. At a weathered bar on the outskirts of Wortham,
just across the railroad tracks from the town, a group
of men in from the farms thought a minute and said to
see the Wafer family at a farm near the old Jefferson
place. One of the men, a thin serious man in overalls and
a mackinaw jacket, was going out to his own farm near
the Wafers and asked for a ride in exchange for direc-
tions. As he got out of the car, he pointed to a white
building on the crest of a low rise and said that that was
the Wafers' house.

It was a Sunday afternoon, and the older people
were in the kitchen, sitting in the light from a narrow
window, talking about their children. Old Alec Wafer
had died, but his widow, Savannah, remembered the
Jefferson children when Lemon was still a baby. Her
daughter, a dark, heavy woman, had driven around
Wortham with Lemon's driver, and she remembered
the fat, noisy Lemon who came to be home with his
mother and walk around the farm where he had grown
up. It had been so cold they hadn't gone to the funeral,
but they had walked over the fields to stay for a few
hours with Classie when the news had come that Lemon
was dead. They sat into the afternoon, recalling the
fat little boy who could run across footlogs, and wrestle

in the yard with his brothers, his eyes blind and closed. "It's been so long since I called that boy to mind, but I can certainly remember Lemon. Oh, yes, I can certainly remember Lemon."

It was windy and cold in the cemetery outside of Wortham. The grass was blowing in the afternoon wind. Except for the breeze and a few distant birds it was quiet. Rabbits burst from small tangles of brush and bounded across the fields. The graves were almost lost in the weeds and grass under two ragged oak trees. There was a stone for one of the sisters, and a crude marker:

*Classie Jefferson*
b. 2. 6. 1865
d. 8. 12. 1947
*at rest.*

There were only rusted metal markers between the stones; the names missing. Lemon's grave was unmarked. Looking across the fields as the thin clouds blew across the face of the sun, it was hard not to think of his simple plea:

There's one kind favor I ask of you,
One kind favor I ask of you,
Now there's one kind favor I ask of you,
Please see that my grave is kept clean.

# 5

## "You Don't See Into
## These Blues Like Me"

People, I've stood these blues 'bout as long as I can.
I walked all night with these blues, we both joined
  hand in hand.
And they traveled my heart through, just like a natural
  man.

In 1924 and 1925, the OKeh Record Company in New
York was advertising, "Don't forget to ask your dealer
for OKeh records, the records that put over real hits
by real race artists every time . . . OKeh Records, the
Original Race Records!" The company was still one of
the largest in the race field, but they were staying away
from country blues. It was not until the Paramount blues
began coming out that OKeh started to use country-
blues men. Their first singer was a man named Sylvester
Weaver, who sang and played either banjo or guitar, but
his records had a small sale. Their second blues singer,

73

a St. Louis singer named Lonnie Johnson, within a year was as popular as Lemon Jefferson.

Lonnie brought to the blues an earnest, plaintive voice, and a superb guitar technique. He was a tall, thin, dark man, clumsy when he was not playing, often brooding and unhappy. He had a very successful, but discouraging recording career. His best records, sensitive blues like "You Don't See Into These Blues Like Me" or "I Just Can't Stand These Blues," sold poorly, but the thin, suggestive or tasteless blues like "I Got The Best Jelly Roll in Town," sold much better. Some of his best-selling records were duets with Spencer Williams and Victoria Spivey that were as obscene as anything recorded in the 1920's. "It Feels So Good," "Toothache Blues," "Wipe It Off," "You'Done Lost Your Good Thing." He was singing for an audience that was more interested in sexual suggestion than in music, and his best blues were too introspective and personal to reach many people.

Lonnie had grown up in a large family, one of eleven children, and in 1915 all but Lonnie and an older brother died of influenza. He became a lonely, withdrawn man. He was born on Franklin Street, in New Orleans, on February 8, 1889, and was carefully trained on both the guitar and violin while he was still a young man. He and his brother James, who played guitar, violin, piano and banjo, played in New Orleans in the first years of the World War, but they seem to have made a very slight impression on the musicians who heard them. Neither of them has been recalled playing in the city by local musicians. Lonnie was performing in the local theatres, and after the death of his family he began to travel. From 1917 to 1919 he performed in a musical revue in London, returning to the United States when the war was over. He returned to the theatres, and was working at the Booker T. Washington Theatre in St. Louis when a local cornet player named Charlie Creath talked him into joining Creath's band.

Lonnie had a successful job with Creath, working on the steamer *St. Paul* on the Mississippi River. He became a fine orchestra musician, and with his brother in St. Louis, he was happier than he had been. In 1922, he and Creath had a falling out and Lonnie had trouble findings jobs. He had to stop playing and take a job in a tire factory in Galesburg, Illinois; then he moved to East St. Louis in 1925, found a job in a steel foundry and got married. In the fall of 1925, the Booker T. Washington Theatre, where Creath had heard Lonnie play, had a blues contest. Lonnie entered and won it.

The OKeh representative in St. Louis, Jessie Stone, was very active in picking up talent for the company and pushing the records through his shop in south St. Louis. Within a few days after Lonnie had won his theatre contest, he did his first record for OKeh, "Mr. Johnson's Blues" and "Falling Rain Blues" on OK 8253. OKeh was still afraid of the guitar accompaniments; so a friend of Lonnie's, De Louise Searcy, played violin and John Arnold played piano. The record was released in January, and the company advertised that Lonnie would appear at an "OKeh Recording Artists Dance and Concert" at the Chicago Coliseum, February twenty-seventh. He was recorded again in the St. Louis studios during the last weeks of January and his brother, James, recorded with him. The records were actually confusing displays of versatility. De Searcy played the violin for the first side, while Lonnie played guitar; then the latter switched to piano for the second side. De Searcy dropped out for the next four sides while Lonnie's brother played piano; then Lonnie and his brother recorded a guitar duet with the improbable title of "Nile of Genago." Lonnie played violin and kazoo for the next side, with De Searcy playing piano and James playing banjo: then they finished with "Johnson's Trio Stomp." Lonnie and De Searcy played violins and James played the piano. The records were released with the instrumentation printed on the label, otherwise it would be very difficult to identify all the musicians.

Lonnie was not raised in the country-blues tradition, but he had adopted the style and sang the blues easily and naturally. He took theatre engagements during the spring, becoming more and more popular as the months passed. He recorded again in May and August, finishing the year's recording activity on August fourteenth with a guitar solo "To Do This You Gotta Know How," released with the "Nile of Genago" on OK 40695. His records were selling very well, and the OKeh advertisements printed his picture, playing either the guitar or violin, every three or four weeks. In the spring of 1927, he made his first records with added accompaniment. The striking sound of his guitar was very prominently recorded, and his new records sold even better than the St. Louis recordings of the year before. He was playing one of the new metal-front guitars, and it had a sweeter, more sustained tone than the usual instruments. The tone had a tendency to become unpleasantly "twangy" if the strings were played hard, but Lonnie only had trouble once, when he was recording later in the year with Duke Ellington's orchestra, and had to play louder than usual.

He decided to move into New York for a few months in the summer of 1927, and he and his wife, Mary, found an apartment in Harlem. He recorded at the New York studios throughout the month of August, doing several blues, and accompanying a new OKeh singer named Texas Alexander. Alexander was in his late forties, a country singer from outside of Leona, Texas, who still sang freely rhythmic field shouts and work songs. He was very difficult to follow, but he and Lonnie worked together for several days and between August eleventh and August seventeenth recorded nine blues, including the difficult "Levee Camp Moan Blues" and "Section Gang Blues," released together on OK 8498. Lonnie's accompaniments were among the handful of successful musical solutions to the difficult problem of staying in a rhythmic relationship to the singer. He played an almost entirely melodic background, in a simple rhythmic imitation of Alexander's deep voice. The recording was musically among the finest OKeh releases for the year.

The same day that Lonnie had done the first recordings with Alexander, he had recorded his own "Mean Old Bed Bug Blues," released with "Roaming Rambler Blues" on OK 8497 in September. It was one of his biggest hits, and he was in constant demand as a singer, guitarist and entertainer. He was thirty-eight years old, at the height of his success and musical abilities. In December, 1927, he was on four sides with Louis Armstrong's Hot Five, and recorded some of his most striking solos. He and Louis seemed to inspire each other, and two of the blues they recorded, "I'm Not Rough," on OK 8551, and "Savoy Blues," on OK 8535, are among the Hot Five's classic performances. For "I'm Not Rough," Lonnie played an insistent doubled rhythm, playing almost a drumming chord, and continued the rhythmic idea in his solo while Johnny St. Cyr, the group's banjo player, played the chords softly behind him. During Louis's vocal, Lonnie, with St. Cyr very much in the background, was the only accompaniment, and he played a rhythmic variation that emphasized the rough, shouted quality of Louis's hoarse singing. The group finally seemed to give way to Lonnie's rhythmic intensity, and as the record ended, they broke into a fierce double rhythm. As if to demonstrate his versatility, for the recording of "Savoy Blues" Lonnie didn't play until after a beautifully lyric solo by Armstrong and a gentle ensemble strain by the group. With St. Cyr playing a second guitar behind him, Lonnie answered Armstrong's lyricism with an almost songlike solo. His reputation as a jazz guitarist was secure.

Lonnie was on the road most of the winter. He recorded in San Antonio in March, 1928, doing five solo blues and accompanying Texas Alexander again. On April twenty-eighth there was a story in the Dallas papers:

> Lonnie Johnson, OKeh record artist, has closed a very successful three weeks engagement at the Ella B. Moore's Theatre. Mr. Johnson was booked for one week, but having proven so popular he was given an extension of two weeks. On the third and last week a blues contest was given with Lonnie Johnson, Mag-

gie Jones, Columbia artist, Texas Alexander, OKeh artist, and Lillían Glenn [sic] the new sensational Columbia artist. Miss Glenn won as she is a local favorite, with Lonnie Johnson giving a close second.

He was in New York again in the fall, and he and Baby Cox, a popular young cabaret singer, recorded with the already very successful Duke Ellington and his orchestra. To avoid contract difficulties, Ellington had the record released under the name, "Lonnie Johnson and his Harlem Footwarmers."

It was during these months that Lonnie recorded some of his finest blues—the muted, personal blues that failed to reach a large audience. The blues were similar to many of the city-blues songs that the women singers were recording, but he sang with the emotional depth of a country singer, accompanying himself with an individual style based on the rural traditions. The blues were fine poetic achievements:

I've been blue this blessed day, and a angry feeling
all night long.
I've been blue this blessed day, and an angry feeling
all night long.
I have lost my best job, and now my best woman done
gone.

I work in the rain and snow to put shoes on her feet.
I work in the rain and snow to put shoes on her feet.
Now she's got all my money and left me standing in
the street.

But that will be all right, sweet woman, your troubles
will come some day.
That will be all right, sweet woman, your troubles will
come some day.

There will be another good woman laying on the pil-
low where you once have laid.

His blues were filled with the sexual insecurity of the
young urban group that was buying his records, but his
earnest style seemed to give the overworked blues attitudes a new emotional vitality.

I'll tell you, sweet woman, like I told my used to be.
    (repeat)
Stay off these whoopee parties and you won't have no
    trouble with me.

I'm a hard working man and baby I don' mind trying.
    (repeat)
If I catch you making whoopee on me then you don't
    mind dying.

I don't want you for no prisoner, but stay home with
    me sometime.
    (repeat)
When you go out night and day you got a graveyard
    on your mind.

A man lets you women go out, you never know when
    to come back home.
    (repeat)
But when you go out and stay on me you can bet your
    time ain't long.

Didn't I tell you, not to stay out all night long.
    (repeat)
Give your size to the undertaker, 'cause hell is your
    brand-new home.

On November 16, 1928, a few weeks after a series
of tasteless records with Victoria Spivey, he recorded
a single record that was one of his finest achievements.

"Careless Love" and "When You Fall for Someone That's Not Your Own," on OK 8635. "Careless Love" in successively bitter verses blamed love for an entire life of troubles; finally turning on the personified image of desire with:

> . . . damn you, I'm going to shoot you,
> Shoot you four—five times.
> Then stand over you until you finish dying.

"When You Fall for Someone That's Not Your Own" was an almost despairing statement of the emotional pain of an adulterous relationship.

> Blues and trouble, they walk hand in hand.
> (repeat)
> But you never had no trouble, 'til you fall for the wife of another man.
>
> When it begins raining, you're looking out your window pane.
> (repeat)
> Thinking of that other man's wife, it's enough to drive you insane.
>
> You say blues and trouble have followed you all the days of your life.
> Blues and trouble—they have followed you all the days of your life.
> You never had no trouble, 'til you fall for another man's wife.
>
> A married woman is sweet, the sweetest woman ever was born.
> (repeat)
> Only thing wrong with her, every time she has to go back home.

He finally had another hit in the winter, when he and Spencer Williams covered the Tampa Red-Georgia Tom success "It's Tight Like That" on Vocalion. Lonnie and Spencer had joined the rush to record something as close to "It's Tight Like That" as the singer could come. They called their version "It Feels So Good." It wasn't any better than the original, but then it wasn't any worse either:

> Said the chicken when she ate the worm,
> It makes me wiggle when you start to squirm,
>     'Cause it feels so good.
>     Oh, it feels so good.
> I like good bait, because it feels so good.
>
> The funniest thing I ever seen
> Was a wampus cat with his eyes of green
>     Cryin', It feels so good,
>     Oh, Lord, it feels so good.
> Lord, I'll tell the world it feels so good.

There were more solo blues and accompaniments in 1929, and the first of his duets with Eddie Lang was released in January. Lang was a fine white guitarist, who recorded with Lonnie under the name Blind Willie Dunn. He was one of the few guitarists in Lonnie's class and they were very exciting together. Lang was the finer musician, and had probably more knowledge of the guitar's harmonic possibilities than any musician of his period, but Lonnie had an emotional sense and emotional intensity that shaded Lang's brilliance. Their duets were always marked with a careful respect for each other's abilities.

Many musicians in the 1920's used pseudonyms for

occasional recordings, just as Lang had done for his duets with Lonnie. Lonnie himself seems to have used the name George Jefferson for a series of recordings on Gennet in 1927. He was under exclusive contract to OKeh, and used the other name to protect both himself and Gennet.

As the record business found itself in trouble in 1930 and 1931, Lonnie began recording more and more blues like "I Got the Best Jelly Roll in Town," "Don't Wear It Out," or "Jelly Killed Old Sam." OKeh was drifting into bankruptcy. His last records for the company was released by Columbia Records in September, 1932. "Unselfish Love" and "My Love Don't Belong to You" on Co 14655D. OKeh had been a Columbia subsidiary since 1926, but there had been no use of the same artists on both labels until the business was nearly at a standstill. Two earlier records of Lonnie's had been released on the 14000 series under the name Jimmy Jordan. Lonnie joined Putney Dandridge's Orchestra and went to Cleveland. He stayed in Cleveland with Dandridge until 1937, doing occasional radio shows for stations WJAY and WHM. In 1937, he was offered a night-club job at the Club 3 Deuces in Chicago and he decided to take it, working in an upstairs room with the drummer, Baby Dodds.

In Chicago he began recording again, first for Decca, then for Bluebird. His first record more or less picked up where he had left off, "Man Killing Broad" on De 7445. His new records were even more popular than his old ones had been. After the 3 Deuces burned in 1940, he went to the Boulevard Lounge on E. 51st St. He was working with a string trio of his own, two guitars and a bass, and the group had a light, swinging sound, very much like the popular recording group, the Spirits of Rhythm, but with Lonnie's distinctive style. The group never recorded commercially, but private recordings made of the three, at the Lounge, caught the fine spirit of Lonnie's playing and singing.

In the years that had passed since his great recordings of the 'twenties, Lonnie had become more conventional in sound, and the Bluebird house accompaniments that were used on most of their records made him sound even less distinguished. He had the misfortune to be recording when blues were becoming a kind of "jump" music. "Jive" was about the latest fad and the blues were going along with it. His biggest hit was a thing called "He's a Jelly Roll Baker," released on Bluebird B9006 in 1942:

> She said Mr. Jelly Roll Baker, let me be your slave.
> When Gabriel blows his trumpet then I'll rise from
>     my grave.
> For some of your good jelly roll.
> Yes I love your jelly roll.
> It's good for the sick, yes,
> And it's good for the old. . . .

> She said Can I put an order in, for two weeks ahead.
> I'd rather have your jelly roll than my home cooked
>     bread.
> I love your jelly roll.
> I love your good jelly roll.
> It's just like Maxwell House Coffee,
> It's good two times in my soul.

Other records were about the same. Speaking of this period, Lonnie once remarked that he had copyrighted 148 songs, all with the same melody.

In 1945 or 1946, Lonnie began playing electrified guitar, and his distinctive tone was completely obliterated. He recorded with some success for the King Record Company in Cincinnati, but he was dropped by King in 1952, and his scattered records since 1952 have sold poorly. His great reputation carried him to England for a series of concerts in 1952, but he has been unsuccessful in adopting any of the stage styles that other blues singers have developed to interest an intellectual white audience. His name is almost unknown to the young colored audience that still occasionally buys blues records.

Lonnie is living in Cincinnati, not well, and doing very little musically. A close friend saw him on the streets of Chicago in 1958, a sick man, shabbily dressed. He tried to make an arrangement to meet Lonnie later in the day, but Lonnie was too ashamed to meet him and went back to Cincinnati. There is a chance that he may receive some of the attention that he deserves, but he is not a young man, and the opportunities for someone to break into the teen-age rock-and-roll craze that dominates the industry are very slight. For Lonnie it has been a long road, without much of an end.

# 6

## "... The Noisiest Damn Place in the World"

By the spring of 1927 the excitement over the country blues was beginning to interest the major companies in blues recording. The smaller companies had the best singers under contract; so Victor and Columbia at first were forced to do the best they could with the second-rate music that was left. Finally they both tried sending out field units to record the music where it was being played, in the rural South. They recorded hundreds of blues singers and they recorded the raucous, haphazard singing of the little dance bands or the Saturday-night shows in the country towns. The singing of these little "hamfat" bands never reached the artistic intensity of men like Blind Lemon or Lonnie Johnson, but it had an infectious exuberance, and it was just right for noisy political barbecues or farm auctions or Sunday picnics, with children and parents and grandparents dancing

86

beside a picnic table set with ham and potato salad and piled high with steaming sweet corn and sun-ripened tomatoes.

Victor was the first company to do extensive "field" recording, and their technicians set the pattern that was followed by most of the other companies. It was not field recording in the present-day sense. They carried enough equipment with them to set up sketchy but complete studios, and if there was any kind of equipment in the city they usually rented the local studios while they were recording. The engineers still remember some of the difficulties they had to contend with thirty years ago. They leased General Electric equipment for the field trips, as most of the other companies did, and used two Western Electric condenser microphones, but in New Orleans it was so hot and the humidity was so high that the microphones shorted out. They had to use old-fashioned carbon microphones, but the heat made them "sizzle"—hum while they were being used—so they had to pack the microphones in ice until they were ready to record. They used both microphones for most of their work, which was quite advanced for their day. The Victor engineers said that they were the only ones in the field using two microphones. ". . . the competition only used one microphone." The "competition," the Columbia engineers, confirmed this: ". . . we only used one microphone but the competition used two."

They often had considerable difficulty setting up a studio. In Dallas, on one trip, they tried renting a suite in a hotel, but the management wouldn't allow the colored artists in the building. They moved the equip-

ment into a church and when members of the congrega-
tion heard the kind of music they were recording, there
was a riot. The recording director had to hold off the
irate church members while the engineers rushed the
equipment out the back door and onto a truck. The next
day they tried a roller-skating rink, despite its booming
echo: ". . . it was the noisiest damn place in the
world." A fight broke out between some of the skating-
rink customers and the artists Victor was trying to record, and the engineers were backed up against the wall
by some drunken customers who were using knives.
They finally had to use a banquet hall. Even when they
had the studio set up, they sometimes had trouble getting the singers and musicians to the studios. At El Paso
there was trouble getting a Mexican orchestra through
immigration; so the engineers had to wait until their
musicians could wade across the Rio Grande outside of
town and change into some dry clothes. It was hard,
exasperating work. They had to record whenever they
could locate the artists, if it meant going until two in
the morning. Victor advanced them five thousand dollars for a year's recording expenses, with a five-thou-
sand-dollar letter of credit in case they got into trouble,
and they had to keep track of their own expenses, along
with their other worries.

They usually relied on local musicians to find their
singers, but they would make a test of anybody who
wandered in, no matter what kind of music he played
or how drunk he was. If they thought he could get
through three minutes of anything musical, they made
a test. If somebody happened to think about it he was
paid ten dollars for his time. If the director liked a man's

singing, he was usually signed to a year's contract, with an option to renew and a guarantee of eight sides. Sometimes the singers would get so excited the engineers would have to make them take their shoes off so the foot-tapping wouldn't ruin the record. For some of the men, they had to put pillows under their stockinged feet to keep the noise down. A few of the musicians were pretty careful about the length of the tunes, but usually, with a country group, it would take so many tests to get the time correct that the men burned themselves out, in spite of the large quantities of liquor that were usually kept around. In Memphis the engineers had a terrible time handling the jug instruments. The heavy vibration produced a very wide groove that was hard to master successfully. They finally had to put the jug on the dead side of a directional microphone so that it was often almost inaudible. The engineers never even listened to most of what they got. They just shipped it back to New York to let the office men try to decide what to do with the recordings.

The Victor field recordings were under the supervision of Ralph Peer, the man who had begun the race-recording industry with his Mamie Smith recordings for OKeh in 1919. When OKeh became a part of Columbia Records in 1926, Peer began working for Victor, handling their race series. In January, 1928, he and Victor set up the Southern Music Publishing Company to handle the copyrights for much of the company's music. The capital came half from Peer and half from Victor. Robert Gilmore, a young man in the Victor copyright office, was transferred to the new subsidiary and became one of Peer's assistants in the field recording. In

1927, when the field recording was becoming very important to Victor, Peer was thirty-five, with years of experience in the record industry.

Ralph Peer was one of the most interesting personalities in the record business in the 1920's. He had a genuine interest in the country music and he recorded everything, of both white and colored artists, that interested him. There was a flurry of intellectual interest in Negro musical styles in the mid 1920's, and Peer seemed to have been in the middle of the sudden enthusiasm. One of the few contemporary reviews of a blues record, in a literary journal, *Bookman,* July, 1928, mentioned his recording activities.

> Rabbit Brown, colored, sang to his guitar in the streets of New Orleans, and he rowed you out into Lake Pontchartrain for a fee and sang to you as he rowed. It is the pleasant occupation of Ralph S. Peer to go on expeditions throughout the South, looking for such as Rabbit and inducing them to sing their songs for Victor Records on the spot. You may hear Brown's song of the Titanic, secured by Peer, on Victor Record 35840, and you should do so, for his work has character:
>
> T'was on the ten of April, on a sunny afternoon
> The Titanic left South Hamilton, each as happy as
>     a bride and groom.
> No one thought of danger, or what their fate may be,
> Until a gruesome iceberg cost fifteen hundred per-
>     ished in the sea.
>
> It was early Monday morning, just about the break
>     of day.

Captain Smith called for help from the Carpathia and
it was many miles away.
Everyone was calm and silent, asked each other what
the trouble may be;
Not thinking that death was looking, there upon that
northern sea.

Nearer, my God, to thee, Nearer to thee
Nearer, my God, to thee, Nearer to thee,
Though like a wanderer, as the sun goes down,
Though will be over me . . . Just then the Titanic
went down.

The reviewer was a New Hampshire lawyer named
Abbe Niles, who had written the introduction for W. C.
Handy's book *Blues,* which had been published in 1926.
There was a sudden interest in the music of the rural
South and both Handy's book, with stunning decora-
tions by the South American artist Miguel Covarrubias,
and the poet Carl Sandburg's collection *The American
Songbag,* published in 1927, included dozens of blues
from country and city sources. There was much more
interest in background sources for the new blues and
jazz than the record companies realized, and the intel-
lectuals who were interested in the songs seemed to be
only vaguely aware of the rich hoard of rural material
that Peer was tapping. There were three scholarly collections, White, Scarborough and Odum, but they mentioned the extensive blues recordings of the city type,
without any discussion of the raw country material that
was being recorded. Peer was out to find blues that
would sell, but he was a man of exceptional taste and
discrimination, and he had a marked ability to bring

out warm personal performances from many of the singers. The finest body of ethnic music collected in the South was that collected by the commercial recording directors in the South in the late 1920's, and Ralph Peer was one of the best of them.

The Southern Music Corporation, of which Peer was the president, published very little of the material that was recorded. The copyright cost was only a dollar for unpublished manuscripts; so a staff copyist transcribed the melody, wrote the words with it, and sent off the rough sheets to Washington. The songs of the Carter Family or Jimmy Rogers, popular white folk singers that Peer was recording, were published in special songbooks and sold very well, but written music was of very little interest to the Southern colored singers. Peer was a tireless salesman for Victor and Southern music, taking popular recording artists on short trips with him around their parts of the country. They would play on the sidewalk outside music stores and when a crowd had gathered, Bob Gilmore would edge into the crowd, trying to sell phonograph records and sheet music.

Rabbit Brown, the singer who had been reviewed in the *Bookman* article, was only one of several fine blues singers that Peer recorded for the Victor lists. The Memphis singer, Frank Stokes, did a series of recordings that were much more individual and moving than the records he did for Paramount as one of the Beale Street Sheiks. There was a particularly good blues, "Shiny Town Blues," with Will Bast accompanying Stokes's heavy voice with his fine country fiddling. Luke Jordan, from western Virginia, recorded in the summer of 1927 and in the fall of 1929, and his first recording, "Church Bell Blues," on Vic 21076, sold fairly well. The song still turns up on modern rhythm and blues recordings. Occasionally Luke sold on the folk-music series and in December, 1927, Victor advertised his "Pick Poor Robin Clean."

> I picked his head,
> I picked his feet.
> I would have picked his body,
> But it wasn't fit to eat.
>
> Everybody knows some snappy version of this roving song of the gambler.

As more and more singers began to hear about the field recording units they began coming into the cities where the company was working. Both Ishman Bracey and Sleepy John Estes were recorded in Memphis; although neither of them were from Memphis. Bracey came up from the Mississippi delta with young Charlie McCoy playing mandolin accompaniment on most of his records. Estes came in from Brownsville, Tennessee, where he was working as a caller on the track gangs. A mandolin player named Yank Rachel came in with him. Even Blind Willie McTell, the Georgia singer, recorded for Peer. McTell was a brilliant, but elusive blues singer, with an almost indestructible quality about him. He recorded for almost everybody, using pseudonyms to keep out of contract troubles. He was "Blind Sammie" for Columbia, "Georgia Bill" for OKeh, "Blind Willie" for Vocalion and Bluebird, and "Barrelhouse Sammy— the country boy" on Atlantic. The Atlantic record, "Broke Down Engine Blues" and "Kill It, Kid" on

At 891, was one of the most perplexing records in the blues field. He simply walked into the Atlantic studios in 1949, auditioned and recorded without any reference to his remarkable past. Then he walked out and has been as elusive ever since.[1] He was singing in his same style, accompanying himself with his whining, biting twelve-string guitar playing, almost as though the twenty years had stood still for him. His blues were even more distinctive and savage, becoming blasphemous on "Broke Down Engine," one of the few instances of this kind of outcry on blues recordings. The recordings for Victor were McTell's finest work, and "Mama, Tain't Long 'Fo Day," "Three Women Blues," or "Statesboro Blues" were probably his best Victor sides. He seemed to be almost crying to himself, half singing, half chanting the irregular verses:

> Wake up, mama, turn your lamp down low.
> Wake up, mama, turn your lamp down low.
> Have you got the nerve to drive Papa McTell from your do'?
>
> My mother died and left me reckless, my daddy died and left me wild.
> Mother died and left me reckless, daddy died and left me wild.
> No, I'm not good lookin', but I'm some sweet woman's angel child.

[1] In 1940 John Lomax was in Atlanta, recording music for the Library of Congress archives, and he recorded seventeen selections by McTell, including a monologue, "Monologue On Life As Maker Of Records," on record 4072A2. Neither John or his son, Alan Lomax, who edited the material for release, liked McTell's strong singing and the material has not been made available.

Big 80 left Savannah, lord, and did not stop.
You ought to saw that colored fireman when he got
  that boiler hot.
You could reach over in the corner, mama, and hand
  me my traveling shoes.
You know by that I got them Statesboro Blues.

Sister got 'em, daddy got 'em
Brother got 'em, mam got 'em, I got 'em.
Woke up this morning, we had them Statesboro Blues
I looked over in the corner,
Grandma and grandpa had 'em too.

It was singers like McTell, Stokes, Jordan and
Rabbit Brown that Peer seemed most interested in; men
with a stylistic individuality and a literary sense to their
material. He seemed to try to avoid the endless blues
using the sexual clichés that were popular with the
Northern audiences. Richard "Rabbit" Brown was one
of the most interesting singers that Peer recorded. As
Abbe Niles had described in his review, Peer had found
Rabbit working out along Lake Pontchartrain, but he
was from James Alley, in a New Orleans neighborhood
known as "the battleground."

The alley—James Alley, Janes Alley, Jane Alley—
is a narrow street between Perdido and Gravier, just
behind the city jail. The prisoners can shout to anyone
turning into the alley, and if she's pretty enough they
usually do. The railroad tracks are just beyond the end
of the alley, and it is a poor, ramshackle neighborhood.
In the early days of New Orleans brass-band parading,
the section was called "the battleground" because the

gangs of boys that followed their favorite bands would meet at the boundaries and fight to see who would follow the music into disputed ground. Many of the buildings in the alley have been torn down in recent years, and the empty ground is used for parking. It is unpaved, muddy or dusty, depending on the weather. There are trees in front of one or two of the yards, but running feet have worn most of the grass away, and the few skimpy flowers in front of the houses struggle in listless halfheartedness with the shade, the dogs and the children.

There have always been children in James Alley, playing noisy games of ball against the thin wooden sides of the houses, or arguing shrilly among themselves. On hot summer afternoons they sit in the shade, giggling over little jokes and children's games. Old men still shuffle down the alley selling vegetables or peanuts and candy, singing over their wares, and people will come up to a stranger and ask if he wouldn't like to buy a four-foot alligator. The great New Orleans trumpet player, Louis Armstrong, grew up in James Alley, and in three or four of the houses women will show visitors, for a small fee, the room where Louis was born. The street sign says "Jane Alley," but New Orleans people call it James Alley or Janes Alley as often as they call it by the city's name.

Rabbit Brown came out of James Alley to sing in a New Orleans gaudy red-light district when he was still young. He was a short, brown-skinned man, always ready to sing any song that was requested, accompanying himself on an old guitar. He made a poor living, but

Cordially yours
Blind Blake

**BLIND BLAKE**

*Photo from John Steiner*

# Paramount
# Advertising
# Leaflets—1928

THE BEALE STREET SHEIKS
## Frank Stokes and Dan Sane
*Material from John Steiner*

BLIND LEMON JEFFERSON
AND PAPA CHARLIE JACKSON
*Material from John Steiner*

GUS CANNON
*Material from John Steiner*

## "We had something in those years then..."

GUS CANNON
Photograph taken in Memphis
about 1925.
*Photo from Gus Cannon*

Gus Cannon and Charlie
Burse recording for the author
December 5, 1956.
*Photo by S. B. Charters*

A VOCALION ADVERTISEMENT,
JUNE, 1928—FURRY LEWIS
*Material from
New York Public Library*

FURRY LEWIS, 1959
*Photo by S. B. Charters*

WILL SHADE playing
a homemade wash-
tub bass. *Photo by
S. B. Charters*

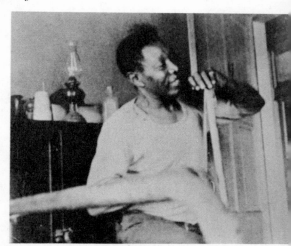

he had friends all over the city, and he was well known in the district.

The Southern red-light districts gave work to many singers of Brown's age. In the stately mansions where the jeweled madams and countesses entertained the city's sporting gentlemen with their refined young ladies, there were expensive mechanical pianos or "professors," who played requests or dance music. The dance halls used three- or four-piece dance orchestras, but the saloons let singers come in from the street and entertain customers for whatever they could make in tips. Sometimes a prosperous saloon would pay a favorite entertainer a little salary to come around, but usually they worked on tips. The singers didn't sing much blues, unless someone requested a song like "Memphis Blues." They sang anything. In New Orleans there were favorites in the district: "The Death of Ella Speed"; "Someone's in the Parlor, Honey, Better Come on Down Stairs"; or "If They Could See You Back at the Plantation What Would They Think of You Now?" Most of the South's red-light districts had their own songs about the loves and quarrels of the local people. Of all the songs only one has survived, the St. Louis favorite about Frankie Baker and her lover, Albert. It is known today as "Frankie and Johnny."

Rabbit Brown was popular around the district because he could sing all the songs, and he could "rhyme-up," little songs about customers in the saloons, using their names. He had a little song of his own that was liked because it expressed some of the wry attitudes of the men in the district toward their women:

> I'm not jealous, I'm not jealous,
> But I just don't like it, that's all.

Standing in the streets, singing to the loitering crowds that strolled through the district on warm summer evenings, the city musicians heard the country singers playing and singing, and the two learned from each other. After his years in the district, Brown could sing a country blues with intensity and conviction. The district was closed in 1917 and life was never easy for Brown again. In the uptown colored districts he was already considered a little old-fashioned. He could still entertain people with his little rhymes and songs, but some of the younger men used to ridicule his old-fashioned guitar style, and they'd chase him off a corner playing blues duets in the new style they were hearing on the first blues records. The years were poor, and Brown became bitter and antagonistic toward his old friends. In the spring of 1927, when he was in his late forties, the Victor field unit was in New Orleans to record Louis Dumaine's small jazz orchestra. In an improvised recording studio—there is some confusion as to whether it was in a garage or in a downtown office building—Rabbit Brown set in front of the microphone, playing his old guitar in his old style, and sang of his life and hard times, the poignant "James Alley Blues":

> "Times ain't now, nothing like they used to be.
>   (repeat)
> And I'm telling you all the truth, oh take it from me.

> "I done seen better days, but I ain't putting up with these.
>   (repeat)

Now I'd have a much better time but these girls now
they're so hard to please.

" 'Cause I was born in the country she thinks I'm easy
to rule.
(repeat)
She tried to hitch me to a wagon, she tried to drive
me like a mule.

"You know I buy the groceries, and I pay the rent.
(repeat)
She tried to make me wash her clothes, but I got
good common sense.

"I said if you don't want me why don't you tell me so.
(repeat)
Because I ain't like a man that ain't got nowhere to
go.

"I've been giving you sugar for sugar, let you get salt
for salt.
(repeat)
And if you can't get along with me, it's your own
fault.

"Now you want me to love you and you treat me mean.
(repeat)
You're my daily thought and my nightly dream.

"Sometimes I think that you're too sweet to die.
(repeat)
And another time I think you ought to be buried
alive."

Rabbit Brown never recorded again. He died poor and
alone in 1937.

# 7

## *Dr. Stokey, Dr. Benson, Dr. C. E. Hangerson . . .*

Since the days of West Dukes and Jim Turner, country fiddlers who had taken dance orchestras out of Memphis after the Civil War, the city had been a center for colored entertainment groups. Many of the tent minstrel shows made up in Memphis, and there were a large number of medicine shows traveling out of the city to Mississippi, Louisiana and northern Alabama. Some of the medicine shows were run by quacks of the worst type, but others were run by well-known "doctors" like Dr. Stokey, Dr. Benson, Dr. C. E. Hangerson, Dr. W. B. Milton and Dr. Willie Lewis, who traveled with small shows including the best country entertainment they could find. The shows played on a wagon, lit up with lanterns or a dangling electric bulb and usually included some banjo and guitar playing, a novelty band, singing, a buck dance, maybe a magic trick or two. There was

**100**

no subtlety in this kind of work. The entertainers sang loud, mugged ferociously, and relied on slapstick to get them through the show. When they were finished, the "doctor" would begin his sales pitch, trying to charm hard-earned money out of overall pockets and into his cashbox. The musicians hung around, helping him with the sales and passing out bottles. They were a hard living, independent bunch. They slept wherever they happened to be, with anybody handy; drinking, gambling, getting run out of the county for chasing the wrong married woman, or getting a royal treatment for singing a song that went over big. They didn't even play many small towns. They stayed out in the country, out at country stores or big farms where there were two or three hundred people to buy bottles of salves and syrup. It was lonely territory, and they were always welcome at least to try and entertain people.

The medicine-show idea has continued in the South until recent years, despite noisy protests over the contents of some of the medicines. As late as 1954, a caravan with a jazz band and some dancers was touring Mississippi and Alabama selling a patent medicine called Hadacol. In the 'twenties the singers and instrumentalists were still playing in the old country styles. The most popular were men like Jim Jackson, who knew hundreds of old songs; or Gus Cannon and his partner, Hosie Woods, singing old minstrel songs, or Furry Lewis, who sang the ballads, "Billy Lyons and Stock O' Lee," "Kassie Jones," and "John Henry." There were always novelty bands. The first man Gus Cannon saw playing a jug was Chappie Dennison, who was with a novelty band in Dr. Milton's show. Chappie was from

Nashville, and somewhere he'd learned to play a piece of water pipe like a trumpet. The singers were in and out of Memphis during the summer and fall months, when the crops were coming in and there was some money around. Many of the singers recorded in Memphis, but a few of the younger men, like Mississippi John Hurt, came to the Northern cities to record. Hurt was a brilliant guitarist and a singer with a fine sense of phrasing and emotional communication. His "Frankie," on OK 8560, "Louis Collins," on OK 8724, and his "Spike Driver Blues," on OK 8692, were deeply moving examples of the Mississippi blues style.

The Victor distributor in Memphis, O. K. Hauk, was able to sell records of the medicine-show singers, and he asked Ralph Peer to record as many of them as he could. The Victor distributors had a standard arrangement with the company to encourage local sales. If the distributor would agree to take five thousand copies of the record, just about enough to cover Victor's costs, the company would record almost anybody. The leader of the pit orchestra at the Palace Theatre, on Beale Street, was a popular young musician named Charlie Williamson, and he was scouting for Victor in Memphis. He missed Jim Jackson, who went to Chicago and recorded for Vocalion, but most of the other singers that Peer recorded for Victor were sent to him by Williamson. Jim Jackson had gone up to Chicago with Furry Lewis, the ballad singer, and both of them had recorded for Vocalion, but Vocalion failed to pick up Furry's optional contract in 1928 and Peer signed him with Victor. He was one of the most popular Memphis blues singers.

Furry was born in Greenwood, Mississippi, March 6, 1900, but his family came to Memphis in 1906 and he grew up in the city. His name was Walter, but other children in school started calling him "Furry," and the name stayed with him. He lost a leg in a railroad accident in Illinois, in 1917, and he learned to sing and play the guitar to make some sort of living. Furry traveled for years with the medicine shows, and he learned many guitar styles from other singers. He worked out a special accompaniment for most of his songs, using many of the Mississippi guitar styles. He even used the famous "Mississippi bottle neck" on several records. He broke the neck off a bottle, heated it in a fire so the broken edge would melt smooth; then he put it on the little finger of his left hand and slid it along the strings to play a melody.

Furry met Jim Jackson with the Dr. Willie Lewis show, working through Mississippi, selling "Jack Rabbit" salve. They played together in a small jug band, Jim Jackson or Will Shade playing guitar, and Gus Cannon playing banjo and jug. Furry and Jim usually sang together, and went over big with a blues of Jim's called "Goin' to Kansas City." It was Jim's biggest hit for Vocalion. They went up to Chicago in May, 1927, and auditioned for Vocalion, singing Jim's blues together; but the company decided to record them separately, and Furry came back to Memphis a few days later. He went up again in October and recorded six more sides, including the fine "Billy Lyons and Stock O' Lee" on Vocalion 1132 with "Good Looking Girl Blues"; then came back to Memphis and took a job as a helper in the city garage.

He was still at the garage when Peer got in touch with him the next August. He took an afternoon off from work, went home and changed his clothes, carried his guitar over to the studios in the McCall Building, and recorded until the engineers were ready to have dinner. He had never had an exciting voice, but he had changed the songs until he was almost talking his way through the verses, using subtle rhythmic emphasis to bring out emotions of his blues. With the carefully elaborate, busy guitar accompaniments, he sounded as though he was holding back in his singing and the records had a beautiful quality of restraint and understatement. Vocalion realized their mistake in losing him to Victor and recorded him again at studios in the Peabody Hotel in September, 1929. At the session he recorded one of the best versions of the ballad "John Henry," released on both sides of Vocalion 1474. He sang most of the well-known verses, but he also sang less familiar verses and brought new interest to a very overworked song:

> John Henry looked at the sun one day,
> The sun had done turned red.
> He looked back over his shoulder, lord,
> He seen his partner falling dead.
> > My partner's falling dead.
>
> Baby, where did you get your pretty little shoes?
> The dress you wear so fine?
> I got my shoes from the railroad man,
> My skirt from the striker in the mine, lord,
> My skirt from the striker in the mine.
>
> Baby, who's goin' to shoe your pretty little feet?
> Who's goin' to glove your hand?
> Who's goin' to kiss your rose-red cheeks?

When I'm in some long distant land,
When I'm in some long distant land?

My Mama's goin' to shoe my pretty little feet,
My sister's goin' to glove my hand.
My striker he's goin' to kiss my rose red cheeks,
When you're in your long distant land,
When you're in your long distant land.

John Henry had a little woman,
The dress she wore was red.
Started down the track,
And she never did look back.
I'm going where John Henry fell dead,
I'm going where John Henry fell dead.

One of Furry's favorite blues was a fine variation of the separate woman for each day theme:

My Monday woman lives on Beale and Main,
My Tuesday woman brings me pocket change.
My Monday woman lives on Beale and Main,
My Tuesday woman brings me pocket change.

My Wednesday woman brings me daily news,
My Thursday woman buys me socks and shoes.
My Wednesday woman brings me daily news,
My Thursday woman buys me socks and shoes.

Lord, my Friday woman put me on the shelf,
My Saturday woman give me the devil, she catch me
hell.
My Friday woman, she put me on the shelf,
My Saturday woman give me the devil, she catch me
hell.

Furry has not recorded commercially since the depression finished the market for country blues. Victor recorded singers for its Bluebird subsidiary, and Vocalion became one of the most active companies recording blues in the 'thirties, but Furry's quiet singing was out of style. He still works for the city of Memphis, wearing a wooden leg that makes it difficult to remember that he's crippled. He plays and sings even better than he did thirty years ago, singing in the same beautifully halting country style, but he doesn't own a guitar, and he moves from one furnished room to another. The few people he bothers to tell about his days as a successful recording artist don't really believe him. He sits on his bed in the evenings, a small gray-haired man, reading or writing letters while the children of the house play around him, laughing and singing. They call him "MISTER Furry," and he laughs with them.

Along with the singers like Furry and the medicine-show entertainers, Charlie Williamson managed to get Peer to record his Palace Theatre Orchestra. The records are among the most colorful sounding items on the Victor lists, "Memphis Scrontch" and "Bear Wallow" on Vi 20555 and "Scandinavian Stomp" and "Midnight Frolic Rag" on Vi 21410, by "Charlie Williamson's Beale Street Frolics Orchestra," but they were just as colorfully unsuccessful. Of all the people that Charlie Williamson brought to Victor, the most important were the two instrumental groups, the Memphis Jug Band and Cannon's Jug Stompers. He introduced Peer to an exciting country-music style and to the most distinctive musical sound in the city of Memphis, the sound of the jug bands.

# 8

## The Memphis Jug Bands

The Mississippi is muddy at Memphis. Sand bars and low mudbanks let the river sprawl against them on either side. Across the bridge from Memphis the country is low and wet, the roads up on banks to keep them out of the mud. On the Memphis side, a grass-covered levee holds the river off, turning it from the city. Most of Memphis is up on the bluffs, but there are warehouses and railroad sidings going to the wharves along the water. A small park downstream is marked with a stone monument to a Negro who took his small boat into the river's heavy current to save the survivors of a ship disaster. There are a few trees and a stretch of river grass.

Beale Street runs up from the river, crosses Main Street at the top of the bluff, goes downhill two or three blocks to a square called W. C. Handy Park; then gradually rises toward the hilly parts of the city. It is the heart of the colored business district, lined with furniture stores, markets, beauty parlors, pawnshops, insurance offices and barrooms. Along the street past the business district are crumbling mansions, once the homes of Memphis's wealthier families, but now taken over by schools and churches. The men of the Memphis jug bands came from the crowded neighborhoods around Beale Street.

The first of the bands, the Memphis Jug Band, was organized by a man named Will Shade and his wife, Jennie Mae Clayton Shade, who sang with the band. Shade was born in Memphis, February 5, 1898, and he grew up running with the other boys on Beale Street. He was, and still is, always called "Son," because he was raised by his grandmother, Annie Brimmer, and her friends called him "Son Brimmer." He started playing the guitar when he was still in his teens, following a singer named "Te-Wee" Blackman around the streets, watching his fingers when he played. The first song Son learned was "Newport News," a blues about the embarkation of the troops for France from Newport News, Virginia. Tee-Wee showed him how to play the blues in A and E and Son decided he didn't need to learn any more, but after he tried to learn new keys himself he had to go back to Tee-Wee and get more lessons. After four or five years of serenading along Beale Street, he started going into the country with the medicine shows in the summer and fall.

When Son came in from a show in 1926, he and Jennie started playing and singing in the bars along Beale Street. One night a man named "Roundhouse" came up to them and asked if he could join their band. Son said it was all right and Roundhouse started blowing on a bottle. Everybody at the bar started shouting, "Jug Band! Jug Band!" and they went along the street from bar to bar shouting and laughing. The next day Son decided to get up a band ". . . something like the boys in Louisville." He was talking about one of the first jug bands to record, Clifford Haye's fine Dixie Jug Blowers. He got a friend, Ben Ramey, to play kazoo, and another, Charlie Polk, to play jug. (The jug isn't actually played as a musical instrument. The player makes a buzzing sound with his lips and holds the jug up close to his mouth. The jug acts as a resonator for the sound.) They were both young, about Son's age, with more enthusiasm than experience. Son played harmonica or guitar; so they needed a second guitar player. They talked an older, more experienced musician, Will Weldon, into joining them, and they started playing along the street. Charlie Williamson, at the Palace, heard them and got them an audition with Ralph Peer. Peer came down to the theatre on Saturday morning and they played for him on the stage. He liked them and told them to have four blues ready for him when he got back from a recording trip to New Orleans.

On February 24, 1927, they made their first recordings for Victor. They had been up all night rehearsing, but after a little to drink, Peer got them relaxed enough to play. In the middle of their second song, Williamson came into the studio to hear how they were doing. Son remembers that Charlie was always a fancy dresser and that morning he had on a gray suit, gray spats, a green paisley waistcoat and a white derby. Charlie strolled in, took off his derby and put it down on the piano. There was a hollow bang when he put it down and Son was sure the test was ruined. He looked at the control-room window and Peer was standing there laughing at the whole scene. Victor issued "Stingy Woman Blues" anyway, with the incidental noise by Charlie William-son.

Victor brought them up to Chicago to record again in June, and they added a tall, thin harmonica player named "Shakey Walter" for the trip. They recorded on the ninth of June; then they had an offer from the Grand Central Theatre in Chicago to appear with the Butterbeans and Susie review. They decided to do a jungle act with everybody in jungle costumes and "Shakey Walter" holding a large rattlesnake. They got the snake and pulled its fangs, but when they were having the dress rehearsal the snake got loose and started for a rat hole in the wall of the auditorium where they were rehearsing. Shakey caught it behind the neck and they finally got it back into its box, but they decided that they'd better not feed it much so it wouldn't have the strength to wiggle. They opened at the Grand on Monday, June 20, 1927, wearing their grass skirts and playing their guitars. Shakey and a girl from the chorus took turns holding the snake and sing-ing. Son sang "Newport Blues" and they played some instrumental numbers and the audience seemed to like it very much. Ma Rainey heard about the act and booked them into Gary, Indiana, for her show the next week.

At Gary the act came to a disastrous close. One of Ma's chorus girls was from the country and she felt sorry for the snake because nobody was feeding it. She gave it some food without bothering to tell anybody.

In the middle of the show the revived snake began inching out of the hand of the little chorus girl who was dancing with it. It finally got its head free enough to turn around and nip her. It didn't have any fangs, but it had small teeth, and she screamed and let go. The snake immediately started for the footlights, since everybody was on stage, and the theatre panicked. The first ten rows of the audience climbed over the back of the seats, the orchestra scrambled under the stage, and Ma, fat as she was, jumped on top of the grand piano. Shakey made a dive for the snake and got it just as it was going into the orchestra pit. He scrambled to his feet, waving the snake, pretending to talk to it in a nonsense dialect. He started to dance around the stage with it and Son finally came to enough to start playing. After a moment of hesitation the audience gingerly started back to the seats and finally decided it was all part of the act. They got a rousing ovation. From Ma, herself, they got considerably less than an ovation. "If you bring that ——— snake on this stage again I'll have every one of you put in jail." Without the snake their act wasn't very exciting, and they went back to Memphis.

The Memphis papers ran a picture of the "Memphis Jug Band," when the first records came out. They were all young and a little wide-eyed for the picture, but the records sold very well. They got an Atlanta trip the next spring, and recorded again for Victor. The recordings were long blues, with occasional instrumental interludes, still rather tentative. One night in February, 1928, Son was walking along Beale Street, stopping to say hello to friends, and dropping in most of the bars to keep warm. There was another recording session scheduled with Victor the next morning, back in the studios in the McCall Building. In one of the barrooms, Yardbird's, a man was entertaining in the back room. He played a four-string tenor guitar, using the swinging rhythms of country dances, rather than the blues rhythms that the six-string guitar players like Son used. He was short and thin, dressed in loud clothes, laughing as he sang. His name was Charlie Burse, a country musician from Decatur, Alabama.

Son liked his playing and his singing and he asked Burse if he wanted to record the next morning. Burse was willing; so Son took him home and they rehearsed all night, while Jennie slept in the other room. Burse gave the band an excitement and style that it had never had before. His laughter on the shouted vocal duets he and Shade did became one of the band's trade-marks. They stayed together for the rest of the band's recording activity, making a tour of Chicago, and recording hundreds of songs for several record companies. Their music and their blues compositions had a raucous quality and a rich vein of country humor:

> I know they're going to write to me
> When they get across the sea,
> Every chance,
> When that Washington lands in France
>
> (how you say it—oh, sugar baby)
>
> Now mama, don't you weep and moan
> Uncle Sam's got your man and gone,
> Now he's doing the lindyberg across the sea.
>
> Now mama how can it be,
> You went way across that sea,
> Just to keep from doing that lindyberg with me.

(oh, babe, I done told you)

When I got my uniform on
I'll be living sure as you're born
Then I'll do that lindyberg across the sea.

She asked me for a bottle of beerola
I said mama let me play it on your victrola
Then I'll do that lindyberg with you.

(how you say it—oh, sugar baby)

I asked her for a piece of banana
She said could I play the blues on your piano
Then I'll do that lindyberg for you.

This started out as a tribute to Captain Charles A. Lindberg, but before the singing was over there had been introduced parts of the old "Newport News Blues" and some country sexual imagery. Both Son and Burse insist that doing the lindyberg only refers to the dance, the Lindberg Hop, but the jug player, Jab Jones, sang the words and it doesn't sound as though they remembered to tell Jab.

They were a rough, noisy group, but there was an intense sadness in some of the slower blues. Son sang the moving "I Can't Stand It" in 1929, on Vic V38551:

> What you going to do, Mama,
> When your troubles get like mine.
> Take a mouthful of sugar
> And drink a bottle of turpentine.
> I can't stand it.
> I can't stand it.
> Drop down, Mama,
> Sweet as the showers of rain.

One of their finest recordings was the old train blues, K. C. Moan, on Vic V38558:

I thought I heard that K.C. when she moaned,
I thought I heard that K.C. when she moaned,
I thought I heard that K.C. when she moaned,
She moaned like my woman's on board.

When I get back on that K.C. road,
When I get back on that K.C. road,
When I get back on that K.C. road,
I'm going to love my baby like she's never been loved
before.

Victor put Son on a royalty advance basis, paying him twenty-five dollars a week for nearly four years. His job was to arrange the sessions, write the tunes, and rehearse the Memphis Jug Band. He worked hard, and the number of records they made is impressive. For an actual recording they were paid fifty dollars a side, and the money was split up among the men on the session. Son's composer's royalties were as high as six cents a record if he had composed both songs, and the royalties were even higher on Canadian or European sales. Son had more money than he really knew what to do with. Peer talked him into investing in the Victor Company, helping him buy some common stock, and Son and Jennie Mae bought a house in Memphis, but they still were living high.

In their four years with Victor, the men with Son recorded over seventy songs, and they did other things besides the jug-band work. Son and a piano player named "Hatchet" accompanied a singer named Kaiser Clifton for some recording; the entire band accompanied Hattie Hart on her recordings, and Son accompanied the Memphis Sanctified Singers for recordings playing the guitar and harmonica.

Son remembered that when the singers got warmed up they wouldn't stop in time, and the recording director, an assistant of Peer's named Watkins, gave up on them. After they had gone past time on the tenth try he threw his stop watch across the room. It smashed on a chair with enough noise to make them stop, just in time to save the take. After that the session went without any trouble. Peer would usually write Son about two months in advance of a recording date, giving him time to rehearse the band. They'd go over to Son's house and work all day on a tune, singing it over ten and fifteen times, until they had it right. Jennie would write down the words and when they had timed it, Son would write his "ok" on the words, put the title on the top and his name on the bottom, so that Peer's Southern Music Corporation could copyright it. He is very proud of the fact that he always came within a few seconds of the three-minute deadline. At a later session, for Champion in 1932, he was fifteen seconds short, but when he went to apologize, they looked surprised and told him not to worry.

The Memphis Jug Band was together for almost seven years and nearly a dozen musicians recorded with Son at one session or another. He got his old guitar teacher, Tee-Wee Blackman, for one recording, "K. C. Moan." He used the piano player and entertainer of the "Steamboat Bill from Louisville" show, Charlie "Bozo" Nickerson. Bozo even got a jug-band date of his own, and he and Milton Robie, violin, and Hambone Lewis, jug, both of them out of the Memphis Jug Band, recorded for Brunswick in the Memphis City Auditorium in March, 1930. But it didn't matter who the others were, the heart of the Memphis Jug Band was the musicianship and the enthusiasm of Son and Charlie Burse. They drank hard together, played hard together, and created a new musical style.

Peer had started a rush to record jug bands in Memphis. There weren't any others, but the companies that followed him South had no difficulty talking other medicine-show men into organizing little "hamfat" bands. An entertainer named Jed Davenport, who played half a dozen instruments, working the tent shows with Dub Jenkins and Al Jackson, was in town long enough to record for Vocalion with his "Beale Street Jug Band," and a blues singer for Perfect, Jack Kelly, recorded with his "South Memphis Jug Band." Peer himself wanted to get more of the music, and in January, 1928, began recording probably the finest of the Memphis Jug Bands, Cannon's Jug Stompers.

The Jug Stompers were led by a banjo player and jug player named Gus Cannon who had been playing in the medicine shows for years. He was older than Shade, from the Mississippi hill country. He was born in Red Banks, Mississippi, on September 12, 1883, and grew up on a poor farm, working from the time he was a small boy. He loved music and wanted to learn how to play the banjo, so he made himself one out of a bread pan that his mother gave him and a guitar neck. He put the guitar neck through holes in the side of the dough pan, then covered the pan with a raccoon skin, scraped thin. A lot of country boys made their own banjos this way. The only unsatisfactory aspect was that there were no elaborate drumhead arrangements, with bolts and screws, to keep the skin head tight in damp weather. Cannon always traveled with his pockets full of crumpled newspaper, and before he was going to play he would make a fire with the paper and hold the banjo over the heat until the head was tight enough to play.

When Cannon was a boy, the blues were still just a part of the work songs or field cries, and the music he learned was that of the old dance songs and reels. The first song he learned was the little dance tune, "Old John Booker, You Call That Gone," and he "strummed" it on the banjo. That is, played with a syncopated finger-picking, down-stroking, and thumb-picking style that is similar to the older banjo frailing style. Then he followed around after one of the men who could really play, Bud Jackson, from Alabama, and he learned to finger-pick a little jig in 6/8 time. Cannon laughed. "When I had them two songs down, you couldn't teach me nothing, 'cause I knew it *all*." He kept playing, got himself a real banjo, and when he was fifteen, he was working along the delta, chopping cotton and playing for parties and dances.

About 1901, when he was seventeen or eighteen, he was in Belzoni, Mississippi, a small town between Yazoo City and Clarksdale. Some people came to his cabin and asked him if he wanted to make a record. He didn't even know what they meant. They told him to bring his banjo and they took him into town where a man had a cylinder recording machine. After getting over his nervousness, Gus played a dance song, singing into the crude metal horn. He remembered the picture of the dog looking into the horn, and he thinks it was somebody from the old Victor recording company. He was paid for playing and went back to his cabin, still wildly excited at having heard himself play. The early catalogs of Victor, Columbia and the Berliner gramophone companies do not list anything specifically as by Cannon, but there are cylindrical recordings of banjo songs and dances one of which could be his cylinder. He may have been recorded by a pioneer field collector whose recordings have been lost, but if the material should ever be found, it would be a priceless collection of Negro country music.

Cannon stayed with cotton farming and worked in the delta for the next eleven or twelve years. In 1913 he came up to Memphis for the first time, and spent days down along the river watching the stevedores sweating over their loads. He got a little job so that he could stay in town, and he tried to take some banjo lessons from Professor W. C. Handy. After a few hours they both gave up. Handy couldn't understand any of the country music Cannon was playing and Gus couldn't understand any of the formal music that Handy was trying to show him.

He finally got a poor piece of land out on the Macon Road and "made a cotton crop," but he couldn't find himself any better land to work. He went across the river into Arkansas and started farming outside of Chatfield. The next summer he tried farming outside of Cairo, Illinois, at the junction of the Mississippi and the Ohio, but when the winter came, he went back into Tennessee. In the summer of 1916, he worked some land outside of Ripley, Tennessee, and when he wasn't busy on the farm he was playing in a little country band that worked for Saturday-night dances in Ripley. He

played his banjo; a boy named Noah Lewis, the harmonica; and another boy, Ashley Thompson, the guitar.
They played together until they could produce almost
any country-dance tune anybody wanted to hear. Cannon liked the country around Ripley, but he couldn't
make much money; so in 1918 he came into Memphis
and got a job as a plumber's helper. He still played
dances at Ripley, going up for weekends. By this time
he was working regularly with the medicine shows that
went out every year in the summer and fall. He toured
the South for years, working with Dr. Stokey, Dr. Benson, Dr. C. E. Hangerson and Dr. E. B. Milton. He had
his own specialty: he would start playing "Old Dog
Blue," then he would suddenly swing the head of the
banjo out over the heads of the people standing by the
wagon. He was still holding it with his left hand, and
as the banjo swung back he would change the chord
with his left hand and pick the strings with his right;
then swing it out again. He would finish playing the
song with the banjo swaying wildly in front of him.
People watching him were completely taken by surprise
and he usually got a big hand. It took him weeks to
learn how to do it. He put a mattress down on the
floor of his house in Memphis, so the banjo wouldn't
get too badly damaged when he dropped it.

Gus usually worked the shows with a friend named
Hosie Woods. For years they met at the first of the
season, did a little rehearsing; then went out with the
first show that wanted to use them. Hosie was about
Cannon's age, from Stanton, Tennessee. He played a
little of everything, but was best on the guitar, violin,
or cornet. He was a fine singer and kazoo player, and he

and Cannon did all the minstrel-style duets that were still popular with the country crowds. After Cannon saw Chappie Dennison playing on his piece of pipe, they decided to get a "jug" themselves, and they added a third man who blew into a railroad coal-oil can. The medicine shows passed each other in their wanderings, and any new acts or any new comic ideas were soon used by everybody around. If the audience had seen an act the week before and liked it, they usually told the men about it, shouting and calling. Cannon's coal-oil jug band was a big success, but the man blowing the coil-oil can blew so hard the bottom of the can kept bulging out and he finally split the seams open. Gus finally had a jug made for himself out of sheet metal, with a harness that went around his neck and held the jug up so he could blow into it and play the banjo at the same time. Gus and Hosie Woods played together off and on for over twenty years, singing their old-fashioned songs and accompanying themselves with a rushing, raucous country jug band. Gus would drift back into Memphis with a new box-back tailored suit, patent-leather button shoes and a gold watch chain hanging in front of his lapel.

Son Brimmer heard Gus serenading on Beale Street and got him to go up to Chicago and try the studios there. Gus went up with Jim Jackson and Furry Lewis in October, 1927. Mayo Williams liked his playing, but he couldn't use him by himself; so he sent him over to the Paramount studios. Paramount auditioned him, brought in Blind Blake and told him to work something out with Cannon that they could record. The two of them went to Blake's apartment and started rehearsing. They took three or four days.

> We drank so much whiskey! I'm telling you we drank more whiskey than a shop! And that boy would take me out with him at night and get me so turned around I'd be lost if I left his side. He could see more with his blind eyes than I with my two good ones.

The first week in November they finally got to the studio and recorded seven sides for Paramount, including Gus's favorite banjo solo, "Madison Street Rag." Paramount issued six of the duets as "Banjo Joe with guitar accompaniment by Blind Blake." "Banjo Joe a 'wiz . . . good all the way . . . Banjo Joe is a winner." The odd blues, the fourth song they recorded, was one of Blind Blake's songs, "He's in the Jailhouse Now"; so it was issued with another of his sides with his name on both titles.

When Gus got back to Memphis, Charlie Williamson called him and told him that Victor was going to be down in January, and they wanted him to get a little jug band together. The Memphis Jug Band was selling very well, and they wanted to get something like it if they could. Gus and his wife had a house at 1331 S. Hyde Park, just outside of Memphis; so they drove up to Ripley in January, picked up Noah Lewis and Ashley Thompson and brought them back to the house. They rehearsed some of their old songs that night, then recorded the next morning. Ashley Thompson sang "Minglewood Blues," on Victor 21267, and "Big Railroad Blues," Victor 21351. Cannon sang "Springdale Blues," on the other side of Ashley's "Big Railroad Blues," and talked and played his way through a hilarious "Madison Street Rag" on the other side of "Minglewood." When he listened to the record years later, he insisted, ". . . that's just how it was."

> The first time I was in Memphis, with Ten with the C, I was walking up Main Street. I met an old friend of mine. He said, "Hello, Joe," I said, "Hello." He said, "What's that you got there in that suitcase?" I said, "That's a banjo." He said, "Can you play the 'Madison Street Rag'? I said, "No, man, I don't know nothing about the 'Madison Street Rag.'" He said, "Supposin' I whistle it for you. . . ."

As the record ended, Gus was playing a furious version of "Madison Street Rag."

When they finished recording, they bought a gallon of corn whiskey, went off to some cabins south of town and drank until they passed out. They woke up the next morning lying on a wooden porch, their clothes covered with dust, and their instruments and cases all around them.

The Jug Stompers' recordings had the strong country-dance beat of the old "hamfat" bands, with a deep blues feeling. They brought the jug-band sound to a complete fullness, and their first records had an assurance that the less experienced Memphis Jug Band never quite achieved. They brought their own rhythms to the blues. The banjo couldn't sustain a tone as long as a guitar; so they played the blues accompaniments in a rushing 4/8 rhythm, instead of the slower 4/4. Cannon played with an alternate stroke on a middle string with his first finger; then a stroke on the two outside strings with his thumb and second finger. He was the only Negro five-string banjo player to record with a country group, so it is impossible to compare his style with other colored banjo players; but recordings by white groups made about the same time used a similar banjo picking for the slower tempos.

As much as Cannon liked their first records, he wasn't satisfied with Ashley Thompson's playing. Ashley didn't play a strong enough bass line for him. When Victor got in touch with Gus about recording the next summer, he was out on a show with a friend of his named Elijah Avery, a six-string banjo player from Hernando, Mississippi. Elijah lived around the corner from him in Hyde Park, and they'd known each other for years. For the recordings, Gus used Elijah, playing a six-string banjo, and he sent for Noah Lewis again. They recorded September 5, September 9, and September 20, 1928, doing all the recording at the studio in the McCall Building. Avery's strong banjo was more to Gus's liking, and one of the sides, "Feather Bed," Vi V38515, made at the second session, was one of the best records the Jug Stompers ever made. Cannon sang a long, impassioned vocal about his troubles in Memphis during the war, using the melody of an old country-dance tune, "Lost John," for the chorus. "Lost John" is a harmonica tune, and Noah played it with fierce exuberance.

Hosie Woods got into town about the middle of September, and Cannon managed to get him in on the last session. Hosie played kazoo and they tried a riotous

instrumental version of "Bugle Call Rag," with Gus
playing the bugle calls on the jug. There was no recording in the spring, so after they'd come in from their
medicine show the next summer, Hosie and Gus decided to try the companies in Chicago. Brunswick
picked them up, and they did two sides, "Last Chance
Blues" and "Fourth and Beale," Brunswick 7138, as
"Cannon and Woods—The Beale Street Boys." When
they got back to Memphis, Ralph Peer was in town,
looking for them to do some recording for Victor. They
got Noah Lewis and recorded October 1, and 3, 1929.
Noah sang a beautiful slow blues, "Goin' to Germany,"
on Vi V38585, but most of the songs recorded were
from the material that Hosie and Gus used on the medicine shows. They had such a good time singing together
that Gus didn't even remember that Noah had showed
up. Gus had to listen to the records. "I believe that boy
*is* on there after all."

The best of the songs they recorded were their old
favorites, "Whoa! Mule Get Up in The Alley," Vi
V38611, and "Walk Right In," on the other side. They
had been singing the duet "Walk Right In" so long
they had just about forgotten what it meant, and Cannon is still confused about it.

> Walk right in, sit right down,
> And Daddy let your mind roll on.
> Hey, walk right in, stay a little while,
> But Daddy you can't stay too long.
>     'Cause everybody's talkin' 'bout a two-way woman,
>     See, you don't want to lose your mind.
> Hey, walk right in and sit right down,
> And Daddy let your mind roll on.

Someone in the studio was shouting encouragement, probably Sleepy John Estes, who had to come back to the studio to record the next morning.

With the market for race records dwindling, Victor began doing less recording in Memphis. Peer returned in May, 1930, to record Son's group, the Memphis Jug Band, but he skipped the Jug Stompers. In November, 1930, he recorded in Memphis for the last time. The old studio in the McCall Building had closed up and they had to use a banquet room at the Peabody Hotel. Peer was interested in selling new names; so recordings by the Memphis Jug Band were issued as either by the "Memphis Sheiks" or the "Carolina Peanut Boys." For the first time there was a mixing of the two bands. The Jug Stompers were recorded on the twenty-fourth, and Noah happened to be in the studio two days later, when the Memphis Jug Band was recording. He made two harmonica solos; then a guitar player, a mandolin player and a jug player, probably Son, Vol Stevens and Bozo Nickerson, accompanied him for two other blues that were issued as "Noah Lewis and his Jug Band." On the twenty-eighth of November, Peer had the last recording sessions with the Memphis jug bands. Noah Lewis and his Jug Band, Cannon's Jug Stompers and the Carolina Peanut Boys made their last records for Victor. Peer regretfully settled the Victor account with Son and said goodbye to all of them as they left the studio.

Cannon had his job as a plumber's helper, so he worked as best he could around Memphis until the shows went out in the summer. He was forty-seven, and the recording had been only a small part of his musical life. For Son and Burse, younger men without any kind of a job, the recording had been very important, and they tried to keep some kind of a band going. They got Jab Jones to play piano and added a drummer to modernize the band; then they went up to Chicago. They got a recording date with Champion in July, 1932, and did twelve fine sides, but Champion was in financial trouble. They kept touring, playing as a novelty band at dances and night clubs, but the depression was making it harder and harder to survive. In November, 1934, they did a large group of recordings for OKeh, using Charlie Burse's younger brother, Robert, on washboard, but despite the success of some of the sides—"Tear It Down, Bed Slats and All" or "Take Your Fingers Off It" or "Boodie Bum Bum"—the Memphis Jug Band never recorded again.

Son had managed to buy nearly three thousand dollars' worth of Victor stock with his royalties, but he had to sell it at a fraction of its face value. He and Jennie finally had to give up their house, and they began moving from one furnished apartment to another. He had been one of the most conscientious men who had ever recorded for Victor Records, but he wasn't much suited for anything else. Burse got a job as a house painter and went into business for himself during the war. In 1939, he was able to land a contract with Vocalion, recording fourteen sides with a band of his own called "Charlie Burse and his Memphis Mudcats," but they weren't successful enough for Vocalion to renew the contract.

Son and Charlie often got little jobs outside of

Memphis, still going on their reputation from the Victor and OKeh days. In 1940, they had a job working as a novelty band at a dance at Natchez, Mississippi. The young, popular Chicago band leader, Walter Barnes, was bringing down his large swing band, and the dance was to be the biggest event of the year for Natchez. Son and Charlie; a drummer, Otto Gilmore; and a piano player, Robert Lee Lesters, drove down from Memphis, but they had a flat tire, and had to stop to get it fixed. They were nearly three hours late getting to Natchez. As they approached the dance hall, they could see a dull glow in the sky and began to hear the sounds of screams. When they got there, the hall was enveloped in flames, the terrified crowd trying to jam through the single narrow exit at the end of the hall. Son and the others stood watching, horrified, as two hundred people burned to death. Walter Barnes and his band were playing "Dixie," trying to calm the crowd, when the roof fell in on them.

In the winter of 1956, Son was working irregularly in a tire-recapping plant a few blocks off Beale Street. He was drinking, but he kept his job because the owner of the business had liked his old records. He and Jennie had a small, poor room in an unpainted building on Mulberry Street. An old booking agent had known where to find him. "You interested in those old jug bands? They're still playing." Son was happy to talk with someone who knew about his old records, and he had Burse's address. He hadn't seen Gus Cannon for nearly a year, but he knew that he was still living somewhere in the southern part of the city. He said that

Noah Lewis had been stabbed to death by his wife in the late 1930's.

That evening, Charlie Burse was sitting watching television with his wife, but he began talking about his "new" jug band the moment he realized that someone had come to talk with him about music. He even had a studio test the band had made of a song he wanted to record the summer before. Son was playing washtub bass with the band, a heavy rhythm and blues styled group, for the recording. Burse said he'd seen Cannon a few weeks before and that he was doing yard work for a room and meals at a private home on South Park Avenue. He said that he would go over to Son's in the morning and they'd try to find him. In the morning all three were there. A friend had seen Cannon going into a laundry and told him Son was looking for him. Cannon was a tall, straight, brown-skinned man, wearing gold-rimmed glasses, talking excitedly with the others.

After a few minutes of talking over old times, they wanted to record together; so they split up what little money there was for recording, about twelve dollars, and Cannon and Burse went to Beale Street to buy some whiskey and get Son a harmonica. They came back with a cheap American harmonica; Son tried it and said it wasn't good enough. After a long argument they finally went back to get him a genuine "Marine Band." They recorded until it was too dark to see the instruments. At first they were tight and nervous, but Son, despite quite a bit of wine, began to pull the group together, just as he must have done at many recording sessions thirty years before.

It was exciting to feel his influence on these men,

who in the world outside of the dingy, cold room were more successful than he had been. It was not his musicianship—he was a limited musician. It was his earnest, deep sincerity. He had never been a great harmonica player and he hadn't had a harmonica in twenty years, but he began playing with fierce determination, sitting in a low chair, the harmonica almost hidden in his scarred hands. Before the afternoon was over, he and Charlie created the wonderful "Harmonica-Guitar Blues" that was included in the Folkways record of the session. While the others were outside, he played on an old guitar that Cannon had brought until he was able to re-create some of the magnificent blues he had recorded years before.

Son has finally lost his job, and he and Jennie live on public welfare in a slum apartment behind Beale Street. Burse is still working as a house painter, getting along as best he can. The old violin player who recorded the "Mississippi River Waltz" with them, Milton Robie, is still living on College Street, but the others from the band are dead. Son and Charlie were on a local television tribute to W. C. Handy in the spring of 1958, but even the Christmas jobs they have been playing for years have been dwindling.

> "Me and Charlie work up and down the floors at the McCall Building. Every Christmas we play it, you know, for contributions. This year we didn't hardly make more than $12."

Gus Cannon is still working out on South Park, and still plays and sings. Last year, at the age of seventy-five, he married again. When his wife heard his old records, she kept asking excitedly, "Is that my hubby on there?" For Gus, the records brought back memories of a long, full life of playing his banjo for small, laughing crowds at a country crossroads, or singing with Hosie Woods in improvised theatres in poor cotton towns. He shook his head. "Me and Hosie sung that song more years than I can name. We had something in those years then."

# 9

## *"Goin' to Kansas City"*

The director of the race series at Paramount, Mayo
Williams, was too ambitious to be satisfied with the
shortsighted business view of the Wisconsin Chair
Company. He reasoned that if he had been successful
in finding talent for Paramount, he would be even more
successful in finding it for his own record company. It
was a mistake that Mayo was to make from time to
time for the next twenty-five years. In March, 1927, his
Chicago Record Company began issuing "Black Patti"
records, named for the famed Negro concert singer,
Sissieretta Jones, who was often compared with Adelina Patti, and usually advertised herself as "The Black
Patti." Williams used the Gennet recording facilities
and began with a series of newspaper advertisements
in the spring. He lasted only a few months. He found
that most of the good blues singers were under contract to someone else, and that his capital was insuffi-

**131**

cient to keep the business going until he built up a
catalog. He gave up in August, 1927.

When Mayo realized that his Black Patti venture
was going to be somewhat less than a success, he began
looking for another job in the industry. The Vocalion
Company had put out a number of race recordings in
1923 and 1924, but they had hesitated to begin advertising a race series. By 1926 they realized that there
was considerable money to be made in race recordings,
and on May 1, 1926, they announced that they would
begin a series of recordings by popular race artists, the
first releases to be in the early fall. Their first release,
Vo 1007, "Snag It," by King Oliver and his Dixie Syn-
copators, was a hit, and they followed it with King
Oliver's most successful record, "Someday Sweetheart,"
on Vo 1059. By the next summer, Vocalion was selling
thousands of records to the race market, but they still
hadn't done much in the vocal blues field. Mayo Williams retreated from the wreckage of Black Patti and
went to work for Vocalion.

Vocalion had been recording blues singers like
Henry Thomas—"Ragtime Texas"—a gentle, tasteful
singer, who played on a set of shepherd's pipes between
the verses of his song, accompanying himself on the
guitar. He was not too successful, and after a few
months they stopped advertising his records. When
Jim Jackson, the Memphis medicine-show entertainer,
drifted into town with Furry Lewis in October, Mayo
was with Vocalion. He picked Jim up and recorded his
blues "Goin' to Kansas City." It was released as "Jim
Jackson's Kansas City Blues," Parts 1 and 2 on Vo 1144

in December. Jim's little song sold and sold and sold. It was one of the biggest race records in years. On March 17, 1928, there was a full-page ad for the record, with illustrations for all the verses. There wasn't much to the song, but it had a catchy refrain, and soon everybody was ". . . going to Kansas City."

> If you don't want my peaches, don't shake my tree
> I ain't after that woman, but she sure likes me.
>
> I've got to move to Kansas City, mama, sure as you're born
> I've got to move to Kansas City, mama, sure as you're born
> I've got to move to Kansas City, honey, where they don't 'low you.

Jim was an older, balding man, who had been singing on the shows or around the Memphis cabarets most of his life. He was a good guitar player, and there was a fine sensitivity in his singing, but most of his records were like his "Kansas City Blues"—there were "Kansas City Blues" Parts 3 and 4 and "Going to Louisiana" Parts 1 and 2. He knew many of the older country songs, and when Ralph Peer was able to get him away from Vocalion early in 1928 Jim recorded some of his country songs for Victor. Jim's "Old Dog Blue," recorded in February, 1928, on Vic 21387, was not as popular as "Kansas City," but it was one of the most imaginative of the country songs recorded in the 1920's. Abbe Niles, at *Bookman,* noticed it, and in September, 1926, between articles on E. E. Cummings and Virginia Woolf, there was a note about "Old Dog Blue . . . a wholly fascinating story of a hound who treed his possums anywhere he found them, from a holler stump to Noah's Ark." Jim had been singing the song for years.

> Had a old dog his name was Blue
> You know Blue was mighty true
> You know Blue was a good old dog . . .
> Blue treed a possum out on a limb
> Blue looked at me and I looked at him,
> Grabbed that possum, put him in a sack,
> Don't move, Blue, til I get it back.
> Here Ring, here Ring here,
> Here Ring, here Ring here. . . .
>
> When old Blue died and I dug his grave
> I dug his grave with a silver spade.
> I let him down with a golden chain
> And every link I called his name.
> Go on Blue, you good dog you,
> Go on Blue, you good dog you.
> Blue lay down and died like a man
> Blue lay down and died like a man
> Now he's treein' possums in the promised land.
>
> I'm going to tell you this to let you know
> Old Blue's gone where good dogs go.
> When I hear old Blue's bark
> When I hear old Blue's bark
> Blue's treed a possum in Noah's Ark
> Blue's treed a possum in Noah's Ark.

Vocalion was dismayed at having lost Jim to Victor, and the newspaper advertisements reflected the struggles over Jim's artistic endeavors. On April twenty-first, only a month after Vocalion's full-page advertisement for "Kansas City Blues," Victor announced that Jim was now an exclusive Victor artist, and they advertised his first two records, "The Policy Blues" and "Bootlegging Blues" on Vic 21268, and "My Monday Woman Blues" and "My Mobile Central Blues" on Vic 21236. Three weeks later Vocalion advertised Jim's newest Vocalion record. To no one's surprise, it was "Jim Jackson's Kansas City Blues" Parts 3 and 4, on Vo 1155. In May, Victor was back with its newest Jim Jackson record, and Peer finally managed to keep him for the rest of the year.

Mayo Williams was having the same kind of success at Vocalion that he had had at Paramount. On November 24, 1928, he advertised another novelty record, "It's Tight Like That," by "Georgia Tom" and "Tampa Red" on Vo 1216. The ad said, "You'll say it's the catchiest and snappiest tune you've heard in a long, long time." Presumably to find out whether it was the ". . . catchiest and snappiest tune you've heard in a long time," nearly a million people bought "It's Tight Like That." Tampa remembers people lined up outside southside record shops trying to get copies. It even outsold "Kansas City Blues." The tune had a simple melody, like Jim Jackson's big seller. The words were more suggestive, but no more imaginative:

> Now the girl I love is long and slim,
> When she gets it it's too bad, Jim.
> It's tight like that, beedle um bum,
> It's tight like that, beedle um bum.
> Hear me talkin' to you, it's tight like that.

The song made Tampa Red; a young guitar player from Atlanta named Hudson Whittaker; Georgia Tom, Ma Rainey's accompanist, and Thomas A. Dorsey. But Dorsey found the song a little embarrassing. In the early 1930's, Tom began singing and composing religious songs, and he was continually being reminded of his records with Tampa Red. He has since said that he always intended to write religious songs, but he liked his job with Ma Rainey, and he helped Tampa with his "Tight Like That" only after much persuasion. He said that Tampa brought the words over to his house one night and asked him to help write a melody. Tampa says they both wrote the words and stole the melody from Papa Charlie Jackson, which is probably closer to the truth.

A few singers, including Lonnie Johnson, had tried to record "Kansas City Blues," but everybody tried to record "It's Tight Like That." There was such a rush on the tune that Mayo Williams tried to cover it with Vocalion artists. Tampa Red did it again with his "Hokum Jug Band," and Frankie Jaxon sang a version that must have curled Georgia Tom's hair. Williams advertised it in January, 1929, six weeks after the release of the first record. Three weeks later he was advertising "It's Tight Like That" #3 and #4 by Georgia Tom and Tampa; then in April he advertised:

FIVE RED HOT RECORDS!

*It's Tight Like That*
by Georgia Tom and Tampa Red,
#3 and #4 by Georgia Tom and Tampa Red.

Jimmy Noone's Apex Club Orchestra
Tampa Red's Hokum Jug Band
Tampa Red—guitar solo.

No matter how you wanted to hear "It's Tight Like That," you could find it on Vocalion.

There were so many versions of the tune, it became the most over-recorded melody in the blues and country field. Dance orchestras, singers and white hillbilly bands all rushed to record some version of "It's Tight Like That." Despite his embarrassment, Tom made a small fortune out of the song. His first royalty check came to $2,400.19.

In the summer of 1928, before the excitement over "Kansas City Blues" had died down, and the excitement over "It's Tight Like That" had started, another singer had begun recording for Vocalion. He was a quiet, wistful blues singer from Nashville named Leroy Carr. Despite the noisy success of Jim Jackson and Tampa Red and Georgia Tom, it was Leroy Carr whose singing was to change the style of the blues, and his first record, "How Long How Long Blues," released in September, 1928, was one of the most enduring blues compositions of the 1920's.

# 10

## Leroy Carr

Nashville is a rough, dirty town in the hills of central Tennessee. Most of the buildings are red brick, darkened with haze and dirt until there is a sombre cast to most of the older streets. The spires of Fisk University, erected in the 1890's with money collected by the Fisk Jubilee Singers, rise above the city on a hill near the outskirts of town. The state buildings sit in grimy splendor at the top of a long rise from the railroad yards and the largest colored district. Many homes still use soft coal for heating, and on winter days there is a dark haze over the lower sections of the city. A run-down neighborhood near the railroad tracks seemed the right part of town to ask about a blues singer. There was a place to park in front of a new welfare-board workshop, and there were three or four men in a tailor shop a block and a half down the street, who looked old enough to have known a man living in Nashville in 1927. It was late afternoon; a bitter wind was sweeping

138

along the darkening street. The lights had been turned on and a gas stove in the corner of the shop was turned up as high as it would go. A heavy man in a ragged sweater was working at a pressing table, while a smaller, serious-looking man was busy with a sewing machine. Two older men were sitting near the stove, still wearing heavy coats and gloves, talking quietly. The man at the sewing machine looked up.

"I'm trying to find someone who might have known a blues singer named Leroy Carr."

"Leroy? Leroy Carr? He and I grew up together. You know that Welfare Board Building right down the street?" ·

The car was parked right in front of it.

"Yes."

"His family had a house right on that spot."

A man beside the stove looked up. "I haven't heard anybody ask about that boy since his father passed. His father and mother passed during the war."

The man at the sewing table thought a minute. "What happened to that girl he left here?"

"Lottie?"

"What became of Lottie?"

"She passed just about the time Leroy did."

The man beside the stove shook his head. "Wouldn't that surprise you, somebody asking about Leroy?"

In the late 1920's, Leroy Carr almost completely changed the style of popular blues singing. He was a city man, playing the piano, and his singing was much less intense than the singing of the country-blues men.

It was an easy style to imitate, and singers who were influenced by Leroy dominated the blues field until the Second World War. Leroy's singing was simple and direct, almost understated, and he played a quiet accompaniment on the piano. His emotional mood was an appealing wistfulness that made him immediately popular.

Leroy was much better educated than men like Blind Lemon, and he was able to approach the blues as a musical form, rather than as a recollection of work songs, blues, or party songs from many sources. His blues were marked by their thoughtfulness and the records were remarkably consistent in style. The guitarist on the records, Scrapper Blackwell, was almost as influential as Leroy, and their accompaniment style—a full, relaxed rhythm, with melodic solo passages by Scrapper—was imitated as much as Leroy's singing. Their first record was so successful that their reputation was made a few weeks after they began working together. It was the very popular "How Long How Long Blues" on Vocalion 1191:

How long, how long, has that evening train been gone?
How long, how long, baby, how long?

Standing at the station, watch my baby leaving town.
Feeling disgusted, nowhere could she be found.
How long, how long, baby, how long.

I can hear the whistle blowing, but I cannot see no train,
And it's deep down in my heart, baby, that I have an aching pain,
For how long, how long, baby how long.

Sometimes I feel so disgusted, and I feel so blue,
That I hardly know what in the world just to do,
For how long, how long, baby how long. . . .

Leroy was almost immediately popular. A few
weeks after the release of "How Long," on September
first, Vocalion was advertising, "Here he is again! Leroy
Carr, exclusive Vocalion artist who is fast becoming
the greatest blues singer in the land" for his next record,
"Broken Spoke Blues," released the last week of October, 1928. They advertised free copies of his pictures
to anyone who sent in his name. He was with Vocalion
until December, 1934, recording over a hundred blues,
including six versions of "How Long How Long." The
later records sounded as though he were getting a little
tired of it himself.

How long, baby, how long,
Must I keep my watch in pawn?
How long, how long, baby, how long?

I'm going to the pawnshop, put my watch in pawn,
I don't want it to tell me that you've been gone,
For so long, so long, baby, so long. . . .

I can look and see the green grass growing up on the
    hill,
But I haven't seen the green back of a dollar bill
For so long, so long, baby, so long. . . .

Sometimes he complained about Chicago, but he
married a girl in Indianapolis and stayed in the North.
One of his popular records was about his home:

I'm just sitting here thinking of dear old sunny Ten-
    nessee,
        (repeat)
And wondering if my baby is waiting there for me.

I'm going where the Northern crosses the L&N
   (repeat)
And catch me a freight train to go back home again.

I'm going back South where it's warm the whole year
'round.
   (repeat)
I'll be so glad when my train pulls up in town.

But the last time he came back to Tennessee it was to die.

Leroy was born in 1899, the only child of Will Carr and his wife, Susie, who was always called "Sis" Carr around the neighborhood. Will Carr was a short, friendly man who worked for years at Vanderbilt University, in Nashville, as a laborer and porter. They had a one-story brick house on Charlotte Avenue, near N. 13th. There was a small alley beside the house, running between the backyards of the houses on 13th and 14th, and Leroy grew up playing outside with the boys in the neighborhood or going down toward the tracks into the rougher section. He did well in school and graduated from high school in 1915. He worked as a delivery boy for a drugstore after school; then got a job in a clothing store when he graduated.

In 1918, a man named Ollie Akins drifted into town, playing the piano at a place called "The Pot Roast." He was a country musician from Greenwood, Mississippi. His little specialty, a shimmy dance called "Tell 'Em About Me" was whistled and hummed all over town. Leroy started hanging around Ollie, watching him play, then going home to try playing like Ollie on the piano in the front room. His friends remember him sitting up straight, hitting away at the piano so he'd at least look like Ollie, even if he didn't sound like him. He continued learning from piano players around town, and in 1922, when he was twenty-four, he started playing Friday and Saturday nights at the Gold Star Dance Hall, on 12th Avenue, a few blocks from his home. Leroy played the piano and a man named Jack Wiley sang.

In the spring of 1925 or 1926, Jack Wiley, who was pretty versatile, gave up singing at the Gold Star to become a professional baseball player. At first Leroy tried to find another singer, but he couldn't find one he liked; so he started singing himself. He was nervous about it, but when he saw nobody minded, he kept singing and was soon very popular. He started buying expensive clothes at the store where he was working, and for two or three years he always wore gray flannel suits, with gray socks and a gray flannel cap. He always had his cap with him, even wearing it sometimes when he was playing. He had a steady girl named Lottie and he got drunk occasionally, but he was still living at home, working at the store and helping his mother and father. So many of his friends encouraged him to try the recording studios in Chicago, that he finally took the train north in the spring of 1928. The first word they heard from him was the record "How Long How Long Blues."

Scrapper Blackwell—his real name was Francis Black—had been playing the guitar and singing around Chicago for two or three years when he met Leroy. He had been recording for Vocalion and it may have been Mayo Williams's suggestion that he and Leroy work together. His first records, "Kokomo Blues" and "Pineal Farm Blues," Vocalion 1192, and "Trouble Blues" Parts 1 & 2, Vocalion 1213, had not sold well, but Blackwell was a superb guitarist, and his playing seemed suited to Leroy's simple piano style. Playing together over the years, they developed the piano-guitar duet into a distinctive blues accompaniment style. Leroy stayed in the background, letting Scrapper bridge the pause between the lines of his blues with improvised melodies on the upper strings of the guitar. There were often breaks for the guitar, and they played so well together it was often difficult to tell when Scrapper was playing by himself and when Leroy was playing softly behind him. Scrapper and Leroy only sang together once, with other singers on a noisy "Be-Da-Da-Bum" and "Non-Skid Tread," released on Vocalion 1276 in 1928, but Leroy's singing was so restrained that his records would probably not have been so successful without Scrapper Blackwell. He felt this himself, and both names were usually printed on the record label.

After the success of "How Long How Long," Leroy became an exclusive Vocalion artist. He did some theatre work and occasional night-club appearances, but after his marriage he lived quietly in Indianapolis, coming into Chicago to record or to see friends. He did a Christmas record for Vocalion's 1929 Christmas promotion, "Christmas in Jail-Ain't That a Pain," Vocalion 1432, but the record was not one of his best. Vocalion continued to record him during the worst years of the depression, recording the contract minimum of eight sides in 1931 and 1932; then after the worst of the depression had lessened, began recording him again in 1934. Despite a cut in theatre engagements, he was doing pretty well. The royalties from "How Long How Long" were enough to take care of his family. He was well liked by the other blues singers and they always stopped by his house when they were in Indianapolis. Big Bill, Tampa Red, Bumble Bee Slim and Little Bill Gaither were very close friends of Leroy's. Gaither recorded as "Leroy's Buddy," and both he and Bumble Bee Slim did memorial records after Leroy's death. Scrapper was still with Leroy, but he was doing some recording by himself, a group of blues for the Gennett subsidiary, Champion, in 1931, and a guitar solo record for Bluebird in 1932. No one realized it, but the relationship between Leroy and Scrapper was becoming strained.

Tampa Red was recording for Bluebird, and when Leroy's contract with Vocalion ended in 1934, Tampa talked him into leaving Vocalion and recording for Bluebird. Leroy and Scrapper got to the Bluebird studios, but when they were signing the contracts, the antagonism flared up. Scrapper swore that Leroy was getting all the fame and money from their recordings, and wasn't giving Scrapper his share. Scrapper had become jealous. Leroy was too hurt to say much, but after they had done a little recording, Scrapper got angry again and finally had to be physically thrown out of the studio. Leroy went on and recorded without him, but the records were very poor. There was to be one of the usual parties after the recording at the club where Tampa Red was singing. Scrapper came and joined the party, feeling very contrite, but about nine P.M. Leroy phoned to say that he didn't feel like a party and that he wasn't going to be there. Tampa never saw him again.

There is still some mystery about Leroy's death. A few weeks after the Bluebird session, Tampa heard that Leroy was in the South doing some night-club shows. Sometime after that he heard that Leroy had died of tuberculosis in Memphis. The death stunned everyone. Most of his friends refused to believe he had died of tuberculosis; since they hadn't been aware that he was sick. After this there was a story that it had been pneumonia. He seems to have been staying in a kind of brothel and dance hall in Memphis, drinking a little heavier than usual, when he died. Chicago blues singers said that "somebody put a spider in his whiskey," either he was poisoned or somebody put a curse on him. Bluebird had photographed him sometime during the afternoon when he and Scrapper separated and on the back of the photo of Leroy sitting alone, smiling, there is a penciled note: "Died, June, 1935." [1]

The blues sung for him were simple songs made up by his friends. Bumble Bee Slim recorded "The

[1] The most comprehensive listing of Carr's recordings, in Dave Carey and Albert McCarthy's *Jazz Directory,* Volume 2, published in London in 1955, lists a recording session by Carr in Jacksonville, Florida, on October 18, 1935, some five months after the time of his death as indicated on the Victor photograph. The master number series is a Jacksonville series, and is difficult to place in the Vocalion numerical sequence, but the release number indicates a release sometime in the spring of 1935. The record, "Can't Anybody Tell Me Blues" and "Black Widow Blues," does not include Blackwell. The number of recordings relating to the death of Carr, all recorded in the summer of 1935, indicate that the listing is in error and that the Victor notation of June, 1935, for Carr's death is correct.

Death of Leroy Carr" on Decca 7098 and Little Bill
Gaither recorded "The Life of Leroy Carr" on OK
05770.

> Bumble Bee Slim has told you about the death of
> his closest friend.
> (repeat)
> But I'm going to tell you from the beginning to the
> end.
>
> Leroy was born in Nashville, down in dear old Ten-
> nessee.
> (repeat)
> In the Smokey mountains, right close by the East
> Tennessee.
>
> Leroy came into the world in 1905.
> (repeat)
> He was only seven years old when the blues arrived.
>
> In 1928 he made the How Long and Prison Bound.
> (repeat)
> He had lots of luck and success and the cash came
> rolling around.
>
> So many women came around to hear the poor boy
> sing,
> (repeat)
> He would spend his money because money did not
> mean a thing.

There was a final blues to Leroy, recorded for
Champion in July, the month after his death—"My Old
Pal Blues" by Scrapper Blackwell.

# 11

## *The 14000's*

Columbia was the slowest of the major record companies to make a serious effort to record music from the rural areas. Their race series, with artists like Bessie Smith and Ethel Waters, was the most successful in the business; so they stayed out until the country blues began to sell as well as the city blues. Their first recordings of Southern talent were done as early as November, 1926, when they recorded Peg Leg Howell in Atlanta, but not until the spring of 1927, in March, were a large group of recordings made. The recordings done in the South were issued as part of Columbia's black-label race series, the 14000 series that had begun with Bessie Smith's "Chicago Bound Blues," on Co 14000, in 1924. There was a corresponding list of white country recordings, a black-label 15000 series. There seems to have been several individuals or groups out recording, and master numbers may have been recorded in a single

day in three or four cities or towns. There were vaudeville performers, blues singers, church choirs, hillbilly-
like string bands, religious singers—almost every kind
of music in the South. It was the period of the novelty
blues and no one in the record business had any real
idea of what might be the next hit record. Most of the
companies tried to guess. Ralph Peer, at Victor, tried
for an evenly balanced line which would reflect his own
musical sensibilities, and if he didn't have a hit, he had
a line that sold fairly steadily and did very well for the
company. At Columbia nobody wanted to even guess;
so the company pressed anything. There was only one
similarity in most of their new records—they were resounding commercial flops. Somehow Columbia managed to turn out the greatest collection of uninteresting
music recorded in the rural South.

Columbia made an intensive effort to sell their
blues material, and in addition to their regular newspaper advertising, they were the first company to use
press releases to advertise their race country material.
In March, 1928, several of the newspapers reaching a
colored market carried a short press release:

> The Columbia Phonograph Company has added three
> new Race stars to its catalog. Coley Jones, a Texas
> singer of blues, has been called the new Bert Williams
> for his personal magnetism, though he has a style all
> his own. Lewis Black, another new find, came from a
> logging camp in Arkansas. He wears a coonskin cap
> all the time and is called the Daniel Boone of the
> blues. The Dallas String Band is a unique little or-
> ganization of stringed instrument players from in and
> around Dallas. All the boys in the band sing and they

play engagements varying from dance halls to street concerts.

Abbe Niles, at *Bookman,* did the best he could. In June, 1928, he wrote:

> . . . give me a jazz record with strangeness and humor, or with wit, or with honest slapstick, and while it revolves I'll lump the noise and do without the sweetness. A fat comedian, bouncing downstairs, is worth a thousand tootsie rolls. Therefore I shall holler for such fox-trot records as Columbia's (r.) of the raucous, ginny voices and the felonious fiddling of Peg Leg Howell and his Gang in "Two Tight Blues."

In a footnote he added:

> "Race Records", here indicated by the letter 'r', are those made for colored consumption. Most dealers haven't them, but all can contain [sic] them. Listening to race records is nearly the only way for white people to share the Negroes' pleasures without bothering the Negro.

Columbia should have been advertising in *Bookman.* The Atlanta recordings of Peg Leg Howell and Barbecue Bob—Niles mentioned him "whaling his guitar and singing 'Motherless Chile Blues' "—sold fairly well, but the three artists advertised in the Negro papers had a bleak reception. Coley Jones sounded so much like a hillbilly performer that his records sold better to white listeners than they did to colored; though they didn't sell in any number to anybody. "The Daniel Boone of the Blues," Lewis Black, sold so poorly he was never recorded again. The Dallas String Band did much better for Victor under the name "Bobby Leecan's Need More Band."

Despite its persistence in the rural recording, Columbia had very poor success with the records. Peg Leg Howell and Barbecue Bob sold well on the blues lists and the religious singer Blind Willie Johnson sold very well in the first years of the depression, but the rest of the series sold very poorly. The original recordings, because of their poor sales, are very rare, and the 14000 series has become legendary among record collectors, but the country recordings in the series are only occasionally interesting. The singing usually seems heavy and constrained, and there are few moments of relaxed playing. The recording engineers may have had a poor approach to the man they were recording. Most of the singers sound a little unnerved. There is none of the fine subtlety that Peer seemed to be able to bring out and none of the unabashed exuberance that Mayo Williams was getting from his singers. Something seems to have been wrong with Columbia's approach.

A local musician, Dan Hornsby, was scouting for Columbia in Atlanta, and he had the most success finding singers. The first singer that Columbia recorded in Atlanta, Peg Leg Howell, had been playing around the city for four or five years when Columbia picked him up. He was an older man, in his forties, from outside of Cordele, Georgia, south of Macon. Somewhere he'd lost his right leg and got around with a wooden brace. He was a heavy, white-haired man, well known and well liked in Atlanta.

The colored district in Atlanta is shabby and poor today, but in the 1920's it was a colorful, noisy section. Along Decatur Street, the business district right off Peachtree Street, there are old saloons, barbershops, several shabby night clubs, and a colored theatre run by the Baily Theatre chain. The singers hung around either in the pool hall on one side of the theatre or the barbershop on the other. Peg Leg used to sing in front of the theatre or down a block outside two or three restaurants. There is a Pawnee Indian trading post in the middle of the block, and there is something very touching about the old Indian sitting outside his dingy store, its windows filled with trinkets, stretched hides and rusted traps hanging from nails along the wall. Children come up to him, asking shyly for medicinal roots and bits of bark and he gravely goes into the shop, finds what they want, and wraps the little bundle in newspaper. Peg Leg used to pass his shop every day.

Most of Peg Leg's songs were noisy, simple blues, and they were fine for his "gang," usually another guitar and a mandolin or violin.

> . . . I got a sweet jelly, I got a sweet jelly roll,
> It takes a sweet jelly to satisfy my worried soul.

But occasionally his songs were more interesting. "Coal Man Blues" was made up of cries used by vendors to sell their coal, and he accompanied the song with an involved accompaniment picked with his fingers, rather than with the pick he used on many of his recordings. One of his best blues was the fine "Low Down Rounder Blues," recorded on April 20, 1928, and released in June on Co 14320D:

Just a worried old rambler with a troublesome mind.
Just a worried old rambler with a troublesome mind.
All burned up from hardship, fate to me has been
   unkind.

I wouldn't listen to my mother, wouldn't listen to my
   dad,
   (repeat)
With my reckless ways I put myself in bad.
   (spoken) I wouldn't listen to nobody—mama
   tried to talk to me, I wouldn't listen to her.

I ain't trustin' nobody, I'm afraid of myself,
   (repeat)
I've been too low down, liable to put me on the shelf.

My friends has turned against me, smiling in my face,
   (repeat)
Since I been disobedient I must travel in disgrace.

I cannot shun the devil, he stays right by my side,
   (repeat)
There is no way to cheat, I'm so dissatisfied.

Ain't nobody wants me, they wouldn't be in my shoes,
   (repeat)
I be so disgusted, I got those low down rambler blues.

The depression ended Peg Leg's recording career
and he left Atlanta in the early 1930's. He was in New
York for a year or two, but he has not been seen in
either city since the war years.

After Peg Leg, the most successful of the country-
blues singers on the 14000 series was another Atlanta
singer, Robert Hicks, who recorded under the name
"Barbecue Bob." The fifty-six blues he recorded were

often almost primitive in their musical style, and there is every type of blues song in the group. He accompanied himself on a twelve-string guitar strung in a Spanish tuning, and played with a knife or bottle neck. His records were often stiff and poorly played, but blues like "Mississippi Heavy Water Blues" on Co 14222D, from his second session, June 15, 1927, had a vividness of detail and a sense of personal involvement:

> I was walking down the levee with my head hanging low,
> Looking for my sweet mama but she ain't here no mo'
> That's why I'm cryin', Mississippi Heavy Water Blues . . .
>
> I'm sittin' here lookin' at all this mud,
> My gal got washed away in that Mississippi flood,
> That's why I'm cryin', Mississippi Heavy Water Blues . . .
>
> I think I heard her moan on that Arkansas side,
> Cryin' how long before sweet mama ride,
> That's why I'm cryin', Mississippi Heavy Water Blues . . .
>
> Listen here you men, one more thing I'd like to say,
> Ain't no women right here, they all got washed away,
> That's why I'm cryin', Mississippi Heavy Water Blues . . .

Others—"Goin' Up the Country," "Poor Boy Long Ways From Home," or "Yo-Yo Blues"—were more conventional, but he sang with an earnestness and directness that was often moving. Except for Charlie Lincoln, another Columbia singer recording in Atlanta, Hicks had a singing style different from almost any

other recording artist. Lincoln sounded so much like
him that they may have been close friends or from the
same area. They did one record together, "It Won't Be
Long Now," on Co 14266D, so they may have been
traveling together. The depression finished Hicks's recording career, just as it had finished Peg Leg's, and he
died a year or so later.

Columbia recorded extensively in New Orleans
and Dallas, but the most successful New Orleans releases were the jazz-band recordings by Sam Morgan's
band, and the blues singers, including young T-Bone
Walker—"Oak cliff T-Bone"—recorded in both cities
had a poor reception.

Of the other singers on the Columbia 14000 series,
the religious singer, Blind Willie Johnson, is the only
other important figure. Perhaps he does not belong in
a discussion of the blues, but as has been said by
jazz historian Frederic Ramsey, Jr., to justify including
a recording of Blind Willie's with a group of blues recordings, he seems to belong with these men. Like them
he was an itinerant guitar player, a blind street beggar;
his music a personal expression of the singing he had
grown up with in the Central Texas cotton country. He
was one of the most intense singers to record in the late
1920's, and his style left a deep imprint in the singing
of both sacred and secular singers who heard his records. Blind Willie Johnson was one of the last of the
singers from the South of the 1920's to continue to sell
records after the depression struck the nation in 1929.

# 12

## *Blind Willie*

The country is very dry in central Texas—ragged, dusty country, with narrow creeks running through twisted sandstone channels and a rough growth of trees and brush. Blind Willie was born on a farm outside of Marlin, Texas, a small town east of the Brazos River. His father was a farmer named George Johnson. When Willie was three or four years old, about 1905, his mother died and his father married again. About the time he was seven years old, his father caught his second wife with another man and beat her. To get even with Willie's father she threw a pan of lye water in the little boy's face, blinding him. For Willie, a blind boy in poor farming country, there was the same choice that the blues singer, Blind Lemon Jefferson, had faced, to become some kind of beggar.

The country along the meandering, shallow Brazos is even more lonely than the country around Wortham where Lemon had been raised. Willie had felt himself to be alone even before he was blinded, and he would say to his father that he was going to be a "beecher," trying to say "preacher." As he began singing and playing the guitar, a harsh desolate sense of loneliness came into his music. He began going into Marlin when he was still a young man, playing in the windy, open streets. Marlin is a flat, colorless town, with an emphasis on religion and propriety. Willie sang in the churches and for religious meetings on the outskirts of town. In the winter months he would stand in the wind, playing an incessant, rasping guitar accompaniment to his rough voice, until his fingers were stiff with the cold. A tin cup was fastened with wire to the neck of his guitar so people could drop coins in while he was playing.

In 1925, he was singing in the streets in the town of Hearn, Texas. His father was farming outside of town. He would bring Willie in from the farm and Willie would sit under an awning singing as the crowds of people, in from the farms to shop, would walk past. Toward the end of the afternoon, the shopping done, they would stand listening. Hearn was a brickyard town, with nine yards working. There was money for street beggars and singers. Blind Lemon often came down to Hearn, and on some Saturdays they would both be on the streets.

Willie's wife, Angeline, met him in Dallas in June, 1927. He was singing the religious chant "If I Had My Way," and she walked along behind him singing the same song until he noticed her. She invited him to come to her house and sing hymns with her. She had a piano, and when he sat down she started singing "If

I Had My Way" and Willie shouted, "Go on, gal, tear it up."

After she had fed him some gumbo, breaking up the lobster claws for him, he asked her to marry him. "That was what I wanted."

They were married the next day, June twenty-second. Willie was twenty-five years old, a tall, gangling man with a thin mustache; a dark, intense man.

The Columbia recording unit was in Dallas in December and recorded Willie on December third. He sang with deep emotion and feeling, one of the songs almost a cry of pain:

> Motherless children have a hard time,
> Motherless children have a hard time,
> Mother's dead.
> Haven't got nowhere to go,
> Wandering 'round from door to door.
> Motherless children have a hard time,
> Mother's dead.
>
> Your wife and husband may be good to you,
> When mother's dead.
> May be good to you,
> Your wife and husband may be good to you,
> But come another they'll prove untrue.
> Nobody treats you like mother will,
> Mother's dead.
>
> Some people say that sister will do
> When mother is dead.
> That sister will do when mother's dead.
> Some people say that sister will do,

But soon as she's married she'll turn her back on you.
Nobody treats you like mother will.

Father will do the best he can,
When mother is dead.
The best he can when mother is dead.
Father will do the best he can,
So many things a father can't understand,
Nobody treats you like mother will.
Mother's dead.

Motherless children have a hard time.
Have a hard time,
Mother's dead.
They haven't got nowhere to go,
Wandering around from door to door,
Motherless children have a hard time,
When mother is dead.

The Dallas recordings, as a group, were among his best. The retelling of the Samson and Delilah story, "If I Had My Way"; the raw, shouted "Nobody's Fault But Mine"; and the haunting wordless chant, "Dark Was the Night and Cold the Ground," were recorded in Dallas.

The first record by Blind Willie was released a month and a half later, in the last week of January, 1928. It was "I Know His Blood Can Make Me Whole" and "Jesus Make Up My Dying Bed" on Co 14276-D. "The new sensation in the singing of sacred songs—and what guitar accompaniment!" "Nobody's Fault But Mine" and "Dark Was the Night" were released in May on Co 14303-D. Abbe Niles mentioned the record in his June review:

> A few unusual singers should be mentioned . . .
> Blind Willie Johnson's violent, tortured and abysmal
> shouts and groans and his inspired guitar in a prim-
> itive and frightening Negro religious song "Nobody's
> Fault But Mine!" . .

The last of the recordings, "Motherless Children" and
"Nobody's Fault But Mine" were released on Co
14343-D in the fall. The label was misprinted and the
title of the first song was given as "Mother's Children
Have A Hard Time." The advertisements were clumsy
examples of misplaced sentimentality:

> A very popular artist sings a wonderful song of
> mother love. Everyone who loves mother will love this
> record. . . .

Abbe Niles, at *Bookman,* was still having difficulties with Blind Willie's style.

> . . . also for connoisseurs, the extraordinary guitarist,
> Blind Willie Johnson, apparently a religious fanatic,
> singing "Mother's Children Have A Hard Time" and
> a Samson fantasy "If I Had My Way I'd Tear This
> Building Down." . . .

The recordings made little change in Willie's way
of life. He and Angeline moved to Waco, then to
Temple, then to Beaumont, where they bought a little
house. In December, 1928, the couple recorded four
songs together in Dallas. They sang in a rough antiph-
onal style for part of the songs and in unison for the
other verses. There was still the unrelenting harshness
and passion that Niles had noticed, without even the
softening of harmony:

OKEH ADVERTISEMENT,

BRUARY, 1928—

LVESTER WEAVER

typical blues ad from the late

20's. *Material from New York*

*blic Library*

A COLUMBIA ADVERTISEMENT.

DECEMBER, 1926—

PEG LEG HOWELL

An early Columbia ad for its

Atlanta recordings. *Material from*

*New York Public Library*

THE COLUMBIA RACE CATALOG—

PEG LEG HOWELL

*Material from*

*Record Research Magazine*

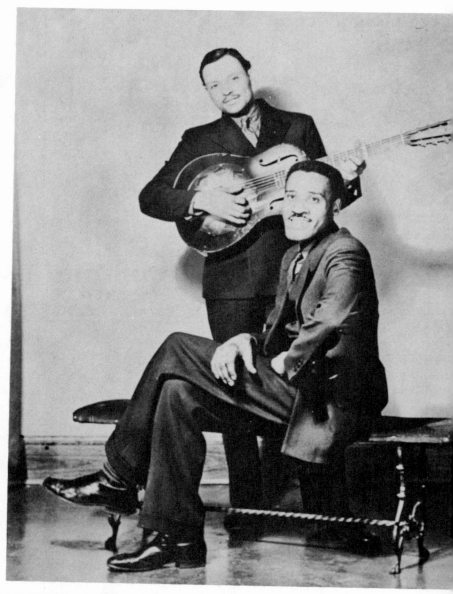

LEROY CARR AND SCRAPPER BLACKWELL

*Photo by Henry De Lorval Green. Courtesy of RCA Victor*

## BLIND WILLIE JOHNSON

# *"Trouble soon be over,*
# *Sorrow will have an end..."*

A COLUMBIA ADVERTISEMENT,
FEBRUARY, 1928
This is the only known photograph of
Blind Willie Johnson. *Material from
New York Public Library*

### BARBECUE BOB
Fred Boerner, who handled
the mail-order promotions
for Paramount, sent out
photographs of many pop-
ular blues singers, and this
Columbia Record Com-
pany photo of Barbecue
Bob was among Boerner's
stock. *Photo from
John Steiner*

## "That Sun's Gonna Shine..."

BIG BILL BROONZY, *Photo by David Gahr*

ADVERTISING HANDBILLS
FOR BIG BILL
RECORDS—1937
*Material from Record
Research Magazine*

I just can't keep from cryin'
  Sometime.
I just can't keep from cryin'
  Sometime.
My heart's full of sorrow,
And my heart's filled with fear.
And I just can't keep from cryin'
  Sometime. . . .

A drawing of Willie made from the photograph that had appeared in the first ads was used in later ads as part of a scene including the clouds of heaven and members of the heavenly host. ". . . touchingly beautiful songs." The first record, "I'm Gonna Run to the City of Refuge" and "Jesus Coming Soon," on Co 14391-D, was released in February, 1929, and the second, "Lord, I Just Can't Keep From Crying" and "Keep Your Lamp Trimmed and Burning," on Co 14425-D, was released in June.

Columbia was still interested in recording him for the next year, and brought him from Beaumont to New Orleans in December, 1929. He recorded on December tenth and eleventh, using a woman from one of the New Orleans churches to sing soprano. Angeline had stayed in Beaumont with the first of their children. In New Orleans he recorded one of his most widely imitated songs, "Let Your Light Shine on Me," on Co 14490-D. He began singing in a slow, quiet voice, then the guitar doubled the beat and the song became a fervent chant.

He stayed in New Orleans nearly a month, and there is a story that he was nearly arrested for trying to incite a riot. He was in front of the Custom House, on Canal Street, near the river, singing "If I Had My Way." A policeman walked by as Willie was singing Samson's cry, "If I had my way, I'd tear this building down" and tried to arrest him, thinking Willie was referring to the Custom House. He went back to Beaumont, on his way spending a few days with his father in Lafayette, Louisiana. George Johnson had left the woman who had blinded his son, and he was living alone in a small community of older Negro families.

As the depression deepened, Willie's records, with their anguished cry to God, began to sell widely. There was a widespread return of religious enthusiasm. Columbia recorded him again in Beaumont four months later, using improvised facilities on College Avenue. He and Angeline sang together, recording ten songs. She sang her first solo verses on the well-known revival hymn "If It Had Not Been for Jesus," released on Co 14556. The best selling of the last records was "Trouble Will Soon Be Over," on Co 14537.

> Trouble soon be over,
> Sorrow will have an end.
> Trouble soon be over,
> Sorrow will have an end.
>
> My burden may be heavy,
> Almost crush me down,
> Someday I'll rest with Jesus
> And wear a starry crown.
>
> He proved a friend to David,
> I heed him and I pray.
> The same God that David had,
> Will save me, come that day.

Trouble soon be over,
Sorrow will have an end.
Trouble soon be over,
Sorrow will have an end.

The records were released within a few weeks after the recording, the first, "John the Revelator" and "You Gonna Need Somebody on Your Bond," Co 14530-D. "You Gonna Need Somebody on Your Bond" was one of their most deeply moving songs, and with it—it was the last song recorded—Blind Willie's recording ended.

The thirty songs that Blind Willie recorded in his three and a half years with Columbia were a magnificent body of music, "violent, tortured . . . and frightening." Sometimes he sang in a clear, strong voice, but most of his songs were sung with a rasping false bass voice. The chanted songs like "If I Had My Way" were so intense they were almost unintelligible and he often seemed to cry out during the long solo guitar passages, "well, well . . . oh Lord." He was one of the finest country guitarists to record, and the interplay between the voice and the guitar was an astonishing series of exchanges as the guitar ended vocal phrases or the voice finished a melodic phrase that had been started on the guitar. He played with finger picks in an open-E chord tuning for the longer chants, playing an insistent, drumming rhythm over and over on the bass strings. For most of the other songs he used a pocket knife, playing in the "Hawaiian style" that had been introduced into the United States by the Hawaiian troops that toured the country before the First World War. It was these recordings that were the complex exchanges between the voice and guitar.

The songs came from many sources. Some of them were written by Willie; others were folk hymns from central Texas. A few, like "Let Your Light Shine on Me," are from white sources. "Everybody Ought to Treat a Stranger Right" had been taught to him by Blind Butler. "Dark Was the Night and Cold the Ground" is a wordless chant used in Baptist Church services in east Texas. Willie's wife, Angeline, taught him many of the songs he sang. She learned them from old songbooks that were in a trunk in the back of their house. A typical one was the "Redeemer's Praise, for Sunday School, Church and Family" by T. C. Okane, published by Walden and Stowe in 1881. It had words and music for more than five hundred songs.

With the depression, recording ended. Willie's recordings were very successful, and he was widely imitated, but Columbia was in serious financial difficulties. He lived in Beaumont with Angeline and their children, singing along Forsythe Street. He was heavier, his head usually shaved close. He dressed as neatly as he could, and the storekeepers along Forsythe remember him as a gentle, dignified man. During the winter, Angeline would lead him into the business district, and they would sing together in the noise and crowds of downtown Beaumont. Except for religious meetings like the encampment of the "South Texas Missionary Baptist Association" in Houston from August eleventh to eighteenth, 1936, they traveled very little.

Beaumont is on the flat level ground near the Gulf

Coast, railroad embankments the highest ground in the city. It is an uncrowded city, with trees and empty lots. Willie sang at church benefits or accompanied younger "gospel" singers like the Silver Fleece Quartet. With the jazz revival in the Northern cities there was renewed interest in Blind Willie's singing, and in the late 1940's he was a well-known name in jazz circles as one of the greatest of the recorded religious singers. He had become a legend, but he knew nothing about it. He was still living a poor life in Beaumont. His oldest son, Willie Jr., had already left home and was living in Houston. In the winter of 1949, their little house at 1440 Forest was burned. He and Angeline and the children got out safely, losing only a few furnishings and Willie's guitar, but the house was filled with water. Angeline spread newspapers over the soaked bedding and they slept in the house that night. Willie was a restless sleeper, and he turned over onto the wet mattress. He was sick the next morning, but he went out into the streets to try and earn a little money singing. Standing for hours singing in the winter winds complicated his sickness, and within a few days he was dying of pneumonia. Angeline tried to get him into a hospital but she said he was not admitted.

"They wouldn't accept him. He'd be living today if they'd accepted him. They wouldn't accept him because he was blind. Blind folks has a hard time. . . ."

# 13

## "Big Bill Broomsley"

A depression hits the poor the hardest and it hits them first. Within a year after the crash of 1929, the Negro South was destitute. Singers and entertainers touring the Southern vaudeville circuits found themselves playing to empty houses, and some of the most popular blues artists had a difficult struggle trying to get through the long summer of 1930. Ma Rainey's show was stranded and she was forced to join a group called "Boisy DeLegge and his Bandana Girls." They spent a hungry winter in a small town in Arkansas. Bessie Smith took what little money she could find and ran out on her show, leaving the others stranded. As the months of 1931 passed, the situation became steadily worse.

The record companies continued to record blues artists in the early months of 1930, hoping that business conditions would improve, but the race lists were hit with increasingly poor sales. There was an attempt to

**166**

reach some kind of audience with blues that were openly salacious, but everywhere in the South, and in many Northern cities, there was an almost hysterical religious revival. The depression was imagined to be a scourge sent to end the excesses of the 'twenties. The blues were "evil music." By the early months of 1931, advertising in the *Defender* and the *Courier* had almost disappeared. Columbia continued to advertise the religious records of Blind Willie Johnson, and it seemed momentarily that the sales of his records would be able to save the company, just as Bessie Smith's blues recordings had saved it in the 1920's, but the record business was at a standstill. Columbia was forced into receivership in 1932, and with it went its subsidiary, OKeh.

By 1933 there had been almost a complete reorganization of the race record business. The Vocalion label had been a subsidiary of Brunswick Records, both of them owned by the Brunswick-Balke-Collender Co., a manufacturer of bowling alleys and billiard tables. In 1931, the Brunswick-Balke-Collender Co. was forced to sell its record companies. The Warners Brothers Motion Picture Studios took them over late in the year, but sold them a few months later to the American Recording Corporation, a New York corporation selling a variety of cheaper records to the five- and ten-cent stores. A.R.C., as the corporation was usually known, set up a Brunswick subsidiary, with Vocalion Records as a race label. Mayo Williams stayed with Vocalion through the changes in ownership. Victor was in the best position of any of the companies, but it decided to change the sales organization, and set up a subsidiary called Bluebird Records for both its race recording artists and white country artists. The Paramount Record Company simply went out of business.

There was some recording in 1932—Vocalion recorded Leroy Carr to protect their contract with him and there were a few blues releases—but in 1933 even Vocalion was almost inactive. The new President, Franklin D. Roosevelt, was struggling to revive the stricken economy, but it was a terrifying year. The bank closing and the currency devaluation left a deep impression on a frightened nation. The desperation relief measures forced some money into circulation, and in 1934, despite the depressed conditions of most of the people who might be expected to buy records, the companies began recording. But the first releases sold slowly, and many of the recording artists were destitute.

The blues were still popular, but the old country-blues singers, with their endlessly varied vocal styles and guitar accompaniments were no longer commercially successful. The more sophisticated blues of Leroy Carr sold better than the others; although there was no boom in the sale of records. There were a few records that reflected the depression, but the blues were never strong on social consciousness and the ones that tried to make some comment on the bad times—"Northern Starvers are Returning Home" or "Times is Tight Like That"—didn't sell. More "hard times" blues were recorded in 1927 than in 1934. The blues were still expressing the emotional yearnings and unhappiness of the young Negroes that were buying the records. Leroy Carr's first record in 1934 was "Mean Mistreater Mama" and "Blues Before Sunrise," on Vocalion 02657. Leroy's great popularity lasted until his death, but he was already being eclipsed, in 1935, by one of the most successful and popular blues singers of the 1930's, the Arkansas singer, Big Bill Broonzy.

Broonzy had recorded for Paramount in the late 1920's, but the records were very poor. He made a series of recordings for the A.R.C. in March, 1932, but despite aggressive merchandising—the records were released on Perfect, Melotone, Banner, Oriole and Banner labels—he still didn't catch on. 1932 was a bad year for any singer. In March, 1934, he began recording for the new Victor subsidiary, Bluebird, and was finally on his way. Until the Second World War, he recorded dozens of blues for almost every record company in the blues business. When the wartime recording restrictions were eased in 1945, he began recording again, and until his death in 1959 was one of the most prolific blues artists the record business had ever seen.

Bill Broonzy was born in Scott, Mississippi, on June 26, 1893, but his family moved to Arkansas when he was a child, and he was raised in Arkansas farm country. He was one of seventeen children, living a poor, hard life. When he was still a boy, he made a cigar-box violin and he and a friend named Louis Carter, who played a homemade guitar, entertained at parties and picnics. Bill was married in 1915 and began working his own farm. He had decided to become a preacher and had given up his violin two or three years before, but he was offered fifty dollars and a new violin for four days of playing. His wife took the money and spent it so he'd have to play. The 1916 drought destroyed his crop, his stock and his savings; so he went to work in the coal mines until the draft took him in 1917. He was in the army two years; then tried living in Arkansas again. Like many other colored ex-soldiers, he found the South intolerable, and realized that he couldn't live there any longer. In 1920, he moved to Chicago and got a job with the Pullman Company.

Bill found there was more opportunity to make a living in Chicago than there was in Arkansas farm country, but he was ambitious, and needed money. He later said that when he came north he wanted to have everything that a white man had—his looks, his clothes, a big car and a white woman. He "couldn't change what was in his face," but he got the rest, and spent all his money to keep it. He got Papa Charlie Jackson, the Paramount blues singer, to teach him how to play the guitar and got an audition with Mayo Williams. Williams told him he wasn't good enough, but Bill persisted and got a friend of his, John Thomas, to shout along with him, and they went to the studio to record. They got roaring drunk, Bill had to sing into the old-style acoustical recording horn; then raise his head to read the words of his blues. The recording engineer had Thomas up on top of a box. The tests were rejected. Bill got Thomas to try again a few months later and this time Williams okeyed the tests. Their record, "House Rent Stomp" and "Big Bill Blues" by "Big Bill and Thomps," Paramount 12656, was released in 1927. The record was not much of a success, but Bill kept after Paramount. "Big Bill and Thomps" recorded "Down in the Basement

Blues" and "Starvation Blues" on Paramount 12707 in 1928, and Bill recorded by himself in 1930, "Station Blues" and "How You Want It Done," on Paramount 13084. Paramount used his full name on the label, but with its usual carelessness managed to spell it wrong. Bill was listed as "Big Bill Broomsley."

Bill's Paramount recordings were probably the most unpromising first records ever made by any blues singer. He was terrible. Arkansas has never had much of a blues tradition; so Bill had to learn to sing by listening to records. He was trying to imitate Blind Lemon, but he didn't have Lemon's voice, and no one has ever been able to imitate Lemon's guitar style. Bill was five years older than Lemon, but he sounded immature and very unsure of himself. He was thirty-four years old when his first records were released.

By 1930, Paramount wasn't getting anywhere and Bill wasn't getting anywhere. He had a job working as a grocery boy. Lester Melrose, a partner in the Melrose Music Publishing Company and a recording director for Gennet and Champion labels, picked up Bill in the winter and recorded four blues. The records were released the next spring under the name "Big Bill Johnson," but there was very little money around and they sold poorly. In March, 1932, Melrose recorded him again; then later in the month Bill was in New York for sessions with the American Recording Corporation. He had improved as a singer, but his style was still very derivative. He was no longer trying to sound like Lemon Jefferson, he was trying to sound like Lonnie Johnson and Leroy Carr. They were easier to imitate and he sounded a little more sure of himself. The "Big Bill Blues" on Champion 16400 and Superior 2837 is probably the best known of his early records.

> Lord, my hair is a'risin', my flesh begins to crawl.
>     (repeat)
> I had a dream last night, babe, another mule in my doggone stall.
>
> I know some people said these Big Bill Blues ain't bad.
>     (repeat)
> Lord, it must not have been them Big Bill Blues they had.

Bill made some money from his 1932 recordings and his name became better known. The blues recorded for A.R.C. were released on six labels for cheap sales. There were six solo blues, including the popular "Bull Cow Blues" and "Mistreatin' Mama Blues," two sides by "Big Bill and his Jug Busters," and a side by "Big Bill accompanied by Jug Band." He managed to find jobs of one kind or another and began playing around the southside. After he began recording for Bluebird in 1934, he quickly became very popular. He was using piano accompaniment, and his singing was more sophisticated. For three years he recorded with a piano player named Black Bob; then in 1937 he began using Josh Altheimer. They were together until Altheimer's death in February, 1940.

The recordings Bill and Black Bob made between 1934 and 1937 were strong, rhythmic blues, with a fine strutting sound to them. Bill had found his own style. He had been awkward and stiff as a shouter in the grand tradition on his Paramount recordings, but as a warm, entertaining blues singer he had no equal. Even the personable Leroy Carr sounded aloof and distant beside Bill's ingratiating style. One of his most popular recordings with Black Bob was an October, 1935, recording of "Take Your Hands Off Her" and "The Sun Gonna Shine In My Back Door Some Day" on Bluebird 6188. "Take Your Hands Off Her" was Bill's version of one of the old tent-show favorites, "Take Your Fingers Off It." It was usually sung as a duet. The man would beg to see a diamond ring the girl had gotten as a present. She would argue with him until he got too excited, then she would start singing,

> "Take your fingers off it,
> Don't you dare to touch it,
> You know it don't belong to you. . . ."

With a lot of mugging they made it clear to the giggling audience that they were not singing about anybody's diamond ring. It was recorded three or four times as the old duet; then in the late 1920's, as the records were becoming more and more openly obscene, it was recorded by the blues singers and the jug bands. The Memphis Jug Band did a riotous version of the song with Will Shade and Charlie Burse shouting:

> ". . . I got a gal in the neighborhood,
> Everybody knows she treats me good.
> Take your fingers off it,
> Don't you dare touch it,
> 'Cause you know it don't belong to you."

Bill took the song and softened it, singing:

"Take your hands off her,
 Don't you dare to touch her,
 'Cause you know she don't belong to you . . .

"Look her up and down as she goes by,
 The day I catch you with her that's the day you
   goin' to die,

"Take your hands off her,
 Don't you dare to touch her,
 'Cause you know she don't belong to you."

And his singing about his own girl and warning other men to stay away, made it a warm, personal blues song, even though he had changed very few of the words and the melody was not changed at all. The other side of the record, "The Sun Gonna Shine," was the old blues "Trouble In Mind." Bill's only change was to emphasize his personal attitude by singing it in a cheerful voice and repeating two or three times that the "sun was gonna shine in his back door someday." The style was a subtle rephrasing of the older, more austere singing styles, but the sound was entirely fresh, and the full piano accompaniment softened the intensity of the solo guitar accompaniments. The style was as close to being ingratiating as the blues can be.

During the late 1930's, Bill recorded frequently. From December 1935 until October 1937, he worked exclusively for the American Recording Corporation; from March, 1938, until April, 1940, he was with Vocalion, and until December, 1947, he was with OKeh-Columbia. Bill's own recordings were only a part of his domination of the blues scene in the 1930's.

His half-brother, Washboard Sam, and two close

friends, Jazz Gillum and Tampa Red, were recording for Victor's Bluebird series, and Bill wrote many of the most successful blues that they recorded. He played guitar on many of the Washboard Sam dates, being careful not to sing a note or have his name appear on the label except as composer. He was careful to honor his exclusive agreements. Besides his records and his blues, there were men imitating his style, usually working for rival companies. Decca was trying to counter his success with Peetie Wheetstraw, and Bluebird was using Jazz Gillum, younger singers who could be mistaken for Big Bill if somebody was playing a jukebox in a crowded barroom after he'd had a drink or two.

Bill copyrighted more than three hundred blues in his most active years. Many of them were almost taken from the recordings of the 1920's, and he probably would have had trouble defending his copyright in case of legal action, but some of the best, as "Keys to the Highway," and "Looking Up At Down," were Bill's own. He was using his friends on most of his dates, and they were using his songs on theirs. Gillum, added for "Keys to the Highway," recorded May, 1941, had previously recorded the song for Bluebird. Because of his first recording there was some confusion about the copyright, and a later recording by Brownie McGhee was credited to Gillum rather than Broonzy. Bill was using larger and larger groups on his records, and there were many sessions with four- and five-piece jazz and swing groups. The New Orleans trumpet player, Punch Miller, was with him for at least one session, and there was a succession of saxophone players. His singing style was unchanged, a little rougher, but still very pleasant; but both his accompaniments and his attitude toward his personal life had changed. There was a bitterness and cynicism in his blues about the women in his life.

> Don't you ever think your women just belongs to
>     you . . .

> I'm looking for a woman that ain't never been kissed,
> Maybe we can get along and I won't have to use my
>     fist . . .

A close friend, the singer Casey Bill Weldon, wrote a blues "I'm Gonna Move to the Outskirts of Town." Bill's recording of it, OK 06651, was particularly savage.

> I'm gonna move way out on the outskirts of town,
> I'm gonna move way out on the outskirts of town,
> That's why I don't want nobody always hanging
>     around.

> I'm gonna tell you, baby,
> We're gonna move away from here.
> I don't want no iceman,
> I'm gonna buy me a frigidaire. . . .

> I'm gonna bring my groceries,
> Gonna bring them every day.
> That's gonna stop that grocery boy,
> I mean that's gonna keep him away. . . .

> It may look funny,
> Funny as can be,
> We got eight children, baby,
> Don't nar' one of them look like me.
> That's why I'm gonna move to the outskirts of town.

That's why I don't want nobody always hanging around.

Despite the cynicism of the new blues—there were several singers as bitter as Bill—he was more popular than ever. In 1939 he was asked to sing at the second "Spirituals to Swing" concert at Carnegie Hall, and found himself in the middle of one of the emotional, depression-conscious affairs that were being sponsored by liberal groups in the New York area. A singer from the Louisiana Penitentiary who had been brought up from the South by men connected with recording activities of the Library of Congress, a smouldering personality named Leadbelly, was one of the high lights of the concert and the emphasis was on the rural backgrounds of blues and jazz. Bill heard himself introduced, not as a popular blues singer with records being played on thousands of jukeboxes in every city in the country, or as one of the most successful and prolific blues writers of the period, but as an "ex-sharecropper." It was true that Bill had done some farming, but that had been in 1916. There was probably no more startled man in the world than Bill Broonzy when he heard the introduction.

Bill had always been able to get along with people, and he managed to avoid confusion at the concert. When two young enthusiasts cornered him and asked him to sing some sharecroppers' songs, he managed to explain that he didn't want to sing any because he might have to go back to sharecropping. He was taking a chance, since someone might have been aware that he was Vocalion's biggest selling artist—he recorded

thirty-four blues that year, including "Just a Dream"
and "Baby I Done Got Wise," two of his big records—
but he managed to carry it off. In his last years he recorded for many labels as a "folk artist," but the blues
he sang were almost invariably romanticized versions
of his earlier hits. If he ever knew any sharecroppers'
songs, he seemed to have forgotten them in 1916.

Bill enjoyed his money, and after the war, when
his popularity was waning, he took a job as a janitor at
Iowa State College. There was an active enthusiasm
over folk music in the Chicago area, and more and
more young enthusiasts approached Bill as an "ex-
sharecropper." Bill seemed to be endlessly amused by
the entire situation, and with his genius for being liked
and his warm personality, he was soon the center of
a group of young white folk musicians. A singer that
Bill had known in Chicago in the 1930's, Josh White,
was having considerable success singing a sort of thin
blues to night-club and theatre audiences and Bill
realized that he would have to be a success in this new
field to begin recording again. The young folk singers
learned from Bill, but he learned at least as much from
them, and when he made his move into the folk music
world he had a useful knowledge of what the new audience wanted to hear. At first he was overshadowed by
the very popular White, but he changed his style to
sound more and more like Josh and he soon became
one of the most successful concert personalities of the
folk movement.

Despite the pretentiousness of the "folk blues" recordings that Bill made before his death, he still main-

tained his self-respect as best he could. For the notes on an English record, Bill was questioned about his early life. There was an almost complete ignorance of Bill's many years of great popularity; so with a perfectly straight face he told the earnest young woman who was questioning him that he'd been an Arkansas sharecropper until 1946, when he'd finally decided to come north and give his songs to the world. This rather startling information was duly printed on the back of the record jacket. When record collectors would play one of the old records, complete with bleating saxophone, thundering piano and dirty lyrics, for one of Bill's new adolescent fans, there would be a moment of stunned silence and the new enthusiast would finally state in a serious tone, "That's not the same Big Bill. There must be two men using the same name."

There were two Big Bills. There was the Big Bill who described himself as ". . . a well-known blues singer and player and has recorded 260 blues songs up till 1952," and there was the Big Bill who could stand up on a concert stage and sing work songs he'd learned from phonograph records and back country blues he'd picked up from books on country music, and fascinate the audience just talking about himself. They were both the same man, but one was a singer entertaining a Negro audience and the other was a man entertaining a white audience. The difference explains most of what there is to explain about the blues.

Bill had several successful years as a concert performer, and he became widely known for his appearances in France and England, as well as the United States. The young colored audience wasn't interested in his records, but the intellectual folk audience was, and he recorded dozens of albums. They were beautifully designed and decorated albums, with emotional testimonials about Bill's singing, usually written by someone who hadn't heard his old records. Most of the fire was gone from his singing, but the people who were listening to him sing were not listening to the blues as a personal music that they could identify with the emotions and desires of their own lives. They were listening to the blues as an art form, and they expected the same pretentiousness that surrounds the singing of any art music. They wanted pretentiousness, and in the same manner that Josh White had done, Bill gave it to them. His singing became a series of conscious effects and contrived drama. To intensify the dramatic effect, he slowed the songs down and used the guitar less and less. There was none of the easy swinging of his Memphis Five or Chicago Five and there was none of the exhilarating exchange between the piano and guitar that had marked his records with Black Bob and Josh Altheimer. The recordings, almost indistinguishable from company to company, sold well, and there was money again. He even wrote a book, "Big Bill's Blues," published in England, then in the United States, a sensitive and colorful story of his life, his songs and his friends.

At the height of his new fame, Bill began to have trouble with his throat. He was bothered with hoarseness and had to be hospitalized—it was cancer, and he never rallied. An operation to remove the growth left him without his voice. A benefit concert was given for him in Chicago, attended by thousands of his friends.

There were two or three radio broadcasts with Bill's close friend, Studs Terkel, including a sad moment when Bill tried to talk and there was only a voiceless sound. He died in an ambulance rushing him back to the hospital early in 1959. There were memorial concerts for him, and his story was printed in dozens of newspapers and magazines, but in his book he had written his own estimate of his life and career, and it is perhaps the way Bill Broonzy would best like to be remembered.

. . . when you write about me, please don't say that I'm a jazz musician. Don't say I'm a musician or a guitar player—just write Big Bill was a well-known blues singer and player and has recorded 260 blues songs from 1925 up till 1952; he was a happy man when he was drunk and playing with women; he was liked by all the blues singers, some would get a little jealous sometimes but Bill would buy a bottle of whiskey and they all would start laughing and playing again, Big Bill would get drunk and slip off from the party and go home to sleep. . . .[1]

[1] Broonzy, William, "Big Bill Blues," London, Cassell & Company, Ltd., 1955.

# 14

## "I Got the
## Bluebird Beat"

The label on Bluebird Records, Victor's new race subsidiary, was more colorful than the old Victor black
label. It was printed in a light blue on a yellow background, and there was a drawing of a bluebird flying
across the label. The new, brighter design was only
part of the change in Victor's attitude toward its race
series. Ralph Peer was no longer working with the company, and some of the new releases were blues that
Peer would have thought twice about issuing. One of
the first blues singers on Bluebird was the rowdy Bo
Carter, singing some of the blues he had done for
Columbia and OKeh, "Don't Cross Lay Your Daddy"
or "Let Me Roll Your Lemon." Bluebird was off to a
noisy start.

In the years before the Second World War, Bluebird exploited the blues with a persistence and thor-
**182**

oughness that made its blues releases almost as popular as the standard vocal releases on Victor. The country blues were a commercial success. In the 1930's, they became as repetitious as the city blues had been in the 1920's. The personal vocal styles and the intense, personal moods were almost eliminated. Instead of individual accompaniments, there were small groups with piano, bass, guitar and washboard, sometimes even trumpet, clarinet, or saxophone. To make individuality even less noticeable, Bluebird used a group of house musicians who accompanied everybody. The singers were not even singing their own blues most of the time. Big Bill, who was recording for Bluebird in 1934, set the vocal and background style, and he wrote hundreds of blues. If he wasn't responsible for the song, his half-brother, Washboard Sam, probably was. After two or three years of this it was almost impossible to tell one singer from another. Washboard Sam was fairly distinctive, and no one sang with Big Bill's warmth and personality, but the records were easy to confuse. It could be Big Bill, Tampa Red, or Jazz Gillum on many of the records, and the difference, musically, was unnoticeable. The Bluebird blues, with few exceptions, was a stereotyped product.

In the late 1930's, the Bluebird recordings were selling by the thousands. Lonnie Johnson came to Bluebird from Decca in 1939 and recorded some of his biggest hits for the company. By the 1940's, the entire blues record business had "the Bluebird beat." The label reflected the company's new prestige. First, the colorful light blue on yellow label was changed to a rich-looking gold on dark blue, with the bluebird, slightly smaller, sailing over a part of a musical score. Then as the records were selling by the thousands, the bluebird disappeared and was replaced with Victor's standard "His Master's Voice" design. As a final gesture Bo Carter was dropped in 1939, and the "Bluebird beat" became respectable.

Some of the Bluebird singers, like Jazz Gillum, were younger men who began singing in the 1930's, and they probably would have done very little recording if the styles of the 1920's had survived the bleak days of 1930 and 1931. Tampa Red was one of the few popular Bluebird artists who had been successful in the 'twenties. His "Tight Like That," with Georgia Tom, had sold hundreds of thousands of copies in 1928, and many of his early records were very exciting. He was called "Tampa Red" because he had come up to Chicago from Tampa, Florida, in the 1920's, and he was light skinned, but he was a Georgia singer named Hudson Whittaker. He was born in Atlanta, December 25, 1900. Tampa came to Chicago as an inexperienced but talented young singer, playing the guitar with a bottle neck on his little finger and playing it superbly. Some of Ma Rainey's best records were done with Georgia Tom and Tampa accompanying her. Georgia Tom, Thomas A. Dorsey, Ma's regular accompanist, has said that despite the success of "It's Tight Like That," he was dissatisfied with his life as a blues artist, but it took him three years to make up his mind, and he never talked about it with Tampa. Tampa noticed that Tom wasn't as friendly as he had been, but they were doing so well he didn't think much of it. They recorded in New York for Vocalion and Tampa noticed that

Tom was " . . . very smart," wearing his best clothes, and he had a brief case with him that he kept on the floor beside him while he played. When the session was over he didn't feel like going drinking with Tampa as they always did after doing some recording. As he walked away, Tampa realized that something was wrong. He learned later that Tom's brief case was filled with promotional material for the religious songs he had been writing, and Tom spent the afternoon going to churches in New York, talking with choir directors and leaving his songs with them. Tampa saw him occasionally, but they never recorded together again.

Tampa began recording for Bluebird in 1934 with his Chicago Five, a small jazz group similar in style to his old "Hokum Band" on Vocalion. Most of the records were banal popular songs that Tampa had written, and he sang in a style closer to the popular crooners than to the blues. The records sold very poorly and he went back to his blues singing. In later years, the fine blues pianist accompanist, Big Maceo, accompanied him, and they did a few driving instrumentals, but most of the blues were thin and derivative.

> Some women got a habit, I really can't stand.
> Runnin' and Jumpin' from man to man,
> But I ain't for it,
> I strictly ain't for it.
> I ain't for it, none of that old jive at all.
>
> Baby, you gonna miss me when I'm gone,
> Baby, yes you gonna miss me when I'm gone.
> Though you break my heart every day,
> Just to pass the time away,
> But, baby, you gonna miss me when I'm gone.

Baby, I'll never trust your love again,
Baby, I'll never trust your love again,
But if you ever need a friend,
I'll be yours until the end . . .

I can't sleep at night,
I can't eat a bite,
'Cause the girl I'm loving,
Sure don't treat me right . . .

For a long period Bluebird used him to record the dirtier blues that were still selling a little. The blues were usually a series of double meanings with a suggestive title. Tampa's favorite was an unusually vague one called "She Wants to Sell My Monkey," on BB 9024, about a woman he'd given a monkey to who was trying to sell it. For years people would come up to Tampa and ask him just what he meant by that song. One night a man came up to him in a barroom, shook his hand and said, "Tampa, there's one song of yours that was my favorite, "She Always Wants to *Smell* My Monkey."

One of his early Bluebirds, "When I Take My Vacation in Harlem," BB 6166, was one of his best. It had a raffish charm and he sang it with an easy cheerfulness:

"When I take my vacation in Harlem,
What a hell of a time it will be.
With the rhythm of that Harlem hi-de-hi,
And the girls that I know care for me.

"To the jazz of old Duke and old Calloway,
We can love, kiss, and dance 'til the break of day.
I don't care if it's sleeting, raining, or snowing,
We'll be ready when that Harlem fun begins.

"When old Duke sits down to the old piano,
And old Cab shakes his deacon hi-de-ho,
I'll be there with an armful of heaven,
When I take my vacation in Harlem.

"When I take my vacation in Harlem,
What a hell of a time it will be.
With the rhythm of that Harlem hi-de-hi,
And the girls that I know care for me. . . ."

Tampa's pianist, Big Maceo, died in 1953, and Tampa began playing less and less. His wife died in recent years and he is living alone in a small apartment on Chicago's southside. He has none of the shrewdness that helped Big Bill make the change from the race market to the concert audience, and he is not a colorful personality. He tries to get along, hoping that Victor will pick him up again. He doesn't want to talk about the old days, feeling that if anything is written about him he should be paid for the use of his name. He lives quietly, a dignified, gentle little man, usually wearing a buttoned sweater, his shoes carefully polished. He spends his afternoons visiting friends, walking along the rows of brownstone apartments that line the streets in his neighborhood, a scarf carefully folded around his neck and his overcoat collar turned up. He still owns a guitar, but he hasn't played much in recent years. He is proud of his playing and of the songs he has written, and it is his quiet pride that is the heart of Tampa Red.

Victor had been recording a few singers during 1931 and 1932, and one of their most popular new artists was the good-looking young singer, Walter Davis. His first record, "M and O Blues" and "Mr. Davis Blues" on Vic 38618, sold very well. He played the piano and sang in an easy style reminiscent of Leroy Carr. His first records were re-released on the new Bluebird series in 1933 and he was recording for the new label the same year. He was not a colorful singer, but his quiet style was very successful, and he was a popular Bluebird singer until 1945.

One of the most consistently popular Bluebird artists was Bill Broonzy's half brother, Robert Brown, who used the name "Washboard Sam." Sam was from Bill's section of Arkansas, and because of his father's wayward ways, Bill was pretty sure that he and Sam were related. Bill was working in the mills when Sam showed up in Chicago in 1932. Sam was just twenty-two, and he was already doing a little washboard-playing and singing. Bill helped him with his singing, wrote some of the songs he recorded and played guitar on most of his records. They did some recording together for Vocalion, but Sam was signed to an exclusive Bluebird contract; so the Vocalion records were released as "Ham Gravy" or "Shufflin' Sam."

Sam used many instrumentalists on his records, and often the interest is not in the blues lyrics or in his strong yet monotonous voice, but in a flash of brilliant saxophone work or an archaic-sounding clarinet or some good strong blues piano. His most popular records were usually the most swinging ones. "Back Door," BB B-7001, with good piano and clarinet; "Just Got to Hold You," BB B-8599, with good roaring saxophone and piano; "Phantom Black Snake," BB B-7601, with a beautiful clarinet solo based on the "Mecca Flats Blues" melody, and "Come On In," BB B-6870, with good piano, were among his best records. He had particularly good fortune with his piano players, and it is the steady, driving rhythm of the washboard and the piano that is the most distinctive sound of his records. One of his best blues was an earnest recording he did in the late 1930's, "I've Been Treated Wrong," on BB B-9007.

I don't know my real name, I don't know where I
was born,
(repeat)
The troubles I been having seems like I was raised
in an orphans home.

My mother died and left me when I was only two
years old.
(repeat)
And the troubles I been having the good Lord only
knows.

I been treated like an orphan and worked just like
a slave,
(repeat)
If I never get my revenge evilness will carry me to
my grave.

Now I been having trouble ever since I been grown.
(repeat)
I'm too old for the orphan and too young for the old
folks' home.

Sam recorded until 1947, when he decided to give up music and join the Chicago police force. He moved from the tenement building he was living in near the loop, and he and his family are living quietly on the southside.

To some extent, Bluebird needed the heavy accompaniments on most of their records. Partly it was because they were trying to sell the records for the new "vitaphones" that were being installed in barrooms and restaurants, and the heavier sound was more suited to the noisier surroundings; and partly it was because some of the singers, like Washboard Sam, didn't play accompaniment for themselves and needed a small group. Most of the piano players were blues men who had been playing in bars on the southside for years. Their earthy blues styles are as exciting as most of the singing they were accompanying and the records have a rich variety of fine blues playing. Two younger Bluebird singers, Jazz Gillum and Sonny Boy Williamson, both played harmonica, and they used house groups for accompaniment. Gillum—his first name was William—sounded like a younger Big Bill, and Bluebird used him to record many of Big Bill's tunes. Bill had left Bluebird and was recording for Vocalion and OKeh. Gillum played harmonica on many of Bill's records and did a lot of singing for Bluebird. One of his best was an hilarious Washboard Sam tune that he recorded on BB 34-0730, "Go Back to the Country."

> Now you cryin' with your grocery man, 'cause your
>     bill is too high,
> You don't want to pay taxes, you just want to get by.
> You better go back to the country,
> Way back out in the woods.
> I'm tired of hearin' you hollerin' City Lights ain't no
>     good.
>
> You want the finest house in town for two or three
>     dollars a month,
> You seem to think it's alright for you to go out in
>     the park and hunt.
> You better go back . . . ʼ

You wants a whole lot of credit to pay off once a
    year,
But you owe the salary you make for just liquor and
    beer,
You better go back . . .

You decorate the window with your great big rusty
    feet,
You want hogs in your front yard so you can have
    plenty of meat.
You better go back to the country,
Way back out in the woods.
Plant you forty acres of cotton,
And try to do yourself some good.

Sonny Boy Williamson's fame rested on his better-
than-average harmonica style and a blues that he sang
with exultant ferocity on BB 34-0744, "Elevator
Woman."

Elevate me, mama,
Mama, five or six stories on down.
Elevate me, mama,
Five or six stories on down.
Now you know everybody tells me you must be the
    elevatin'est woman in town.

Sonny Boy came up to Chicago from his home in Jackson, Tennessee, in 1932. He was eighteen, playing the
harmonica as well as he ever did. He was stabbed in
the head on his way home from a job at the Plantation
Club in Chicago in 1948 and died before he could get
to a hospital.

Arthur "Big Boy" Crudup, from the east coast, was
an uneven singer, but better than average, and his first

record, "If I Get Lucky," on BB B 8858, has the shouted intensity of an old field song. He is best known for his popular blues "Mean Ole Frisco," on BB B 34-0704.

Well that mean old, mean old Frisco, and that low-
down Santa Fe,
Yes that mean old Frisco, low down Santa Fe,
Done took my babe away, Lord, and blowed way back
at me. . . .

Well my mama she had told me, papa told me, too.
My mama told me, papa told me, too.
Lord, every woman grin in your face, Lord, she ain't
no friend to you. . . .

Well I'm standin', Lord, lookin', watchin' that Southern
whistle blow.
Yes I'm standin', lookin', watchin' that Southern whistle blow.
Well she didn't catch the Southern, Lord, where did
the woman go.

Most of the other singers on Bluebird, and on Vocalion and OKeh, tended to a repetitious use of clichés and a monotonous accompaniment that was as unimaginative as their singing. Often the piano players, especially Big Maceo, Maceo Meriweather and Roosevelt Sykes, were better blues singers than the men they were accompanying and some their own records were fine blues shouts. There were as many colorful names as there had been in the 1920's—William Bunch, "Peetie Wheetstraw, The Devil's Son-in-Law"; Bill Gaither, "Leroy's Buddy," and Minnie McCoy, "Memphis Minnie." There was the usual number of "Slims"— Peter Chatman, "Memphis Slim"; Amos Easton, "Bum-

WALTER DAVIS
*Material from Record
Research Magazine*

BO CARTER
*Photo from Record
Research Magazine*

TAMPA RED
*Photo from Record
Research Magazine*

## JOE WILLIAMS
### (Blues singer with guitar)

B-8738 { Crawlin'
         King
         Snake
         Meet Me
         Around
         the
         Corner

B-8774 { I'm Getting
         Wild
         About
         Her
         Peach
         Orchard
         Mama

B-8797 { Coal and
         Iceman
         Blues
         Mattie Mae Blues

JOE WILLIAMS

SONNY BOY WILLIAMSON

## SONNY BOY WILLIAMSON

B-7059 { Good
         Morning,
         School
         Girl
         Sugar Mama
         Blues

B-7302 { Early in the
         Morning
         Project
         Highway

B-7352 { Suzanna
         Blues
         Black Gal
         Blues

B-7404 { Worried
         Me Blues
         Frigidaire Blues

B-7428 { Up the Country Blues
         Collector Man Blues

B-7536 { I'm Tired Truckin' My Blues
         You Can Lead Me

## Lonnie JOHNSON,
### Blues Singer)

B-8322 Nothing But
       a Rat
       She's My
       Mary

B-8338 Four 0
       Three
       Blues
       The Loveless
       Blues

B-8363 Why Women
       Go Wrong
       She's Only a
       Woman

B-8387 Trust Your Husband
       Jersey Belle Blues

LONNIE JOHNSON

## *"I Got the Bluebird Beat..."*

## TOMMY McCLENNAN
### (Blues singer with guitar)

B-8760  Whiskey Head Man—Blues
        New Sugar Mama—Blues

TOMMY MC CLENNAN

*Material from New York Public Lib*

BLIND BOY FULLER.                    *Photo from Record Research Magazine*

BROWNIE MC GHEE
*Photo by David Gahr*

*Below, at Right*
LIGHTNIN' HOPKINS
*Photo by S. B. Charters*

SONNY TERRY
*Photo by David Gahr*

ble Bee Slim," and Albert Luandrew, "Sunnyland Slim." There was even a "Blues Doctor," Peter Clayton. Their styles were very similar. Even Memphis Minnie, a stunningly handsome woman who was very popular, sounded often like a feminine Bill Broonzy or Washboard Sam. She beat Bill in a blues contest in the 'thirties, but Bill didn't have a reputation as a guitarist and their vocal styles were about identical. After she sang her blues, the judges, Richard M. Jones and Sleepy John Estes, picked her up and carried her around on their shoulders. The prize was a bottle of gin and a bottle of whiskey. Bill stole the whiskey, leaving her to a crowd of admirers, the bottle of gin, and her irate husband, a jealous blues singer named Joe McCoy.

There were a few blues on the Bluebird lists that reflected the miseries of unemployment and the depression years, but they were usually haphazard songs, trying to laugh off the depression more than anything else. Big Bill did "Hungry Man" on BB 5706; then did "W.P.A. Blues" and "W.P.A. Rag" for the American Recording Corporation labels. Washboard Sam did "C.C.C. Blues" on BB 7993 and "Levee Camp Blues" on BB 8909. There were other depression blues by many of the singers, but the lists were still overwhelmingly given over to blues like "My Woman's a Sender" or "Why Did You Do That to Me?" Even the St. Louis singer, Peetie Wheetstraw, who was very successful with "Working on the Project" on Decca 7311, recorded only a few blues with much social consciousness, and they were usually superficial versions of popular blues on other labels.

Despite the success of the "Bluebird beat," there were still men singing in more intense country styles. Sleepy John Estes, the Tennessee singer who had recorded for Victor, was now recording for Decca, and he seemed to get better as the years passed. His "Special Agent," recorded in April, 1938, and released in the summer on De 7491, was a magnificent country blues. His Victor recordings had used a heavy piano accompaniment, but during the 'thirties he was recording with just guitars and a harmonica. He was one of the few singers to consciously return to a less sophisticated style of accompaniment. Even on the Bluebird lists there were still singers from the Mississippi delta country who sang with some of the raw vitality and savage intensity of the old country blues.

# 15

## 49,51,61

In the summer heat, lightning flickers across the sky and clouds throw their heavy shadows across the dusty fields. Men straighten up to wipe the sweat out of their eyes, looking toward patches of shade under the trees. Cars pass by on the sticky roads, shining in the sun until they are a glistening speck in the distance. The delta is a swollen, drowned land along the Mississippi River north of Vicksburg. It is the delta of the muddy Yazoo River, land flooded across spring after spring, until it was buried under the rich earth from the higher ground. Ask a Southerner where the delta begins and he'll laugh, "The delta begins at the lobby of the Peabody Hotel in Memphis, Tennessee."

How far south does it go? Maybe to Vicksburg. Maybe to Jackson. Is Natchez in the delta?

"Never thought about it much. Must be, though. Hell, yes."

The delta begins below Memphis and goes south, as far south as you want it to go.

The delta country is "Black Belt" country. It's hard country for a Negro. The land is good for cotton— flat, rich, easy to work. It was slave country and near-slave country until the depression. It was bad in the delta. There is a rotted kind of Southerner in Mississippi and lynchings were long public affairs with elaborate bestiality. The lynch rate in Mississippi through the 'twenties and the 'thirties was the highest in the South, and every lynching was a hideous spectacle. If the county needed road work done or a levee built, you just didn't walk down the wrong road or get off by yourself in town. You would be "on the chain." No trial, no hearing. Vagrancy, even if you're on your way back home from the store. Disorderly conduct, if you talk back, and there's no white man to get you out. If you're colored, "armed robbery" is having a closed pen-knife in your pocket when you ask a white man for money he owes you. Armed robbery, in Mississippi, is a life sentence. Looking at a white woman is "rape." It was Klan country until the 1940's. It's been Citizens'-Council country since the early 1950's.

The best known of the Mississippi penitentiaries is in the Delta, at Parchman, south of Clarksdale. The prison buildings are set in the middle of flat, well-tended cotton fields. The men still wear stripes, and the guards wait with shotguns for a man to make a break. There's a patch of woods beginning about two hundred yards north of the prison yard, and if a man was in the fields working and the guard wasn't looking his way he could just about get to the edge of the woods before they saw him. But the woods are bare, stripped of brush, and the dogs would be on him before he'd gone a mile. The trees just stand there, across the fields, looking like a place out of Hell. The old slave songs still live in the crowded buildings behind Parchman's wire fences. There is still the cry of heartsick, beaten man.

The delta has always been blues country and there have been dozens of singers recorded from the area. There were blues about the life and the women, and blues about the highways, 49, 51 and 61, running north and south through the state. One of the first written blues, "Yellow Dog Blues," came from the delta country. A man was sitting in the streets singing, "I'm going where the Southern cross the Yellow Dog." The Southern is the Southern Railroad, the Yellow Dog is the Yazoo Delta R.R. They cross in a little town called Moorhead, "Home of Sunflower Junior College," not far from Parchman. Some of the singers came from the Yazoo River towns. The river meanders across the flat country, moving north to flood into the Mississippi at Clarksdale. The towns don't build too close to it; at least not the white sections. The rains swell the river over its banks, across the fields, into the poor shacks that have straggled too close.

From Charlie Patton, Son House, Robert Johnson and Bukka White, to Muddy Waters and John Lee Hooker, there has been an almost unbroken line of great delta singers. Some of the singers feel that the blues came from the delta, and if any one place could have given birth to the entire variety and richness of the blues, the delta could have done it. In the 'thirties, in the relentless repetition of the Bluebird Blues lists, the two singers who managed to bring some life into their blues were from the Mississippi delta, Joe Williams and Tommy McClennan.

Joe Williams was born in Crawford, Mississippi, on October 16, 1903. His father's cabin was near the Knox-ford Swamp. There were sixteen children in the family, eight boys and eight girls, and it was a poor, hard life. Joe hated it. When he was a little boy he decided he ". . . didn't want to plow, didn't want to chop cotton." He made a one-string guitar when he was four and a half, and he learned songs from his mother and father. He started making up his own blues when he was just getting into his teens, and he still remembers one of his early songs, "Crow Jane Blues," about a neighborhood woman named Jane Tripley. He remembers that ". . . she was a good looking woman when I was a child, still is." He didn't do much field work, but hired out instead to the work gangs along the Mississippi levee or along the railroad lines.

The levee camps and the line camps were squalid, filthy collections of tents or shacks. The work was ex-hausting and the living wasn't much easier. In a lumber camp, in the middle of the swamps, the Company would own the honky-tonk, and sometimes they'd bring in women to keep the men from straying. The pay was $1 to $1.50 a day, and a man never saved anything. It just went out on Saturday-night drinking and dancing to the guitar music of men like Joe Williams. "If a man got killed they'd jus' lay him back out the way." Joe drifted from one camp to another, growing up as best he could. In the levee camps they'd work twelve to sixteen hours a day, then crawl onto rotton mattresses laid out under big tents. They'd have to go find people who were living "backwater," in the ground between the levee and the river, to get a meal or a woman.

The railroad camps were a little better. The men lived in boxcars, and they could get into a town or find some dancing and excitement without looking too far. The food was the same in all the camps. Beans. Chicken on Sunday. Joe came out of the camps thin, hard and mean.

Joe finally got good enough playing the guitar to start taking little jobs for dances or picnics. He drifted into Tuscaloosa and made a hit with a local pimp and racketeer named Totsie King. Totsie was king of the Tuscaloosa poor section, "the M & O Bottoms," and he sent Joe out to play dances around the country. Joe played every dance he could get to, drinking as much as he could get his hands on and chasing the women. Sometimes there'd be a fight, maybe a killing, and he'd have to get out the best he could, leaving his guitar. He got into the habit of buying old broken guitars and remaking them with extra strings so he was playing on nine or ten strings instead of the usual six. He came close to getting murdered himself. He saw a pretty woman at a dance and he leaned over and sang to her:

"If that's your woman you better put her to your side,
'cause if she flag my train I'm sure going to let her ride."

The woman's husband came back with a revolver and shot at Joe. He missed, and Joe went out the window before he could get in another shot.

The medicine show entertainers picked Joe up in Crawford, and he got a job playing with a little band for one of the Rabbit's Foot Minstrel shows. Joe, "One Armed Dave," a "Dr. Scott" and Bogus Ben Covington, a fake blind man from Alabama who recorded for Vocalion, all played guitars. Jay Bird Coleman played harmonica, "New Orleans Slide" played washboard and "Honeycup" played jug. Jay Bird was a singer and instrumentalist from Bessemer, Alabama, who recorded for Gennet and Columbia. Jay Bird shouted a line of his blues, then played the line on the harmonica, and the Gennet recordings, without any other accompaniment, were magnificent. He was so popular around Birmingham, that the local Ku Klux Klan began acting as his manager in 1929. Joe believes the jug band recorded for OKeh on Whitehall Street in Atlanta about 1928, but the records can't be identified. Early in the 1930's, Joe finally made it to Chicago and in 1931 recorded six blues for Paramount. They were issued, but for years they were difficult to identify. For some reason he recorded as "King Solomon Hill." The six blues— "Whoopee Blues" and "Down on My Bended Knee" on Para 13116; "My Buddy Blind Pappa Lemon" and "Time Has Done Got Out of Hand" on Para 13125, and "Tell Me, Baby" and "The Dead Gone Train" on Para 13129—were recorded at the studio at Port Washington, and were among the last records issued by Paramount before the company fell apart.

An unidentified friend was in the studio with Joe and shouted comments during the recording. The record "My Buddy Blind Pappa Lemon" was released by Paramount as a tribute to Blind Lemon Jefferson, but

Joe seems to have been confused. The Lemon he knew was a singer from Decatur, Alabama, who'd gotten into trouble over a killing. It was unfortunate that Joe's early recording career was short. He was an exciting singer and his blues were raw delta cries. He sang with a forced high pitch in his voice and on his later records he had to sing in his heavier natural voice.

During the worst of the depression, Joe got along working on the W.P.A. or in the levee gangs. In the late 'thirties, he started singing again and began recording for Bluebird with Sonny Boy Williamson playing harmonica accompaniments. His singing still had the irregular rhythm of the field songs, and he accompanied his shouted verses with an arresting, dramatic guitar style. His "Please Don't Go," on BB B-8969, sold very well, and he did a good blues about the highway that runs from Jackson to Clarksdale, "Highway 49," on BB B-9025.

> Well, I get up in the morning, catch the Highway 49.
> Yes, I'm gettin' up this morning, oh, catch the High-
> way 49.
> I'm findin' my sweet woman, well well, she gonna
> pay for don't you no mind. . . .
>
> I'm goin' to wake in the morning, I believe I miss
> my babe.
> I'm gettin' up in the morning, well I believe I miss
> my babe.
> Well that Highway 49, boys, it be rockin' through
> my head.
>
> Blue this morning, well I be rolling back to town.
> Blue this morning, I be rolling back to town.

I'm tired of layin' 'round, well boys, on that Highway 49.

When the war ended the Bluebird blues recordings, Joe headed back to Mississippi, but thought better
of it and stopped in St. Louis. He found another blues
singer in the city, Charlie Jordan, and they did a lot of
entertaining together. Jordan had come out of Arkansas,
to record for Mayo Williams at Vocalion, and he'd had
a big record, Vo 1511, "Keep It Clean." After two or
three years of recording, he started relying on obscenity
to sell his records, but he was still a fine blues singer.
He and Joe kept in touch with each other until 1954,
when Charlie was shot dead on Ninth Street by a
woman he was involved with. Joe drinks a lot, and gets
along by begging or getting help from women. He has
recorded again, for a small St. Louis company, and the
record should be available early in 1960. His voice is
rougher and his playing is a little ragged, but he is
still a striking singer.

The other Bluebird singer from the delta was a
younger man, Tommy McClennan. He was born in
April, 1908, near Yazoo City, about forty miles north
of Jackson. Yazoo City is a small town edging nervously
toward the Yazoo River. The wealthier homes are on a
high bluff; the road scrambles downhill to the two or
three streets of businesses and stores, levels out in the
shabby colored district, then crosses the fields that cover
the last two hundred yards to the river on a narrow
embankment. Along Main Street there are mostly hard-
ware stores, a few clothing stores and two or three
blocks of cotton factors. Bins of cotton samples fill

the windows, labels tied to each bin to identify the grower.

McClennan worked about nine miles out of town on the J. F. Sligh farm. The farm is at the end of a winding dirt road, marked with a weathered red barn and the lines of cabins for the people working the fields. A car coming to the farm has to pass the main house, and when Lester Melrose went down to get McClennan for Bluebird, he didn't take Big Bill's advice and send a Negro from town to get Tommy. The farm people saw Melrose talking with one of their Negroes, saw the Illinois license plate on his car, and went after him. They chased Melrose all the way back to town.

Tommy lived on the farm, but he came into town every weekend and hung around the Ren Theatre, a red brick building right across the I. C. tracks from the freight station. If he wasn't in the barroom next door to the theatre, he was in the pool room next door to the bar. He was short and thin, very dark skinned, a nervous man who liked to drink and shout. He learned to play the guitar when he was in his teens and was locally famous for his version of "Bottle It Up and Go." After Bluebird picked him up, he never went back to Yazoo City. He went as far as Jackson, lived there a few months, then moved to Chicago. He put his Jackson address in one of his songs.

> Now Bluebird, when you get to Jackson,
> please fly down Charles Street . . .

McClennan was a limited guitar player and his voice was flat and harsh, but he was one of the most

ferocious blues singers to get near a microphone. Every
line sounded as though it was being torn from him;
then between lines he muttered to himself or shouted
into the microphone. He sounded hard and dangerous,
but he certainly wasn't dangerous, just intense. Two
or three bass players tried to accompany him, but Mc-
Clennan cowed them into a nervous, tentative sound
somewhere in the background behind his tortured singing. His old "Bottle It Up and Go" was his biggest hit,
and he had to do it twice. There was a shouted boast
"I'm a Guitar King," on BB B-8957 and he had a fine
highway blues about the highway from Jackson to
Memphis, "Highway 51."

Highway 51 runs right by my baby's door . . .

Here comes that Greyhound, with his tongue hangin'
out on the side.
Here comes that Greyhound, his tongue hangin' out
on the side.
You have to buy a ticket if you want to ride.

Big Bill met McClennan after his first recording
session, and took him to a party where some people
wanted to hear him sing. Bill was worried because
McClennan sang a verse with the word "nigger" in it.
In Mississippi it was used commonly by both white
and colored, but Bill had been in the North long enough
to know that nobody around Chicago wanted to hear
it. He tried to warn Tommy, but McClennan got mad.
"The hell with them. I'll sing my song . . ." McClennan
sang his song, and as Bill expected, there was trouble.
Bill got him out the window with the cord and a piece
of the neck of his guitar dangling from around his neck

and they had to run three or four blocks to get away.
McClennan was finally too much even for Bluebird
and they had to drop him. He was drinking too much
to work. He went to pieces after he stopped recording
and the last time anyone saw him he was a derelict in
the southside slums. His friends in Yazoo City think he
must be dead, and the man, Tommy McClennan, seems
to have died when he stopped singing.

There was another singer, recording for OKeh
from the delta, Bukka White. Bukka brought the same
rough intensity to OKeh that Joe Williams and Tommy
McClennan had brought to Bluebird. He had a heavy,
dark voice, and sounded like an older man, playing
simple accompaniments and singing in a strong, straight
manner. He sounded a little like Charlie Patton, the
heavy-voiced singer from around Clarksdale who had
recorded for Paramount in 1930 and 1931. Like Patton
he was a deeply moving blues singer. One of his OKeh
recordings, "Fixin' to Die Blues," on OK 05588, was a
strange song that seemed to be almost a hymn, and he
sang it in a halting voice while the guitar and a washboard rushed at the beat:

"I'm lookin' far in mind,
    I believe I'm fixin' to die,
    I believe I'm fixin' to die,
I'm lookin' far in mind,
    I believe I'm fixin' to die.
I know I was born to die, but I hate to leave my
    children cryin'.

"Just as sure we livin' today
    So we's born to die,
    Sure we's born to die.

Just as sure we livin',
    So we's born to die.
I know I was born to die but I hate to leave my
    children cryin'.

"Your mother treated me, children,
    Like I was her baby child,
    Was her baby child.
Your mother treated me, children, like
    I was her baby child.
That's why I tried so hard to come back home to die.

"So many nights at the fireside,
    How my children's mother would cry,
    How my children's mother would cry.
"So many nights at the fireside, how
    My children's mother would cry.
'Cause I ain't told the mother I had to say goodbye.

"Look over yonder,
    On the burying ground,
    On the burying ground.
Look over yonder,
    On the burying ground.
Yon stand ten thousand standin' to see them let me
    down.

"Mother, take my children back,
    Before they let me down,
    Before they let me down.
Mother, take my children back,
    Before they let me down.
And don't leave them standin' and cryin' on the
    graveyard ground."

On the Vocalion blues lists there was another delta
singer, a frightening singer from the Clarksdale area,
the tormented Robert Johnson.

# 16

## Robert Johnson

"I got stones in my pathway, and my road is dark as
   night."

The young Negro audience for whom the blues has been
a natural emotional expression has never concerned itself with artistic pretensions. By their standards, Robert
Johnson was sullen and brooding, and his records sold
very poorly. It is artificial to consider him by the standards of a sophisticated audience that during his short
life was not even aware of him, but by these standards
he is one of the superbly creative blues singers.

Almost nothing is known about his life. In 1941,
Muddy Waters, a young singer who was recording for
the Library of Congress, said that Johnson had been
raised near the Mississippi, north of Clarksdale, but he
had never seen him. Will Shade, the Memphis musician, was playing in a roadhouse in West Memphis,
Arkansas, and Johnson came in and played with the
band for a few minutes. He was murdered in San

Antonio, Texas, in 1937, a few weeks after his last recordings. From the little that Muddy Waters and Will Shade have remembered, Johnson seems to have been about thirty years old when he recorded. In the early years of the depression he went into Arkansas, then moved to San Antonio. There is a story that his first recordings were done in a billiard parlor and a drunken fight broke out after he had recorded. Someone threw a billiard ball at one of the engineers and smashed several of the masters. The company ledger sheets for the recordings, November 23, 26 and 27, 1936, list only a single recording for the second session; so the story may be true.

The next spring, June nineteenth and twentieth, he recorded in Dallas; then returned to San Antonio. Sometime during the summer he was poisoned by his common-law wife.

It seemed possible that he might have lived in Clarksdale, about thirty miles south of his home, in the 1930's, but he seems to have moved north, into West Memphis. His name was not known to anyone in Clarksdale. San Antonio is a large, sprawling city, and despite weeks of questioning, no one could be found who remembered him. He is only a name on a few recordings.

In three days of recording in 1936 and two days in 1937, Johnson did twenty-seven sides for the American Recording Corporation. Three were rejected, but twenty-four were released on the Vocalion label in 1937 and 1938, and six sides were used on the cheaper Conqueror label. There were probably other sides released on the A. R. C. labels—Melotone, Perfect, Oriole,

Romeo and Banner—but the records are very rare and it is difficult to determine which sides were used.

There was almost every kind of blues on the records. Robert Johnson is an artist like Blind Willie Johnson; the intensity of his own performance reshaped the songs into a searing, harsh poetry. There is a suggestion of Scrapper Blackwell's guitar style in his playing, but he uses the guitar as a thin, droning undertone or as an extension of his singing, and his style is distinctively his own. For many of his accompaniments he uses a bottle neck to slide on the strings, giving the guitar an insistent, whining sound.

He was consistently brilliant, but there are four or five records that seem to be identified with him. "32-20 Blues" and "Last Fair Deal Gone Down" on Vo 03445; "Preachin' Blues" on Vo 04630, "Stones in My Pathway" on Vo 03723, and "Hellhound on My Trail" on Vo 03623. They are perhaps his finest blues, but many of the other blues have a superb imagery. "Terraplane Blues," on Vo 03416, is an extended sexual image, elaborated until the blues is an imaginative poetic image, rather than a thin series of double meanings, "Come on in My Kitchen," Vo 03563, is another sexual blues,

Come on in my kitchen, it's rainin' outside,

but he sings it in a gruff, heavy voice, as though he were unsure of himself with the girl, then his voice falls and the guitar almost stops, playing a halting series of notes on the upper strings. He mumbles, almost inaudibly,

"Can't you hear that rain . . . don't you hear that rain outside . . . ," and the notes from the guitar suddenly seem to evoke the smell of a summer rainstorm, and the water streaming down a shadowed window pane.

The finest of Robert Johnson's blues have a brooding sense of torment and despair. The blues has become a personified figure of despondency. On "Preachin' Blues" he cried:

"Uunh, Got up this morning, blues walkin' like a man.
Got up this morning, blues walkin' like a man.
Well, uunh, blues, give me your right hand. . . ."

His singing becomes so disturbed it is almost impossible to understand the words. The voice and the guitar rush in an incessant rhythm. As he sings he seems to cry out in a high falsetto voice.

Johnson seemed emotionally disturbed by the image of the devil, the "Hellhound," and he used the image in at least two blues. His last group of recordings included "Hellhound on My Trail" and "Me and the Devil Blues." The figure seemed to be his torment.

Early this mornin, when you knocked upon my door.
Early this morning, uunh, when you knocked upon my door,
I said, Hello, Satan, I believe it's time to go.

Me and the devil, both walkin' side by side.
Me and the devil, uunh, both walkin' side by side.
I'm going to beat my woman, 'til I get satisfied. . . .

You may bury my body, down by the highway side.
(spoken) Babe, I don't care where you bury
my body when I'm dead and gone.

You can bury my body down by the highway side.
Lord, my old evil spirit can catch a greyhound bus
and ride.

"Hellhound on My Trail" was one of his most moving blues.

I got to keep moving, uunh, I got to keep moving.
Blues falling down like hail, blues falling down like
hail.
Uunh, Blues falling down like hail, blues falling down
like hail.
I can't keep no money, hellhound on my trail,
Hellhound on my trail, hellhound on my trail.

I can tell the wind is running, leaves shaking on the
tree, shakin' on the tree.
I can tell the wind is running, the leaves shakin' on
the tree, uunh.
All I need's my little sweet woman, uunh, keep me
company, uunh, my company.

The first of the Dallas recordings, "Stones in My
Pathway," seemed to express the brooding pain of his
short life.

I got stones in my pathway, and my road is dark as
night . . .

I got a bird to whistle, and I got a bird to sing.
I got a bird to whistle, uunh, a bird to sing.
I got a woman don't love me. She don't mean a thing.

# 17

## "Hey, Mama, Hey, Pretty Girl"

There was a sensual side to the 'thirties, and the strain of coarse "party blues" was widened and carried to even greater excess than in the late 'twenties. The Vocalion lists, which included Big Bill and Robert Johnson, also included Blind Boy Fuller, and there was no other major blues singer, except perhaps Lonnie Johnson, who sang as much coarse material as Fuller. He seemed to have a taste for vulgarity that gave his recordings a kind of leering fascination. It was like listening to dirty stories told with style and imagination. Between July, 1935, and June, 1940, Fuller recorded 123 blues for the American Recording Corporation's Vocalion, Melotone, Conqueror and Perfect labels, many of them crudely suggestive. Fuller was a good blues singer and an exciting guitarist, and he sang dozens of blues that were less vulgar, but he was for Vocalion

212

what Bo Carter was for Bluebird, a "party blues" singer.

The party blues had been very popular in the late 1920's and there was a large audience for this kind of singing. Most of the songs were like Tampa Red's "She Wants to Sell My Monkey," a series of double meanings with a suggestive title, but a few singers, like Blind Boy Fuller, were able to bring to them a colorful imagination and an exciting vocal style. The records were very popular for parties. The people would sit around the phonograph trying to guess the meaning of the confusing imagery, and there would be shrieks of laughter and embarrassment when somebody inter-preted a phrase. Fuller recorded dozens of the songs, but his imagery was often so thinly disguised that the titles themselves were very nearly pornographic.

Fuller was one of a number of singers who were playing and singing the blues around the tobacco-mill towns of North Carolina in the depression years. The sales of cigarets had not been as badly hit as the sales of other items, and in towns like Raleigh, Greensboro, Durham and Winston-Salem, there was still work. The singers hung around the mill workers, making a living singing in small clubs or along the streets. Fuller was from Rockingham, North Carolina, his full name Fuller Allen. He was born in 1903 and learned to play the guitar when he was a boy. An accident when he was in his early twenties left him blind. He moved into Dur-ham and began singing on the streets. He made enough money singing to get married, and after three or four years he and his wife, Cora Mae, were able to adopt a little girl.

In 1934, when Fuller was thirty-one years old, he

was in Waver, North Carolina, visiting his sister. A harmonica player heard Fuller was in town, and went up to the house and asked if he could play some blues with him. They played together for three or four hours, and Fuller told him to look for him in Durham and they'd try to get a job together. The harmonica player was the young Sonny Terry.

Sonny, like Fuller, was from North Carolina. He was born outside of Durham October 24, 1911. He was born Saunders Teddell, the son of a farmer named Reuben Teddell. There were three brothers, Willie, Ronald and Asbury. He grew up on his father's twenty-acre farm learning to play the harmonica when he was still a little boy. His father was a good harmonica player and started Sonny on the favorite little songs "Lost John" and "Fox Chase." A well-known harmonica player named DeFord Bailey came through town and Sonny learned a little from him, but mostly he picked it up from his father. When he was just learning, he'd sit for hours imitating the sounds of the trains that passed in the distance.

When Sonny met Fuller he was nearly blind himself. When he was eleven, he was beating a stick against a chair and a piece of it broke off and flew into his eye. The sight in that eye was impaired. Five years later a boy threw a small piece of iron at Sonny and put out his other eye. He realized that he'd have to start playing on the streets to make a living; so he started going into Durham and Raleigh, playing all afternoon; then walking home alone in the darkness. When he met Fuller he was twenty-three, playing in a distinctive wailing style that was a fine contrast to Fuller's dark voice.

They got along in Durham, playing together most of the time, but separating for occasional jobs out of town. They became such close friends that Sonny moved in with Fuller and his wife. Durham is a crowded, drab town, but with the money they made from the workers around town, they got by fairly well. A man from Bullerton, North Carolina, named J. B. Long, was managing a store in Durham, and heard the pair playing on the street. He talked Fuller into letting him be his manager, and took Fuller up to New York City to audition for the American Recording Corporation.

Fuller's audition was successful, and twelve blues were recorded from July 23 to July 26, 1935. "Baby, I Don't Have to Worry" and "Looking for My Woman" were released on Vocalion 02956 in September. Fuller immediately caught on. He played with a sharp, rhythmic beat and sang with a loud assurance. Fuller and a new Decca singer, Kokomo Arnold, had the same kind of self-confidence, and both their records sold well in the middle 'thirties. Kokomo's first record, "Milk Cow Blues" and "Original Kokomo Blues," on Decca 7026, was released the same summer that Fuller made his first records. Kokomo was a fine guitar player, using a bottle neck on his little finger in a frenzied rhythmic style. The basic rhythm was almost lost in a blur of rhythmic elaborations. For two or three years their records sold with about the same success, but Arnold had less variety than Fuller, and Decca was forced to drop him.

Fuller came back to Durham after the recording sessions, and he and Sonny went back to their old life of playing on the streets. Fuller's recording fees had

paid for his and Long's train fare to New York. Long
was one of the few white Southerners who would have
much to do with the blues singers, and he managed
Fuller, and later Sonny, for what he could get out of it.
He even listed himself as a "composer" on most of the
blues they recorded. He'd write down the words; then
stand behind Fuller, whispering them in his ear when
he was recording. Long never pretended that he was
interested in anything but the money and Sonny talks
about him without rancor:

> "Long got us recording, you know, and at the be-
> ginning he got all the money. We didn't care, 'cause
> it got us our start."

Fuller recorded every five or six months for the
next two years, all the recording, with the exception
of two Decca sessions in July, 1937, for the American
Recording Corporation. The washboard player, "Oh
Red," recorded with him in February, 1937, and they
did a series of exciting numbers together. "Mamie" and
"New Oh Red," on Vo 03276, and "Death Valley" and
"Throw Your Yas Yas Back in Jail," on Vo 03420, sold
very well. Fuller was at his best with another musician
to work with him. He let the other man stay on the
rhythm and he played brilliant melodic variations on
the upper strings of the guitar. He used a heavy, steel-
bodied National guitar, with a very loud tone; so he had
no trouble being heard. He often used irregular driving
rhythms in a complex rhythmic variation of the other
man's ideas. Oh Red, whose name was George Washington, worked with Fuller for the next four years.

In December, 1937, Sonny made the trip to New York with Fuller and they recorded nineteen blues, Sonny playing on most of the sides. The Decca recordings by Sleepy John Estes, with Noah Lewis on harmonica, were selling; so A. R. C. was probably trying to cover the idea with a harmonica player of their own. Oh Red didn't make the trip, but he recorded with Sonny and Fuller at the next sessions in October, 1938. The A. R. C. sent a director down to South Carolina to record them there. Some of Fuller's best, and some of his most obscene, blues were recorded over the next two years. His fine "Three Balls Blues," Vo 05440, was recorded in March, 1940, and "Thousand Woman Blues" on OKeh 05657, was recorded at his last session on June 19, 1940.

"Three Ball Blues" was a pawnshop blues with the well-known verse,

> I asked that pawnshop man, what them three balls doing hanging on that wall.
> I asked that pawnshop man, what them three balls doing hanging on that wall.
> He said it's two to one, buddy, you don't get your things out of here at all.

"Thousand Woman Blues" had a long, free shouted line, almost a field cry, suddenly changing into a rhythmic blues as the line ended:

> "I never loved but a thousand women in my life . . ."

He had lost none of his old assurance. In March, 1940, he recorded "Little Woman You're So Sweet," on Vo 05476.

Hey, Mama, Hey girl, don't you hear Blind Boy
    Fuller calling you,
She's so sweet, so sweet,
My little woman, so sweet.

Back in Durham, he and Sonny were celebrities.
Sonny had even been to New York for the 1938 "Spirituals to Swing" concert, standing alone in the middle
of the stage in Carnegie Hall playing his harmonica for
a surprised audience. J. B. Long was still managing
both of them, and his name often appeared with Fuller's
on the label, in the small composer's credit line under
the title of the blues. Sonny's name was on only a few
of the records, but people who saw him with Fuller
reasoned that he must be the other name on the record.
They'd wave to him and say, "Hello there, J. B."
    Sonny had begun recording under his own name,
and he and Oh Red did a breathtaking "Harmonica
Stomp" and "Harmonica and Washboard Blues" on OK
05538. Sonny half sang and half played the blues, singing in a falsetto that picked up the timbre and pitch of
the harmonica. There were two versions of "Harmonica
Stomp," both released as by Sonny and Oh Red, but
Fuller joined in on the second take and it's one of their
best records.

    In the summer of 1940, four or five weeks after
their last recording sessions, Oh Red met a guitar player
named Brownie McGhee and a harmonica player named
Jordan Webb hitchhiking through Burlington, North
Carolina, about thirty miles west of Durham. He liked
their playing and brought them around to Fuller's

house in Durham. Brownie and Sonny got along, but Fuller wasn't as enthusiastic. Brownie was a good guitar player and singer and Fuller realized that they might be competing with each other in the next few months. Oh Red took them to J. B. Long, and Long sent Oh Red, Brownie and Jordan to the OKeh studios in Chicago to record. When Brownie returned to Durham, he and Fuller still saw each other occasionally. They were more impressed with each other than either would admit. Brownie's first records were a success, but he and Fuller never became rivals. Fuller died during the winter. He had not been well for several months, but his death, from a kidney ailment, stunned his friends.

Brownie got Fuller's big National guitar and in May, 1941, he recorded the simple tribute "The Death of Blind Boy Fuller," on OKeh 06265.

He's gone, Blind Boy Fuller's gone away.
  (repeat)
He heard a voice calling, and he knew he could not stay.

He called me to his bedside one morning as the clock was striking four.
  (repeat)
Crying to get my guitar and take my baby home, I won't stay here no more.

Blind Boy had a million friends, North, East, South and West.
  (repeat)
Yes, you know it's hard to tell which place he was loved the best.

Well, all you women of Blind Boy, how you want your
  lovin' done.
    (repeat)
I'll do my best, I'll do my best to carry Blind Boy
  Fuller's business on.

Goodbye, Blind Boy.

# 18

## Brownie McGhee

Blind Boy Fuller was dead, but J. B. Long wasn't. He
realized that if he could find someone to record the
songs that he had copyrighted with Fuller he would
continue to collect a fair percentage of the royalties.
When Fuller died, it was Long's idea for Brownie to
record "The Death of Blind Boy Fuller" for OKeh.
Brownie used Fuller's guitar for the recording, Sonny
Terry accompanied him, and when the record was released the label read "Brownie McGhee (Blind Boy
Fuller #2)." Long was successful in maintaining his
own relationship with OKeh. The most successful of
Brownie's first OKeh records was Fuller's popular "Step
It Up and Go." After Fuller's brilliant recording, "Step
It Up and Go #2" seemed a little unsure, but the entire
idea wasn't fair to either Fuller or McGhee. There were
men who sounded more like Fuller than Brownie did,
but they either were not available or would not work
for Long. Even if Brownie was no Fuller, he was a

warm, personable singer with a distinctive style and a fine ability to put a blues together. The other side of the "Step it Up and Go #2" was "Workingman Blues," not one of the Long collaborations, and Brownie sounded much more at ease. The recording is much more interesting than the Fuller side. After a few months, Brownie McGhee became an artist in his own right with a series of recordings for OKeh-Columbia records.

Brownie was born Walter Brown McGhee on November 30, 1914, in Knoxville, Tennessee. Knoxville is in Eastern Tennessee, and there are only scattered colored families in this part of the mountains. It was not country where there was much need for slaves, and there is little of the country Negro life that is found in the teeming "black belt" in the cotton country to the south. Most of the Negroes in this part of Tennessee live in cities or small towns, doing the laboring and service jobs that keep the towns going. If they farm, they usually have their own small places away from the neighbors. It is beautiful country. The mountains stretch away into the bluish haze, covered with a heavy growth of broad-leafed trees that blaze into a swirl of brilliant color with the early fall weather. The farms are in narrow, winding valleys, worn out of the mountains and leveled by the mountain streams. In most of the valleys small creeks still run through the farm land, a ragged growth of brush and a weathered fence marking its course through the fields. Many of the farm buildings are still built out of boards cut from the trees at the edge of the fields, and some of the sheds are still built of logs. On a spring day, with a wisp of smoke coming out of a stone chimney and a few chickens scratching in the dirt outside the unpainted barn, the land smells rich and there is a heavy perfume blowing from the first wild-flowers and the blossoming trees.

In the towns there are ornate older homes in the "better" part of town, two or three blocks of brick stores and offices, then a ragged Negro section with unpaved streets, most of the homes unpainted. Often colored sections are monotonous rows of wooden frame buildings set along mud streets a half mile or so outside the town limits. The buildings are company buildings, owned by a mill or a lumber company, and the whistle of the mill wakes the people in the houses in the morning and puts them to bed at night. The company building itself is usually behind the trees, down toward a stream where power can be generated by the water's ceaseless rush from the higher mountains. Most of the houses use soft coal for winter heat and the towns are discolored with the coal soot from dozens of chimneys.

Brownie's father, George McGhee, had a farm near Kingsport, in the heart of the mountains, but during the years when Brownie was still a child the family moved from mill town to mill town in the Eastern part of the state or in the towns along the Tennessee River. There were three other children, two sisters and a younger brother, Granville. When he was four, Brownie was crippled with infantile paralysis and his right leg was left shorter than the left, but he recovered within a few months. He grew up with music. His father was a fine country guitar player and singer, and his uncle, John Evans, played the fiddle. The two entertained at country parties or dances, singing blues or ballad songs, or just playing breakdowns. Brownie has called the style of playing "jookin," a stomping, swinging kind of dance music that makes people stand out under the trees and dance until their faces shine with sweat and the party is shouting and clapping encouragement to keep the musicians working over their instruments. There were quilting parties, old-fashioned husking parties, or just good time get-togethers, and the music was traded from white to colored so much that it's hard to tell who made up any particular song. The famous white singer, Jimmy Rogers, a railroad brakeman living in Nashville, recorded dozens of blues that he'd heard in the mountains and the mountain banjo player, "Dock" Boggs recorded several songs that sound as though they must have been from the country quilting parties, or "jookin" parties.

Brownie's father used to go back into the valleys to play for parties almost every weekend during the harvest months, when there was money around and people wanted to have a good time to celebrate the year's crop. Uncle John usually played along with him. John played mostly "country-style" fiddle, but Brownie's father played hymns and dance songs or made up blues out of the old field songs he'd heard as a boy. Sometimes he'd go by himself to one of the levee camps for a pay night, and every now and then he'd let Brownie come along. Brownie remembered there was ". . . no sleeping." His father would play all night. John Evans had a farm in the northeast corner of Tennessee, near Kingsport, near a farm that Brownie's father worked when the jobs along the river or in the mills got a little slack, and Brownie used to go up and help out. It was a small farm, raising corn, tobacco, watermelon and hogs, like most of the farms around. It was natural that Brownie should want to play music like his father and his uncle; so John made him his first instrument, a small banjo with a marshmallow can for the head and a neck made of seasoned poplar. It had a side peg on the neck, making it a country five-string banjo. Brownie learned the first rudiments of music on it.

By the time he was eight, Brownie was learning to play the piano and could play a little on the guitar. The family moved to Lenoir City, a small town down the river from Knoxville, and Brownie was able to play on the old-fashioned foot treadle organ at the Solomon Temple Baptist church. There was a Sanctified Baptist Church in Lenoir City, and Brownie would sometimes join in their shouted services. He had a good singing voice, and he spoke and sang for school functions when he was small. He sang in a quartet at church. When he finished grade school in Lenoir City, the family moved east to a small city called Maryville, near the North Carolina state line, and Brownie started high school. He was entertaining in the Smokey Mountain summer resorts, an earnest, thin boy, playing on a guitar and a kazoo held under his arm. After a year and a half of high school, he decided he didn't want any more school and began roaming over his part of the state, hitchhiking with his guitar over his shoulder, playing wherever it looked like somebody might take him in for a meal or a dollar. He couldn't find many pianos in the ramshackle barrooms where he was playing; so he just worked harder on his guitar. It was 1928 and the first country blues records were coming into the towns where he was, the stage shows were coming through with their blues shouters and Brownie sang along in his excitement.

After traveling with the Hagg Carnival and haphazard medicine shows or minstrel shows, Brownie came back home and relearned the guitar, using finger picks so he could get more noise out of his instrument and save his fingers. In the early 'thirties, the depression years, the family had gone back to the farm at Kingsport, and Brownie was working with his father and singing in a gospel quartet, the "Golden Voices." Kingsport was a small town in Eastern Tennessee and after two or three years on its streets, Brownie got restless and went into Knoxville and started running little bands for picnics and dances. He generally used two guitars, a harmonica, a bass of some kind and a washboard. He was building the same kind of band sound that the Chicago singers were doing for Bluebird, but Brownie had to do without the piano; since there aren't many pianos at an outdoor picnic. He was good, singing like his father, making a little money out of his music, but he still wasn't satisfied. About 1938 or 1939, he started working on the streets again, moving east toward the rich tobacco country of North Carolina. He stayed in Asheville for a few weeks, but Asheville's a town for white singers, not colored, and Brownie kept on going out of the mountains to the rich, hilly country where there were small fields of carefully tended tobacco and curing sheds behind every house, and the people were living with tobacco from morning to night. He had a friend in Winston-Salem, a harmonica player named

Jordan Webb, and when Brownie got picked up by the police for begging they left town together, still moving toward Durham. At Burlington they met "Oh Red." It was almost as though Brownie had known where he was heading. Washington took them into Durham, introduced them to Long, and a few weeks later the earnest boy with the limp who had learned to sing in church meetings and country parties while his father played the guitar was making his first recordings for OKeh.

Since he first began recording, Brownie has had about the same style, a fine rhythmic beat and a warm smooth voice. He is not an intense singer, but his records sold almost as well as the records of some of the men who had been established for years. The biggest hit was the remake of Fuller's "Step it Up and Go," but there was another fine shouted blues from the OKeh sessions, "Double Trouble," and "Workingman's Blues" was very popular.

> Leavin' here walkin', cryin' ain't goin' to make me stay,
> > (repeat)
> Got the blues so bad, it's the only thing that drives me away.
>
> I got the blues so bad 'til it hurts my feet to walk,
> > (repeat)
> I got the blues so bad 'til it hurts my tongue to talk.
> I got the blues so bad 'til I just can't rest at night,
> > (repeat)
> Got the blues so bad 'til it taken my appetite.

I wake up in the morning, blues on the side of my
bed,
      (repeat)
Go in to eat my breakfast find blues all in my bread.

I got the blues in my water, I got blues all in my
gin,
      (repeat)
Everywhere I go, baby, the blues keeps on followin'
me.

For the first records, made in Chicago in August,
1940, he played with Jordan Webb, but for the recordings under Long's direction he used Sonny Terry and
he and Sonny stayed together. There was another group
of records in October, 1941, and Brownie worked with
some of the best washboard and harmonica players
around. Oh Red, and Washboard Slim played wash-
boards, Sonny and Jordan Webb played harmonicas,
and Buddy Moss played second guitar. Buddy was a
Georgia singer who had been recording for Perfect and
OKeh before Brownie wandered into Durham and he
explained to Brownie the importance of getting copyrights on his songs and making sure that he was paid
composer's royalties on everything he did. When the
war ended recording, Moss went back to Dalton, Georgia; then in the early 1950's he moved to Tampa,
Florida, where he still lives and plays, but despite his
brilliant guitar style and fine blues voice he has never
recorded again. Brownie didn't make Buddy's mistake.
He went to New York and stayed.

Sonny was already in New York, and the two of
them managed to eke out a living during the war years
playing "folk-song" concerts with Leadbelly or working

night-club engagements. Brownie even had to do some street singing to make ends meet, but by 1944 recording had picked up and he signed a contract with Savoy and then with Alert in 1945. He was running his "Brownie McGhee's School of the Blues" on 125th Street, giving lessons, renting the studio for rehearsals and occasional recordings, and teaching young blues singers his own guitar style.

With his Alert and Savoy recordings, Brownie's style matured. He sang with an easy smoothness that was more of a crooning style than a blues style. He had lost some of the hot inflections that had made his early records exciting. The style of his blues was changing, too. His most popular record for Alert was his "Sporting Life Blues," on Al 401. It was a sentimental song using the melody of an old Duke Ellington composition, "Rent Party Blues."

> I'm tired of runnin' around,
> Think I will marry and settle down,
> This old night life, this old sporting life,
> Is killing me.
>
> I got a letter from my home,
> Most of my friends are dead and gone,
> I begin to worry, I begin to wonder,
> About days to come.
>
> My mother used to talk to me,
> Young and foolish and I could not see;
> I have no mother, my sisters and brothers
> Won't talk to me.
>
> She used to fall on her knees and pray,
> These are the words mother used to say:

"Brownie, oh, Brownie, please change
Your ways."

I'm going to change my ways,
I'm getting older every day,
When I was young and foolish I was
Easy led astray.

I've been a gambler and a cheater, too,
Now it's come my time to lose,
This old sportin' life is got the best hand,
What can I do?

Brownie was not from a part of the country where blues singing was a natural expression, and he seemed to sing more naturally in this sophisticated style. His biggest hit on Savoy—his biggest hit on a race record —was a popular ballad, "My Fault," recorded in 1947 with Lonnie Scott on piano and Hal Singer on tenor saxophone. It had a familiar sound, the melody was "Rent Party Blues" again, but the words were even less related to the blues than "Sporting Life" had been. His guitar playing was better than ever, and the records deserved their success. "Sporting Life" was helped with the bowed bass accompaniment, and Singer's saxophone work on "My Fault" was some of his finest recorded playing.

In the late 1940's and early 1950's, Brownie was recording for several labels and his name was everywhere. He and Sonny were more popular than they had ever been. Sonny had a hit of his own on the Capitol recording "Leaving Blues." Brownie began using pseudonyms so "people wouldn't get tired of his name." He recorded a group of spirituals for Circle Records as

"The Tennessee Gabriel," and he was "Spider Sam" for Atlantic, "Big Tom Collins" for King, "Henry Johnson" for Decca and "Blind Boy Williams" for Jade. His brother "Globetrotter" played second guitar on the Circle dates; then played guitar while Brownie played piano on the Jade dates. Along with the recording he did as a singer, he recorded as part of accompaniment groups for several of his friends. He was one of the busiest artists in the blues field.

In the last few years, both Brownie and Sonny have been recording for a folk-music label, Folkways Records, and they have become well-known "folk artists," making very successful tours throughout the United States and Europe. Brownie seems at his best on his Folkways recordings, singing his blues songs in a relaxed, easy style, with Sonny's harmonica shrilling a memorable accompaniment. He has become a successful stage personality and has appeared in two major Broadway productions, Langston Hughes's *Simply Heavenly*, and Tennessee Williams's *Cat on a Hot Tin Roof*. He was married in 1950 and has three children. He and Sonny live a few blocks from each other, and are still close friends. Sonny made a successful Broadway debut playing his harmonica for a scene in the musical *Finian's Rainbow*. When Brownie is not on tour he lives quietly in his apartment on 125th Street in New York, working on new songs or visiting his many friends. He is a warm, engaging man for whom the blues have been an introduction to a fine career as a singer and entertainer.

# 19

## "The Mommies and Daddies from Coast to Coast"

Many of the Negro veterans who were discharged from the service in 1945 and 1946 were resentful of the blues and the social conditions that had produced the blues. They had given their hearts and bodies to defend an ideal of social equality, and they returned to find there was little change in the South, and there was still prejudice and discrimination out of the South. In their bitterness, they lashed out at members of their race who seemed to represent the older social patterns. Big Bill wrote:

> Some Negroes tell me that the old style of blues is carrying Negroes back to the horse-and-buggy days and back to slavery—and who wants to be reminded of slavery? And some will say this ain't slavery no more, so why don't you learn to play something else? [1]

[1] Ibid.

232

Young singers reacted to this kind of criticism with a savagely belligerent style of blues singing, but many of the older singers had to answer as Big Bill did,

"I just tell them I can't play nothing else. . . ."

Within two or three years after the war, the recordings by Big Bill, Tampa Red, Washboard Sam and others from the old lists were selling very poorly. There was a restlessness and aggressiveness in the new young colored audience that was much more excited by the fierce shouting of newer singers—Lightnin' Hopkins, B. B. King, John Lee Hooker, Muddy Waters, Smokey Hogg and Bo Diddley—than it was in the more sophisticated styles of Big Bill or Brownie McGhee. There were long months of insecurity for many of the blues singers and most of the older men were eventually forced into retirement.

The young blues singers who crowded Big Bill and the others out of the picture were loud, mean and sometimes magnificent. The beat had slowed down and the guitars were turned up; so that there was an almost unbearable tension to their singing. The piano was used less and less and the accompaniments used shill electrified harmonicas and guitars, with an undertone of monotonous drumming. The records were overpowering in their crude immensity.

The electrified guitar had been used since the late 1930's, but most of the guitar players had used the new louder volume when they were taking solos; then turned the volume down when they were singing. Guitars like the steel-bodied National that Blind Boy Fuller used were almost as loud as the first amplified instruments. After the war, there were more and more young blues artists who used their new electric guitars at an increasingly high volume. The poorer musicians turned it up to hide their weaknesses and the others were forced to go along. The ringing electric guitars became the standard blues sound of the post-war years.

The large record companies, within two or three years after the war, had completely lost control of the blues record business. There were hundreds of companies recording blues, many of them Negro-owned and many of them in the South. The Chess Record Company in Chicago and Savoy Records in New York have recorded some of the best of the post-war blues, with Atlantic Records, in New York, not far behind. Few of the singers signed exclusive contracts; so a singer like Lowell Fulson or Smokey Hogg was often recording simultaneously for half a dozen companies.

In the late 1940's, more and more blues singers began traveling to recording studios in California. Several companies had sprung up in Hollywood and San Francisco to try to catch the new market for blues records among the new Negro populations in West Los Angeles, San Francisco, Oakland, and Richmond. These cities had a staggering influx of workers for the shipyards and aircraft factories. Hundreds of thousands of Negroes left the South for California. They were a rich, clamorous blues market. Alladin, in Hollywood, was the largest of the companies, but there were dozens of small labels, like Pacific, Trilon, Hollywood, Modern Hollywood, Bel-Tone, Philo, Score, Rhythm and Atlas.

It was a tightly competitive, often dishonest business, but the possible returns on a hit record were very

large. Many of the releases were just intended to introduce a song, and the singer was incidental. The companies were trying for composer royalties. A Hollywood
company that specialized in traditional jazz released
blues records on a subsidiary label, and in the spring of
1953 one of their blues began to catch on. By making
the usual concessions, the company got the song up to
eight on the national hit parade. The "usual concessions" meant that by the time the song got to the hit
parade seventeen more people were receiving a share
of the royalties. Nineteen people, besides the obscure
composer who had written the song, were getting a
share of the return. The composer got very nervous
when he realized that his song was making a small
fortune and he was getting very little of it. He and his
mother went to court and proved he was nineteen years
old. Since he was a minor the contracts he had signed
were not valid, and the royalties were turned over to
his mother. Within two weeks his song had disappeared
from the hit parade.

Only a handful of singers have emerged as blues
singers of any stature out of the hundreds of "down-
home" singers who have recorded since the war. One
of the most popular singers of the late 1940's was a
Texan named Aaron "T-Bone" Walker. T-Bone had
grown up around Waxahachie, Texas, and had seen
Lemon Jefferson two or three times when Lemon was
in town or T-Bone was in Dallas. T-Bone's recording
career began when he was sixteen. In 1929, he recorded
for the Columbia 14000 series in Dallas, using the name
"Oak-Cliff T-Bone." He lived in Texas during the 1930's,

singing and playing in local night clubs. He wasn't much
of a blues singer, but he was a hard working entertainer.
He made several television appearances in the 1950's
as ". . . a singer whose singing goes right to the heart
of this thing we call the blues." The curtain would open
on T-Bone wearing a gold lamé jacket and holding a
jeweled guitar plugged into a long chord that T-Bone
had to keep stepping over during his performance. He
usually sang a fast "jump blues" ending up in a rhythm
dance, with a split while he played the guitar behind
the back of his head as the climax.

The blues had already become confused with the
post-war style called "rhythm and blues," a loud, swinging music that had some of the feeling of the old "Bluebird beat," but since the 1950's the blues have been
almost lost in the teen-age craze, "rock and roll." Rock
and roll took the post-war blues singing style and set
it against a slow rhythm of repetitive chords in the
piano or guitar and an accented off-beat on the drums.
The effect was overpowering. The first rock and roll
singer to reach the general public was a white singer
from Tupelo, Mississippi, named Elvis Presley. Presley
had grown up in the South singing rhythm and blues
and he sang with a more swinging beat than many of
the race artists did. His success has left a deep impression on post-war blues styles.

Presley's family had moved into Memphis when he
was still a boy. In high school he learned to play a little
on a twelve-dollar guitar his father had given him. He
graduated from high school in 1953 and got a job driving a truck for the Crown Electric Company for forty

dollars a week. He took his first check and went over to the Sun Record Company studios and paid four dollars to make a record for his mother. He went over on his lunch hour, carrying his guitar in one hand and his lunch in the other. The office manager thought he had possibilities, and got his name and address. A year later, Sam Phillips, president of Sun, had a ballad to record and they thought of calling the singer who had made the record the summer before. Presley had been promoted to answering the phone and when he got the message he was on his way to the studio as fast as he could get there. He remembers that he ran most of the way. They tried him on the ballad and it was almost completely unsuccessful. Phillips finally gave up and had Presley sing whatever he could think of for the next three hours. Still nothing happened. He finally got a bass player and a guitar player and told them to see if they could work anything out with Presley.

When the three of them got back in the studio the next week, they worked all afternoon trying to record a ballad. It just wasn't Presley's style. They finally took a break and he started fooling around with a rhythm and blues number, "That's All Right, Mama." The other musicians fell over themselves picking up their instruments, the engineer turned on the microphone, and an hour later they had a record. Phillips took the first test around to a Memphis disc jockey and he played it on the next morning's show. Within a week they had orders for six thousand copies of the record. Presley's records on Sun sold by the hundreds of thousands, at first almost entirely to a Negro audience. His records were

played over and over on Southern rhythm and blues
shows and on hot afternoons his voice blared out of
the open doors of dozens of bars and restaurants.

In the fall of 1955, Presley played the annual con-
vention of the "Country and Western Disc Jockey Association" in Nashville. Two Victor talent scouts were
in the audience and they offered to buy his contract
from Sun. They later said that they ". . . hadn't seen
anything so weird in a long time." When Presley had
made his first stage appearance in Memphis, he had
started on a fast number to overcome his nervousness
and he didn't notice until the song was half over that
the audience was screaming. He remembers he
". . . went offstage and my manager says it was because I was wigglin' my legs." It was this stage act that
the Victor scouts had seen.

Sun had six unissued sides of Presley's and they
sold them as well as his contract to Victor for thirty-
five thousand dollars. It seemed like a good price when
the arrangement was made, but after the unissued recordings had broken sales records for Victor, Phillips
was asked by reporters why he had sold Presley so
cheaply. He grinned wryly and said that he really didn't
expect his popularity to last.

When Victor brought Presley to New York, he still
didn't have a great deal of stage presence. He began
hanging around the Apollo Theatre in Harlem watching
the rhythm and blues singers, Bo Diddley in particular.
They were all using dance routines similar to the
T-Bone Walker act. Whether he learned their steps and
routines or worked out his own in the same style is not
important. When Presley first became nationally known,

Bo Diddley was asked if he thought Elvis had copied some of his stage routines. Diddley shrugged, "If he copied me, I don't care—more power to him. I'm not starving."

Presley's first television appearances brought him into national prominence. He was a young, good-looking singer, shouting the blues, and shaking his hips and getting around on the stage like a strutting blues singer in a Southern night club. Overnight he was the most controversial entertainment personality since Frank Sinatra had first toured the country. Presley was ridiculed, bitterly attacked and idolized. There was an emotional near revolt of many of the young people throughout the country and they rose to Presley's defense. The new teen-age audience was richer than any juvenile group had ever been before and they spent much of their money on records. In 1956, ten million copies of Presley's records were sold. A television variety show that had first called Presley "unfit for a family audience" was forced to pay his price of fifty thousand dollars for three short appearances and he sang a new balled, "Love Me Tender." By the end of the month, Victor had orders for one million copies of "Love Me Tender" and they hadn't even recorded it yet.

Presley's immense popularity has brought bewildering confusion to the blues field. He was white, but he was singing in a Negro style, and using many of the rhythm and blues stage ideas. The fact that he was still so young brought the new teen-age audience into the picture and the result was a jumble of racial styles, derivative blues, adolescent emotional problems and relentlessly amateurish singing. The audience has tended to be hopelessly unpredictable, following the lead of the noisy teen-age group that seems to be getting through adolescence with the most assurance. For no discernible reason, a record will sell a million copies and another record sounding almost exactly like it will be lucky to sell out the first pressing. Even the standard practice of covering a successful record with versions by other singers has not worked very well. The successful record, no matter how bad, is often the only one the audience is interested in. The blues have almost been pushed out of the picture, and the singers who have survived at all have had to change their style until they sound enough like rock and roll performers to pass with the teen-age audience. The teen-age record audience buys about 90 per cent of all the single records sold; so they are a frighteningly powerful group.

The emphasis on adolescent emotional problems has changed the emotional contents of the blues, but even the changes have not brought the blues back their old popularity. A 1959 "hit parade" sheet from a Harlem record shop listed forty-nine records before a blues record, Muddy Waters's "Mean Mistreater," was listed. The next ten records were blues, but only two of them, Tarheel Slim's "Number 9 Train" and Little Walter's "Key to the Highway," were in an older blues style. Bo Diddley's "I'm Sorry" was sixty-second on the list. The records nearer the top of the list were songs like "A Lover's Question," "Love's Burning Fire," "Teardrops on Your Letter," and "I Kneel at Your Throne." It was the first time that the popular music of the two racial groups had become so similar.

The reaction to rock and roll, which by this time included the blues, was immediate and bitter. In the South, many white groups recognized the strong Negro influence in the music their children were listening to and there were attempts to suppress it. Police in several Northern cities found that the emotional atmosphere was too much for many white teen-agers and they had to ban rock and roll dances. There was further complication within the song-writing industry itself. Ninety-five per cent of the rock and roll tunes were written by composers who belonged to a new composers' guild, B.M.I., Broadcast Music Incorporated, and the rival guild, the A.S.C.A.P., American Society of Composers, Authors and Publishers, did everything in its power to discredit the new style. There was a congressional investigation into radio and television, largely at the instigation of A.S.C.A.P., and Billy Rose, who had been famous in the 'twenties for the song "Barney Google"— "with your goo-goo-googly eyes"—seriously testified that the new lyrics were lowering the literacy standards of the American younger generation. The popular singer, Frank Sinatra, was irritated enough at the excitement over the new singers that he publicly attacked the new style and its suggestive lyrics.

There was some suggestiveness in a few of the lyrics, or "leer-ics" as the A.S.C.A.P. called them, but one of the most intelligently written of the new musical annuals, *Who's Who in Rock 'N Roll*, answered:

> The blues have always had an earthy quality about them, and in fact some of the most popular blues performances of bygone years—for instance Bessie

Smith's classic "Empty Bed Blues"—became popular because of the smut some people found in the lyrics and not because of the qualities as folk music.

Rock and Roll, as a direct lineal descendant of the old-time blues, continued the tradition of earthy lyrics, concerned with love and heartbreak and human frailties. No one, apparently, had minded when these records were aimed at the purely Negro market.[2]

*Who's Who in Rock 'N Roll* made a strong effort to emphasize the blues contribution to rock and roll. The first singer described and pictured in the book was Bessie Smith, and there were biographies of several popular blues singers. Occasionally their enthusiasm led them into some startling errors, but they were doing the best job they knew how. The sketch of the popular New Orleans singer, Fats Domino, began,

> Not since the early days of Satchmo, Kid Ory, and Leadbelly Morton has a New Orleans musician so completely captured the imagination of the public. . . .

The magazines *Rhythm and Blues Songs* and *Rock and Roll Songs* have been the most colorful supporters of the new craze. There are words to the songs, words for many of the blues, and pictures and biographies of blues stars. For the first time, writing was being done on the blues and the singers as they were recording. The magazines are written entirely for the teen-age audience, and occasionally there is some confusion over singers who are over twenty-five. In an article about

[2] Fredericks, Vic (ed.), *Who's Who in Rock 'N Roll*, New York, Frederick Fell, Inc., 1958.

Count Basie's old vocalist, Jimmy Rushing, who has been singing since 1926, the first sentence started, "Here is a lad who's beginning to click with the teen set." The prose style, too, is a little bewildering. An article on Bo Diddley, said, in part:

> The Diddler hit the music columns with his number one type waxing approximately dubbed "Bo Diddley." The tune was a chart member as soon as the Checker Recording Company released it. The mellow strains of the master's guitar seemed to be a natural with every mommy and daddy from coast-to-coast. . . .

But the blues singers who were still popular were getting publicity and some interest stirred up for their records. There were often lyrics for blues that could have been sung in the 1920's.

> Well, things are getting tough, can't even find a dime,
> Well, things are getting tough, can't even find a dime,
> Things don't get no better, I'm going to lose my mind. . . .

The 1950's have been difficult years for the blues singers, despite new activity in the recording companies. Many of the "down-home" singers, as the style is called now, have only a superficial awareness of the backgrounds of the blues and their music is often thinly derivative. The jukeboxes and the radio have made it hard for singers to develop the intense personal styles of the older singers. The best of the singers recording are older men who grew up in country areas where the blues have a strong tradition. Bo Diddley, whose family moved to Chicago from Macon, Mississippi, when he was still a boy, is the only exception to the general rule. Muddy Waters and John Lee Hooker grew up outside of Clarksdale, Mississippi, during the depression and Smokey Hogg and Lightnin' Hopkins grew up in Central Texas. Hogg has been less successful in maintaining a blues style in his singing, despite some early records of promise, and Hooker has been uneven, but both Waters and Hopkins still sing with some of the depth and richness of the country blues.

# 20

## *Muddy Waters*

In the fall of 1958, Muddy Waters toured England with the group that he usually took with him on his Southern tours. They'd just come out of the South, and England was seeing something that very few Americans interested in Negro music ever see, a colored entertainment group that hasn't had time to make the change from the colored standards of performance to the white standards. A critic sitting down near the stage was so stunned by the volume of Muddy's amplified guitar that he found himself retreating, a row at a time, toward the back of the hall. The guitar was amplified, the harmonica was amplified, the bass was amplified, and there was a microphone in the piano. The critic spent the last half of the concert in the men's room, where the sound seemed a little less shrill. He couldn't hear much of Muddy's singing, but there had been so much din on the stage he hadn't been able to hear much of it anyway. After the refined, sophisticated

**245**

singing of Brownie McGhee and Big Bill, Muddy sounded a little barbaric, but there was an unmistakable earthiness and vitality in his music.

The English tour was the last touch to a colorful musical career. Muddy was included in the ethnic recordings released by the Library of Congress Folk Music Archives, has been a consistently popular entertainer in the South, and has finally become a concert artist.

The recording Muddy did for the Library of Congress "I Be's Troubled" and "Country Blues," on record 18, was one of the most interesting records released. He was working on a large delta cotton farm outside of Clarksdale when John Work and Alan Lomax found him. He was still using his right name, McKinley Morganfield, and he had been playing the guitar and singing for about three years. He was a tough, young field hand, singing a little on Saturday nights to make some money. When he was singing, he used his nickname "Muddy Waters." He used an unamplified guitar, using a bottle neck on his little finger to play the melody. "I Be's Troubled" was an ordinary blues, but "Country Blues" was a beautifully poetic, beautifully sung blues performance. He had learned it from Robert Johnson's record, "Walkin' Blues."

Robert Johnson's recordings were one of the biggest influences on Muddy when he was still in Mississippi, and he is one of the few men who ever knew anything about Johnson. Johnson was from around Clarksdale; though he was gone by the time Muddy started singing. Muddy knew other singers in the area, and he had a fine blues background when he began singing himself. Two Paramount recording artists, Charlie Patton and Son House, were from around Clarksdale; though they did a lot of traveling.

Muddy, himself, had been traveling. He was born at Rolling Fork, Mississippi, south of Clarksdale, on April 4, 1915, but his mother, Berta, died when he was three. It was too much for his father, Ollie Morganfield, to take care of the little boy; so McKinley was sent up to Clarksdale to stay with his grandmother. He came down to visit his father from time to time, but when he was in his teens he started working in the fields and stayed close to Clarksdale. When he was twenty-two years old, he started learning to play the guitar and taught himself to play like his friends at the farm. The large farms, like the one where Muddy was working at Stovall, or the one where Tommy McClennan was working at Yazoo City, often have as many as two hundred people living in cabins along the road to the fields. Some of the men handle the heavy equipment, the rest do the hoeing and labor. At picking time, everybody works—men, women and children—pushing along the rows, dragging the sacks on the dirt, stooped in awkward postures while their hands pull at the cotton. At night people sit on their porches talking, while older people rock back and forth in their old rocking chairs. Men walking along the road call out to friends as they pass. The younger men usually sit around outside a store laughing among themselves, playing a little music, and giving the girls a hard time.

After his recording, Muddy stayed on the farm for another season, working Saturday night jobs and playing as often as he could, playing all-night dances for fifty cents just to get a chance to sing. He played a little harmonica and the next summer joined a traveling tent show, Silas Green from New Orleans, when it came through Clarksdale. The show was a vaudeville review interspersed with comedy bits by a pair of comics, one of them "Silas Green." It continued playing the South until the summer of 1957. Muddy got a job playing the harmonica to accompany blues singers in the show, but he occasionally sang a little himself. The show dropped him after a few weeks, and Muddy went back to Clarksdale. He stayed there for a few months, then decided he'd had enough of the South. He was twenty-eight years old, it was 1943, there were jobs in Chicago —he went North.

For three years, Muddy worked at day jobs in Chicago, first in a paper mill; then driving a truck for a venetian blind manufacturer. He was introduced to Big Bill and through him met other Chicago singers. Singing with them nights, and listening to the noisy music of the southside changed his style from the lonely, almost thoughtful style he had in 1941, and he began to sound more like a Chicago blues singer. In 1945, his uncle, Joe Brant, bought him an electric guitar and in 1946 he recorded, first for Aristocrat and then for Columbia. The Columbia sides were never released, and he signed as an exclusive Aristocrat artist. He was out with his truck when Aristocrat tried to reach him to record. A friend found out where he was making deliveries and drove around the streets until he intercepted Muddy's truck. He took the truck and delivered the venetian blinds while Muddy was racing back to the recording studio in his friend's car. His first record was a commercial title, "Gypsy Woman" and "Little Anna Mae," but at a session a few weeks later he made the first of his blues hits, "I Feel Like Going Home" and "I Can't Be Satisfied." The songs were his old Library of Congress blues. "I Can't Be Satisfied" was his "Country Blues" and "I Feel Like Going Home" was "I Be's Troubled," a blues that came to Muddy when he was changing a tire. He was working with the pianist Albert Luandrew, who called himself Sunnyland Slim. For Muddy's first records, Slim played piano while Muddy played the guitar and sang; then Muddy played the guitar behind some of Slim's singing.

During the late 1940's, Muddy continued to record with other men and to accompany them on their own dates. It was a situation similar to the Chicago blues industry in the years just before the war, when there were the Bluebird and OKeh artists playing each other's dates. When Aristocrat was taken over by the new Chess record company, Muddy made a final record using simple bass background. Then he began to build his own group. Big Maceo worked with him as pianist for occasional jobs, but Muddy usually used Sunnyland Slim or Little Johnny. Since 1953, his half brother, Otis Spann, has played the piano. Jimmy Rogers played second guitar; "Little Walter" Jacobs, harmonica; Freddy Bellow, drums, and Big Crawford, bass. He made two or three Chess dates with washboard instead of drums, but until 1957 he featured his "down-home" sound. It was a very modern "down-home" sound, almost entirely electrified and featuring a pounding rhythm that swept everything before it. The harmonica and the guitars, for club dates, were tuned up to a deafening pitch, and to be heard over the din, the piano player had to use a microphone behind the strings, and the bass player either used an electric pick-up or had a separate microphone. The drummer had a microphone to sing into, but he usually didn't use a microphone for the drums. He kept the heads slack and relied on a strong right arm. The drumming has always been at a grass roots level so subtleties were unnecessary anyway. It was always a little disquieting listening to the group, because there was always a worry that a fuse might blow, leaving the entire band working over its instruments in a rattling silence broken only by Muddy's none-too-strong voice, a rather clumsy blues piano and the depressing drumming of Bellow. The effect with the electricity working is rather awe-inspiring, the men sweating over their instruments and the sound ringing over the din of the crowd. Some of the Chess records were subdued, moving blues, but his hit records were shouting, colorful songs like the imaginative "Hoochie Coochie Man," with its list of the popular southside love charms.

For the last six or seven years, Muddy has been touring the South with his group, traveling in two or three cars with a station wagon to carry the instruments and electrical equipment. They travel in the summer and fall, when people have a little money and feel like celebrating. There are dozens of groups touring the same areas, and Muddy has had to work hard to keep ahead of men like John Lee Hooker, Lightning Slim, Memphis Slim, or Chuck Willis, all more or less blues artists. Every week the fences in a Southern city bloom with ads about the coming week's attractions. The popular artists like

Fats Domino or Ruth Brown draw the biggest crowds and get audiences from all parts of the Negro community. The religious groups that give joint concerts at the local auditoriums and usually include a local group or singer to bring in a bigger house are next in popularity. Usually a church sponsors the concert to raise funds and they have been out selling tickets; so the religious concerts often draw three or four thousand people in a larger city. The blues men work in the local clubs for a tough, sleek younger crowd that drinks hard, wants its music hard, and fills the small, dark clubs with an intense mood of restlessness and emotion. The blues men have to come across and they have to work hard to earn their money. At the bigger clubs there are occasionally two groups working and the signs will advertise "Battle Of The Blues—Lightning Slim versus Guitar Slim." The clubs are so noisy early in the evening that no one could hear much anyway: so the men don't worry about much more than keeping the beat pounding, and smiling and wiggling. When it gets late and the couples are moving slowly across the dance floor, holding each other close, the music begins to have a slow hypnotic effect and the men seem to play without even seeing the crowd in the shadows beyond the lights. They are drunk and tired, their clothes limp with sweat, and they sit with their faces quiet, their fingers moving over the guitar strings or the keyboard with a sad, mournful blues sound. The music is at its best when it gets toward morning.

At his best Muddy has a fine approach to the blues and he has recorded a number of imaginative blues for Chess. The earlier records, with Muddy, his harmonica player, Walter Jacobs, and a bass or drums, were among the best. Jacobs was a sensitive accompanist and they worked well together, picking up each other's melodic ideas. Muddy was still playing with the bottle neck on his little finger, and despite his limitations as a guitarist his solos and the duets with Jacobs were very effective. Often his records were rather ordinary jump songs, but many of his blues were in the rich stream of blues poetry. One of his best was "Early Morning Blues" on Chess 1490.

> Early in the morning before day, that's when my blues come falling down,
>     (repeat)
> Well you know the woman that I'm lovin' she just can't be found.
>
> I wish I knew if my baby was in this town,
>     (repeat)
> Well you know if I hear about her I believe I'll lose my mind.
>
> Yes, I wish I knew who'd changed my baby's mind,
>     (repeat)
> I'd get all of my money, keep her sitting down all the time.

Muddy has not had a big hit in two or three years, but he is still very popular, and the prestige of his European trip has made him in demand in the Northern night clubs featuring blues entertainment. He has come a long way from the fields outside of Clarksdale, and if his singing has lost some of its sensitivity he cannot be blamed for playing the game according to the new rules. He is not responsible for the rules.

# 21

## *Lightnin'*

Sam "Lightnin'" Hopkins, is perhaps the last of the great blues singers. Like Muddy Waters he grew up in farm country, working to bring in a cotton crop or hiring out on shares to bring in somebody else's crop. When he was eight years old, he was already playing the guitar. There was a meeting of the General Association of Baptist Churches at Buffalo, Texas, and Sam's family drove up from the farm at Centerville for the Sunday afternoon picnic. The children sat on the back of a flat-bed farm truck, and Sam's father drove slowly along U. S. 75 to Buffalo. The road goes through rolling farm country, with little bridges over the occasional streams and small farm towns at the crossroads; then turns under a rusted railroad overpass just south of Buffalo. It was a warm, spring Sunday, and there were hundreds of people under the trees at the picnic ground. When Sam got off the truck, a skinny, dark little boy carrying a large guitar, he heard someone singing. A

**254**

fat blind man was sitting on a platform playing a guitar and singing to the crowd in front of him. It was Blind Lemon Jefferson, hired to sing for the picnic. Sam hung around him all afternoon, until he finally got up enough nerve to try and play along with Lemon. Lemon turned around and shouted, "Boy, you got to play it right." When Sam finally managed to say something and Lemon realized it was a little boy he laughed, and he showed him a little on the guitar, letting Sam play behind him.

Sam was born in Centerville, a small town north of Houston on U. S. 75, on March 15, 1912. When he was growing up, he saw Lemon two or three more times in Waxahachie, when Lemon was down to play for "country suppers," but he kept on playing his own way, learning what he could from the people around him. He had an older cousin who had a farm five miles south of Centerville, at Leona, Texas. He was a singer, one of the best in the county. His name was Alexander, "Texas" Alexander, the singer who left Texas to begin recording for OKeh records in 1927. Sam learned to sing listening to his cousin, and it was the association with Lemon Jefferson and Texas Alexander that colored his own blues style. During the depression, he stayed around Centerville, working a small farm north of town. His hands still bear the scars of occasional tangles with farm machinery and mule lines. His older brother moved to Waxahachie, living near some of Lemon Jefferson's family, but Sam stayed close to home. His mother still lives in Centerville, in a room near the feed store. Sam got married and worked several seasons with his "uncle," a family friend named Lucien Hopkins; then he and his wife hired out to a landowner named Tom Moore, who had a large farm north of Dallas. The life on Moore's farm was so bad that Sam spent hours in the fields composing a long blues epic about the Moores. He recorded a few verses of it on an early recording, with the name changed to "Tim Moore's Farm" to keep the family off his neck.

> You know there ain't but the one thing, you know this
>     black man done wrong.
>     (repeat)
> I moved my wife and family down on Mr. Tim Moore's
>     farm.
>
>     You know Mr. Tim Moore's a man,
>     Don't never stand and grin,
>     He sees you back by the graveyard
>     Says I'll save you time gettin' in.
>
> You know soon in the morning, he'll give you scram-
>     bled eggs.
> Yes, he's liable to call you so soon you'll catch a mule
>     by his hind legs.
>
>     You know I got a telegram this morning
>     It say your wife is dead.
>     I showed it to Mr. Moore, he says
>     Go ahead, nigger, you know you gotta plow a
>       ridge.
>     That white man said it's been rainin'
>     Yes sir, I'm way behind.
>     I may let you bury that woman
>     On your dinner time.
>
> I told him, no, Mr. Moore, somebody's got to go.
> He said if you ain't goin' to plow, Sam, get up there
>     and grab your hoe.

Some of Tom's brothers heard about the record and came after Sam, but they couldn't find him in the Houston colored district. Sam won't sing much of it now, but there are dozens of verses, an infectiously funny and harrowing account of contract labor in the fields of southern Texas.

Sam had been playing and singing for years, earning a little money at it, and becoming one of the best guitar players and singers in his part of the country. His "uncle," Lucien, finally sat him down, about 1946, and told him to get into Houston and start singing for a living. He helped him buy a new guitar and Sam and his wife moved into south Houston. At first he worked around the clubs accompanying his cousin, old Texas Alexander, who was still singing. There was a piano player named "Thunder" Smith working with them and the three made a recording for a Houston company sometime in 1946 or 1947. Sam's guitar was turned up so loud it almost drowned out his cousin's voice, but Texas sang in his old style, and the record was an interesting blues release. Late in 1946, Sam and Thunder went to Hollywood and recorded a session for the Alladin studios. They called themselves "Thunder Smith and Lightnin' Hopkins" and "Lightnin'" became Sam's professional name. He still forgets and sings about "Sam Hopkins" in most of his songs, but his records have been labeled "Lightnin' Hopkins" since 1946.

The Alladin recordings were not very exceptional, and there were no jobs around Los Angeles. In 1947, Lightnin' was back in Houston, trying to make some kind of living. One afternoon a man working for a local

record company heard Lightnin' sitting on the curb-
stone playing his guitar for a group of children. He
sent Lightnin' around to the company, a small outfit
called Gold Star Records, run by a man named Bill
Quinn. Quinn was a young veteran who had gone into
the record business with a "King of the Hillbillies" idea.
He soon found out that blues singers sold better than
hillbillies and began recording blues artists. He had a
real understanding of what his singers could do, and
despite the rather poor surface quality, the old Gold
Star recordings have been sought-after collectors items
since the company went out of business in 1951.

Lightnin' came out to the studios on Telephone
Road and recorded a few blues, accompanying himself
with an unamplified guitar. The first record Quinn released was Gold Star 3131, "Short Haired Woman," and
a fast "Big Mama Jump." Without much advertising
and with only fair distribution, the record sold between
forty thousand and fifty thousand copies. Lightnin' was
a sensation. Quinn recorded him for the next two years,
selling about forty thousand of every one of the records,
and as high as eighty thousand on hits like "Baby, Please
Don't Go." Lightnin' lived high. Quinn remembered
him coming in a Tuesday afternoon for a four-hundred
dollar advance and coming in on Thursday afternoon
for more money. He'd spent the four hundred dollars
and he'd just bought drinks for everybody in a local
bar. The owner of the bar had given him an hour to get
back with the fifteen dollars for the drinks. Quinn
couldn't find enough money for him. He finally had to
start giving all the money to Lightnin's wife, who
could handle him a little better. Finally in 1948, Light-

nin' went to New York and recorded eighteen sides, still unreleased, for a small New York label. Many of them duplicated things he had done for Gold Star. This is something a record artist can never do, and Quinn immediately fired him.

When radio stations played Lightnin's records on Gold Star, there would usually be an awkward silence after the record was finished while the announcer tried to think of something to say. Usually there would be a nervous laugh and he'd say something like, "That Lightnin', he sure is something, isn't he?" Lightnin' was a little bewildering to most of the people who heard him. He was accompanying himself on an unamplified guitar. There was no piano, no drums, no bass. He was one of the first blues singers to work without a group in ten years. His singing was very free, almost disorganized. Some verses were twelve measures long, some were thirteen and a half, some were ten. Lightnin' sang in the same unmeasured, harsh style that Lemon Jefferson and Texas Alexander had recorded twenty years before. The guitar trailed along, echoing the words, droning in a rhythmic drumming on a lower string, then ringing above the voice between lines and carrying off painfully intense, lyric passages between the verses. Even the blues themselves, rough and direct, were a far cry from the recordings of other blues singers. Lightnin' was one of the roughest singers to come out of the South in years, and his singing seemed almost primitive when his records were played on afternoon record programs, between endless commercials and the singing of popular styles like Billy Eckstein and Nat Cole.

Lightnin's records sold in the South because of the

impact of his personality. He was the last singer in the grand style. He sang with sweep and imagination, using his rough voice to reach out and touch someone who listened to him. The directness of his blues sold them to a colored audience that likes to listen to a man sing and say, "That's right, that man is speakin' the truth." One of his early records was being played in a poor little record shop along the river in Sacramento, California.

> I'm achin' all over, I believe I got the pneumonia this time.

Everyone in the shop stopped to listen, and broke into laughter as he finished:

> I believe I better take a "B.C." to take care of poor me.

"B.C." headache powders are very popular in the South and everyone was agreeing with him as they laughed. Lightnin' was the last singer who could go back and find his blues in the work songs and in the field songs. He had done it that day in Houston, as he sang the field cry, "No More Cane on This Brazos," then built a blues from its moving cry.

In the next ten years, Lightnin' recorded for dozens of companies in New York and Hollywood. The first recordings were for smaller companies, Alladin in Hollywood, and Jax and Sittin' In With in New York, but he was becoming a big seller. In 1951, Mercury, Victor's big subsidiary label, recorded him in Chicago. He sang some of his usual blues, and a blues "Sad News from Korea," on Mercury 8274. The war disturbed him, and in 1953 he recorded "The War Is Over" for Decca, in New York. It was released on Decca 28842. He was usually recorded with a bass, and there was a drummer on the Decca sides. He was losing the feeling of loneliness that had marked his Gold Star recordings. He played in Houston for a few years; then in 1957 he returned to New York. There were records on TNT, Harlem and Ace records, and a single recording on a "Lightnin'" label—"Grieving Blues" and "Unsuccessful Blues" on Lightnin' 104. There were thirty blues and fast shouts for Herald label, but there was heavy drum and bass accompaniment, and the records were rough examples of "rhythm and blues." Despite the record sales, Lightnin' never seemed to perform well in a night club or theatre, and he was forced to live on recording fees and royalties; which are sporadic and usually not considerable. He often did the same thing to other companies that he had done to Bill Quinn at Gold Star —record the same blues for another company while the first company he recorded it for was trying to sell their version. His professional career was a series of clumsy mistakes. He went through the considerable quantities of money he was paid for his hit records with a frightening lack of foresight; then there were months and months of scuffling.

Despite a sudden interest in the earthy side of his playing by collectors and folk music enthusiasts, there seems to be a slim commercial market for his records on the race labels. He would have very poor success trying to sing in the rock and roll styles. Some of the old Alladin sides, done in 1951, have been brought out on an l.p. with a "Score" label, but l.p.'s by blues artists have generally not been very successful. The buyers of blues records are mostly teen-agers, and they aren't much interested in l.p.'s. They want a single record hit, and they don't want to pay for an l.p. to get it; so the Score l.p. has moved slowly. Two of the best Alladin sides are included, "Shotgun Blues" and "Rolling Blues," retitled "Rollin' and Rollin'," but the record is uneven in quality. "Shotgun" was one of the best of his early blues.

Yes I say go bring me my shotgun, boy, bring me back
some shells.
Yes, I say go bring my shotgun, boy, bring me back a
pocket full of shells.
Yes, if I don't get some competition you know there's
gonna be trouble here.

Yes, you know my woman tried to quit me,
When I ain't done nothing wrong,
She done put me out of doors, boy,
And I ain't even got no home.
Yes, if I don't get some competition you know there's
gonna be trouble here.

Yes, you know my mama told me,
The day I left her door.
She says I ain't gonna have bad luck, son,
I don't care where you go.
I said just bring me my shotgun, boy, you can bring
me just one or two shells.
Yes, if I don't get some competition you know there's
gonna be trouble here.

Well I cried bye bye, baby,
You know you done me wrong.

I'm gonna take my little shotgun now,
I'm gonna carry it back home.

I said, goin' in the morning, boy, and carry my shotgun
home.
Yes, I figured the best thing I can do, just leave that
woman alone.

He recorded nearly 190 sides during his most
active years, and he has begun recording as a folk-blues
singer in the last few months. Most of his blues were
so completely in his own personal style that they have
a very distinctive sound. He recorded several songs
usually associated with other singers, Blind Lemon's
"One Kind Favor" on Sitting In With 649, and some of
the dirtier numbers from the late 1920's recordings, but
he usually changed the songs to quite an extent. His
version of Leroy Carr's "How Long How Long Blues,
Ain't It a Shame" on Gold Star 637, changes the chord
structure so that after a first phrase similar to "How
Long" he characteristically fails to resolve the harmony
and goes into his own melodic patterns. The words are
a fresh variation of the "How Long" theme.

You know it's dark and cloudy,
It look like it's goin' to rain.
My baby left me this evening,
On that southbound train,
I been wonderin'—why,
Did you go away.

Look out yonder,
Just look what I see,
So many women standin'
Laughin' at poor me,

I been wonderin'—why,
Did you go away.

Seems like I hear,
Somebody callin' me.
I been wonderin',
Who can it be.
I been wonderin'—why,
Did you go away.

Ain't it a shame,
The way my baby do,
She got up this mornin'
And broke my heart in two.
Ain't it a shame,
Ain't it a shame,
The way my baby do.

He moves from one furnished room to another in Houston, and it's hard to find out where he's living. He and his wife have separated, and he stays close to the club where he's playing if he's got any kind of a job or gets a room close to Dowling Street, the main street of the colored business district in Houston. A bartender thought he was hanging around a girl who was working as a waitress in one of the clubs. She was off for the afternoon, but her apartment was just around the corner. She opened the door a little, a strong, handsome girl in a ragged slip. Had she seen Lightnin'? He'd left two or three weeks ago. Did she know where he was? She didn't know. She said to ask along Dowling Street. A pawnshop owner said he knew a Sam Hopkins, had his electric guitar in and out. He had an address on Webster Street. It was a gray day, looking like rain. The wind was blowing the dust along the street. Above the ramshackle houses the wind rattled the trees. At

Webster Street there was a shabby wooden building back of a littered vacant lot. The bare hallway upstairs had apartments going off it on both sides, the doors pulled to with cheap padlocks, the glass windows painted over. A little boy finally came to one of the doors. Lightnin' had moved. His sister was across the street. Across the street, in a wooden building that had been painted white several years before, a tall, thin looking woman came to a doorway.

"You looking for my brother?"

"Yes."

"He's moved over to Hadley Street. Look for the house with the red chair on the porch. Somewhere down from the corner."

At the house on Hadley Street, a nervous, heavy woman looked out from the darkness of her small living room. A television set was flickering in the corner. Had she seen Lightnin'?

"This time of day he's usually at that barroom at the corner; if he's not there try the one across the street. He'll be at one or the other."

He wasn't at either one. The next morning a green sedan rolled alongside the car at a traffic light on Dowling Street. A thin, nervous man leaned out the window.

"You lookin' for me?"

"You Lightnin'?"

"That's right."

As the cars drove slowly along the street he agreed to record that afternoon.

After he had sung the magnificent "Penitentiary Blues," he went on to sing seven more blues and Blind Lemon's song "One Kind Favor I Ask of You." He sang until he became so tense emotionally that it was impossible to talk to him. He drank steadily, but he seemed to play more brilliantly and sing with even greater intensity. Except for the friend who had been driving the car in the morning, he was almost singing alone in the dimly lit room. Then as he was singing the last songs, people could be heard laughing and joking in the kitchen, just outside his room. When he was finished, the door opened and his sister looked in:

"How's it goin', honey?"

Lightnin' was still subdued from the emotional strain of singing. He shrugged. Three or four people came in as Lightnin' was counting his money. His sister was there, there was a younger girl, his sister's boy friend, a friend of Lightnin's. The landlady was looking over their shoulder. Lightnin' straightened up, looking very tired and alone. Finally all of them left for the small, noisy barroom at the corner, Lightnin' trailing along behind with the man who had been with him during the afternoon.

Lightnin', in his way, is a magnificent figure. He is one of the last of his kind, a lonely, bitter man who brings to the blues the intensity and pain of the hours in the hot sun, scraping at the earth, singing to make the hours pass. The blues will go on, but the country blues, and the great singers who created from the raw singing of the work songs and the field cries the richness and variety of the country blues, will pass with men like this thin, intense singer from Centerville, Texas.

# APPENDIX

*Recorded Blues Backgrounds*

*The Blues Recordings*

# Recorded Blues Backgrounds

In many parts of the South, the older musical styles are still sung and played in lonely cabins away from the cities and towns. The older traditions are passing, but there are still men and women working small farms off dirt roads who sing the work songs as they do the chores around their cabins or "holler" to each other in musical conversations across the fields. The Library of Congress recordings of the 1930's documented much of this music, the background of the blues, and the recordings that have been released are a rich source of musical material. Much of the music recorded was derivative, from religious or blues recordings of the 1920's, but the recordings done in the prison yards or in the fields were often very musical performances, giving a glimpse of the life that produced the music, as well as the sound of the music. The recording was done without studio facilities, and with inadequate equipment, but despite the poor sound, the records give an unforgettable picture of Southern music. The Library of Congress has made material available on a series of long play-

269

ing records which may be purchased by mail from the Music Division, Recording Laboratories, of the Library. Record L3, "Afro-American Spirituals, Work Songs, and Ballads," includes the Texas prison song, "Ain't No More Cane on This Brazos," recorded by a prison group in 1933. Record L4, "Afro-American Blues and Game Songs," includes Muddy Waters's magnificent "Country Blues."

Since the Second World War, the tape recorder has made possible a more complete documentation of Southern musical backgrounds. The Folkways Record Company has, since 1948, released a series of field recordings that have become a definitive study of the music and the people who sing and play it. The records have not been commercially successful, but the recording director of Folkways, Moses Asch, has persisted in issuing as much of the material as he is able. The large research foundations have recognized the importance of recording as much of the music as possible, before the old people who still remember the songs and ballads have died, and they have made available research funds for field recording.

The younger Negroes in the South are not carrying on the music of their parents and grandparents, as much for its social implications as for any other reason. As Big Bill wrote, ". . . who wants to be reminded of slavery?" This has meant that the field recording has had to be done as quickly as possible, and the recordings still reflect the fact that many of the best singers are singing in the newer styles and that the person who remembers the most old songs sometimes is no longer singing his best. On the whole, however, the recordings released on Folkways are a memorable documentation.

In the winter of 1950, Harold Courlander did extensive recording in eastern Alabama, on a field trip sponsored by the Wenner-Gren Foundation, and the material collected has been released on six Folkways records.

| Volume I | Secular Music | –Folkways FE4417 |
| Volume II | Religious Music | –Folkways FE4418 |
| Volume III | Rich Emerson, 1 | –Folkways FE4471 |
| Volume IV | Rich Emerson, 2 | –Folkways FE4472 |
| Volume V | Spirituals | –Folkways FE4473 |
| Volume VI | Ring Game Songs | –Folkways FE4474 |

Rich Emerson, Vols. III and IV, is a storyteller and singer, with a wonderfully imaginative sense of narrative, and the ring game songs have caught the happy carefree sound of children playing in school yards on cold winter afternoons, skipping through their little games. The spirituals, sung by Dock Reed and Vera Hall, are examples of Negro singing at its purest and give an insight to the vocal styles that shaped the singing of a Lemon Jefferson or a Blind Willie Johnson.

In 1954, Frederic Ramsey, Jr. recorded a wealth of musical material in Alabama, Mississippi and Louisiana, on a field trip sponsored by the Guggenheim Foundation. He has edited from this a series of ten records for Folkways, titled "Music from the South." The records, on Folkways Records FA2650 to FA2659, are one of the most satisfactory documentations of the life of the "older songsters" who still sing in the old traditions. Ramsey has somehow captured a feeling of presence that has never been so forcibly presented. It is easy to imagine yourself in a country cabin, in the dim lantern light, as the sounds of a country "buck" dance almost overwhelm the singing or playing of the noisy performers. There are country brass bands, revival religious groups, harmonica players, guitarists, string bands; and through all it, a sort of running commentary as the performers talk about themselves and their music.

Three records, Volumes 2–4, are devoted to an older singer from western Alabama, Horace Sprott. For evening after evening, Sprott and Ramsey sat talking about the blues, or about the old "slavey" songs, or about Horace's wanderings, while Ramsey tirelessly operated a small spring-operated tape recorder that had to be wound up every five or six minutes. Horace sang hundreds of songs, remembering ones that he had learned from people who were old when he was a boy. As they talk, and as Horace sings, the story of the creation of the blues unfolds itself in Horace's deep, halting voice. Horace was learning to sing when the blues were just beginning to be a separate kind of song, and his singing is a moving glimpse of the first blues, when men were "hollerin'" to each other across the fields.

A catalog and the address of local distributors of the Folkways documentary recordings may be obtained by writing Folkways Records, 117 W. 46th St., New York City. A photographic record of Frederic Ramsey's travels in the South, "Been Here and Gone," has recently been published by the Rutgers University Press.

Some of the most memorable recordings done for the Library of Congress in the 1930's were recorded at Parchman Farm, the penitentiary farm in the Mississippi delta country. In 1947, when the improved recording equipment was available, one of the men who had recorded on the first trips, Alan Lomax, returned to Parchman and recorded the music of the men as they worked in the fields and in the prison yard. The material has been released on an overpowering record by Tradition Records, a new company which is documenting American folk music. The music catches the feeling of the men just starting to work, stiff and barely awake, in the early morning hours, or working with an angry ferocity as the sun begins to climb higher. There are the lonely songs a man makes up to sing to his mule and the blues a man makes up when he has hours by himself in the fields. The music is unforgettable, and in many of the cries and songs there is the sound of the raw country blues. A catalog and the address of local distributors may be obtained from Tradition Records, Box 72, Village Station, New York City.

The wealth of recorded blues backgrounds that have become available in recent years have made it easier to study the development of the blues styles, and the documentation of the lives of the people still singing in the older styles has added an important chapter to the study of the American folk traditions. Many of the recordings are not widely known, and it is hoped that this short description will bring them to the attention of a larger audience.

# The Blues Recordings

Since 1952, a collector in New York named Pete Whalen has been trying to find a copy of the blues "Poor Me," a 1931 Paramount recording by Charlie Patton. After two or three years of advertising, he finally went into the South and went from door to door in Columbia, South Carolina, carrying a sign "I Buy Old Records." He spent part of one afternoon trapped behind a screen door by an irate dog, but he kept at it, and finally found a copy of "Poor Me," scratched and almost unplayable, but still a copy. Since then he has been advertising for a copy in better condition.

The country blues records made in the 1920's are among the rarest of the historical recordings made of Negro music. They were often pressed in small quantities for a local distributor and then most of the copies were sold by mail. If copies are found by going door to door they are usually in poor condition. A record sent away for and eagerly awaited was played by everybody in the family until there wasn't much left to it but the label. The late Gennet Records, many of them recorded in Birmingham, Alabama, are so

274

rare that there is a question as to whether some of the records listed in the catalog were ever even released. The scarcity of the records has been very discouraging to blues enthusiasts. The large auction lists of *Record Research* magazine, 131 Hart Street, Brooklyn, N.Y., from time to time include blues records and there is valuable research material published about the early blues recordings, but the records themselves are very scarce.

In an effort to make some of the greatest of the early blues recordings more available, a long-playing record entitled "The Country Blues" has been produced to illustrate the singing and playing of many of the singers. The recording includes:

| | |
|---|---|
| Blind Lemon Jefferson | "Match Box Blues" |
| Lonnie Johnson | "Careless Love" |
| Cannon's Jug Stompers | "Walk Right In" |
| Peg Leg Howell | "Low Down Rounder Blues" |
| Blind Willie McTell | "Statesboro Blues" |
| Memphis Jug Band | "Stealin', Stealin'" |
| Blind Willie Johnson | "You Gonna Need Somebody on Your Bond" |
| Leroy Carr | "Alabama Woman Blues" |
| Big Bill | "Key to the Highway" |
| Sleepy John Estes | "Special Agent" |
| Bukka White | "Fixin' to Die Blues" |
| Tommy McClennan | "I'm a Guitar King" |
| Robert Johnson | "Preachin' Blues" |
| Washboard Sam | "I've Been Treated Wrong" |

The records were taken from the collections of Pete Whalen, Pete Kaufman, Ben Kaplan and S. B. Charters, and have been re-engineered to conform as closely as possible to present-day standards of fidelity. The record may be obtained from Record, Book and Film Sales, Inc., 121 W. 47th Street, New York.

There has been enough interest in the early blues in the last few years that some reissues were released of blues records. The Riverside Record Co., 553 W. 51st Street, New York, has issued a large number of recordings from the old Paramount catalog, and there is a fine reissue of twelve blues by Blind Lemon Jefferson on RLP 12-125, "Blind Lemon." A ten-inch record, RLP 1039, "Backwoods Blues," includes records by the obscure King Solomon Hill, Bobby Grant and Buddy Boy Hawkins, and two records by Big Bill, under the name of Big Bill Johnson. Of interest, too, are the reissues of many of the finest blues recordings of Ma Rainey, including a duet with Papa Charlie Jackson, "Big Feeling Papa."

Folkways has made the most persistent effort to reissue a number of blues performances. Volume 1 of the series, "Jazz," FJ2801, includes Leroy Carr's fine "Down South Blues," and Volume 2, FJ2802, includes Blind Willie's "Dark Was the Night" and "I Just Can't Keep From Cryin'," and Blind Lemon's "Black Snake Moan." The most extensive documentation of the early blues is Folkways magnificent series of six records entitled "American Folk Music." Most of the records were taken from the legendary collection of Harry Smith and the booklet of notes includes pictures of many of the singers, Furry Lewis, Cannon's Jug Stompers, Sleepy John Estes and Blind Lemon, and much information about the recordings themselves. The series is arranged in three volumes, FP251, "Ballads"; FP252, "Social Music," and FP253, "Songs." All three volumes include some of the greatest of the early blues. Some of the most memorable sides were among the rarest of the early recordings. Mississippi John Hurt's "Frankie" and "Spike Driver Blues" were included; "Kassie Jones," by Furry Lewis; "Old Country Stomp" and "Fishing Blues" by Henry Thomas; "Old Dog Blues" by Jim Jackson, "Newport Blues" by the Cincinnati

Jug Band; "John the Revelator" by Blind Willie Johnson; "Minglewood Blues" and "Feather Bed" by Cannon's Jug Stompers; "James Alley Blues" by "Rabbit" Brown; "Rabbit Foot Blues," "Prison Cell Blues," and "See That My Grave Is Kept Clean" by Lemon Jefferson; "Expressman Blues" by Sleepy John Estes; "Poor Boy Blues" by Ramblin' Thomas; "Ninety-Nine Year Blues" by Julius Daniels, and "Bob Lee Junior Blues" and "K.C. Moan" by the Memphis Jug Band. The collection is an excellent survey of the early blues.

Despite the rarity of the early records there have been collectors like Pete Whalen who have been collecting the records in any condition they could find them; so they could list the records, including them in the large discographies which have been assembled by collectors over the last twenty years. The English publication, *Jazz Directory*, includes listings of every blues record known to have been made in the last thirty years and is an invaluable guide to the singers and their music. The *Directory* is available in the United States from Walter C. Allen, 168 Cedar Hill Avenue, Belleville, New Jersey.

In the years of research that have gone into the book, there has been extensive documentary recording. The Folkways record "Blind Willie Johnson," FG3585, documents the search for Blind Willie through Louisiana and Texas and includes reissues of five of his recordings and reissues of blues by other blind singers, Blind Lemon, Blind Willie McTell and Blind Boy Fuller. Folkways record, FA2610, "American Skiffle Bands," includes the best music from the 1956 sessions with Will Shade, Charlie Burse and Gus Cannon, in Memphis. All three of them reminisce about their recording careers and about the musical backgrounds of their own styles.

There have been a number of contemporary recordings of Big Bill, Brownie McGhee and Sonny Terry. The Folkways recordings of all three of them include some of their finest singing. Brownie's first Folkways album, "Brownie McGhee Blues," FA2030, was one of his best records. The Folkways catalog includes the most complete listing of the newer records. There is an interesting record by a young blind singer from the streets of New Orleans. His name is Snooks Eaglin, a fine guitarist and a promising country blues singer. He was recorded by Dr. Harry Oster of Louisiana State University in 1958. The record is "Blind Snooks Eaglin," FA2476. The Lightnin' Hopkins record, "The Legendary Lightnin'," contains some of his best work.

Riverside Records has issued a few interesting recordings of the playing of Sonny Terry and Blind Gary Davis, a singer who first recorded for the old Melotone lists in the early 1930's. The other side of the Davis recordings, which are on RLP 12-611, "American Street Songs," is singing by Pink Anderson, the old singer who recorded for the Columbia 14000 series in 1929.

The amount of recording of the older country blues is still small, but there is an increasing interest in the music and the lists are growing.

There are so many records of the new "down-home" singers on the race labels that it is futile to try to list them. Anyone interested in the blues should go to a Negro record shop and listen to any of the records that look promising. He will find a strong, vital current of blues singing that has continued into many of the modern records, and he will have a better understanding of the spirit and heart of the blues themselves.

# Index

Ager, Milt, 44
"Ain't It a Shame," 263
"Ain't No More Cane on This Brazos," 15
Akins, Ollie, 142
"Alcoholic Blues," 44
Alert Record Company, 229
Alexander, Texas, 77-79, 255, 259
Alladin Record Company, 235, 257
Allen, Fuller, See Fuller, "Blind Boy"
Allen, William, 24-25
Altheimer, Josh, 172
American Recording Corporation, 167, 171, 208, 212, 215
American Society of Composers, Authors and Publishers, 241
Apollo Theater, 238
Aristocrat Record Company, 248
Armstrong, Louis, 77, 96
Arnold, John, 75
Arnold, Kokomo, 215
Arto Record Company, 52
"Atlanta Blues," 36

Atlantic Record Company, 93, 234
Avery, Elijah, 123

"Baby I Done Got Wise," 178
"Baby, I Don't Have to Worry," 215
"Baby, Please Don't Go," 258
"Baby Seals' Blues," 34, 36
"Back Door," 188
Bailey, DeFord, 214
"Banjo Joe," See Cannon, Gus
Banks, Classie, 58
Banner Record Company, 52, 208
Barbecue Bob, 150, 153-155
Barnes, Harrison, 33
Barnes, Walter, 127
"Barney Google," 241
"Barrelhouse Sammy—the Country Boy," See McTell, Blind Willie
Basie, Count, 243
Bast, Will, 92
Beale St. Jug Band, 116
Beale St. Sheiks, 65, 92

**279**

"Bear Wallow," 106
"Be-Da-Da-Bum," 144
"Beggin' Back," 63
Bellow, Freddy, 249
Berliner Record Company, 118
Berlin, Irving, 44
Bertrand, Jimmy, 53
"Big Bill Blues," 170, 172
*Big Bill Blues,* 180
"Big Bill Johnson," *See* Broonzy,
    William
Big Maceo, 185, 192, 249
"Big Mama Jump," 258
"Big Railroad Blues," 121-122
"Big Tom Collins," *See* McGhee,
    Walter "Brownie"
"Billy Lyons and Stock O'Lee,"
    101, 103
Black Bob, 172
Black, Francis, *See* Blackwell,
    Scrapper
"Black Horse Blues," 64
Black, Lewis, 149
"Black Patti," 131
"Black Snake Moan," 64, 70
Black Swan Record Company, 52
Blackman, "Tee-Wee," 108, 115
Blackwell, Scrapper, 140-146,
    209
Blake, Arthur, *See* Blind Blake
Blake, Eubie, 44
Blind Blake, 52-55, 65, 120
Blind Boy Fuller No. 2, *See* Mc-
    Ghee, Walter "Brownie"
"Blind Boy Williams," *See* Mc-
    Ghee, Walter "Brownie"
Blind Butler, 164
"Blind Lemon's Birthday Record,"
    65
"Blind Sammie," *See* McTell,
    Blind Willie
"Blind Willie," *See* McTell, Blind
    Willie
Bluebird Record Company, 83-84,
    106, 168, 175, 182, 197,
    202

"Blues before Sunrise," 169
"Blues Doctor," *See* Peter Clay-
    ton
"Bluin' the Blues," 44
Bobby Leecan's Need More Band,
    *See* Dallas String Band
Boerner, Fred, 54
Boggs, "Dock," 224
Boisy DeLegge and his Bandana
    Girls, 166
"Boodie Bum Bum," 126
*Bookman,* 90, 92, 150, 160
"Booster Blues," 63
"Bootlegging Blues," 135
"Bottle It Up and Go," 203
Bracey, Ishman, 93
Bradford, Perry, 44-45
Brimmer, Son, 120
Broadcast Music Inc., 241
Broadway Record Company, 52
"Broke and Busted Can't Be
    Trusted Blues," 44
"Broke Down Engine Blues," 93
"Broken Spoke Blues," 141
Broonzy, William "Big Bill," 145,
    169-181, 203, 212, 232, 246,
    248
    "Big Bill and His Jug Busters,"
    172
    "Big Bill and Thomps," 170
Brown, Rabbit, 90, 92, 95-98
Brown, Robert, *See* Washboard
    Sam
Brown, Ruth, 251
"Brownie McGhee's School of the
    Blues," 229
Brunswick Record Company, 115,
    124, 167
Buckley's Minstrels, 26
"Bugle Call Rag," 124
"Bull Cow Blues," 172
"Bumble Bee Slim," *See* Easton,
    Amos
"Bunch of Blues," 44
Bunch, William, *See* Wheatstraw,
    Peetie

Burse, Charlie, 112-113, 116, 126-129, 173
Burse, Robert, 126
Butterbeans and Susie, 110

"Cannon and Woods—The Beale Street Boys," 124
Cannon, Gus, 101, 103, 116-129
Cannon's Jug Stompers, 106, 116-125
"Careless Love," 81
"Carolina Peanut Boys," 125
Carr, Leroy, 137-147, 168, 172, 182, 188, 263
Carter, Bo, 212
Carter Family, 92
*Cat on a Hot Tin Roof*, 231
"C. C. C. Blues," 193
Champion Record Company, 55, 115, 126
"Charlie Burse and his Memphis Mudcats," 126
Chatman, Peter, *See* Memphis Slim
Chess Record Company, 234, 249
"Chicago Bound Blues," 148
Chicago *Defender*, 47, 63, 65, 167
Chicago Five, 185
Chicago Publishing Company, 51
Chicago Record Company, 131
"Christmas Eve Blues," 55
"Christmas in Jail—Ain't That a Pain," 144
Christy Minstrels, 26
"Church Bell Blues," 93
Circle Record Company, 230
Clayton, Peter, 193
Clifton, Kaiser, 114
"Coal Man Blues," 152
Cole, Nat, 259
Coleman, Jay Bird, 200
Collins, Sam, 55
Columbia Record Company, 83, 86, 87, 89, 118, 148, 158, 167
"Come On In," 188

"Come On in My Kitchen," 209
"Coming through the Rye," 21
Conqueror Record Company, 208
"Country Blues," 246
Covington, Bogus Ben, 200
Cox, Baby, 79
Cox, Ida, 54
Crawford, Big, 249
"Crazy Blues," 44, 46
Creath, Charlie, 75
"Crow Jane Blues," 198
Crudup, Arthur "Big Boy," 191

"Dallas Blues," 34, 36, 42, 43
Dallas String Band, 149, 151
Dandridge, Putney, 83
"Dark Was the Night and Cold the Ground," 159
Davenport, Jed, 116
Davis, Walter, 187
"Dead Gone Train," 200
"Death of Blind Boy Fuller," 219
"Death of Ella Speed," 97
"Death of Leroy Carr," 147
"Death Valley," 216
Decca Record Company, 83, 175, 194, 215
Dennison, Chappie, 101, 120
"The Devil's Son-In-Law," *See* Wheatstraw, Peetie
Diddley, Bo, 233, 238, 243
"Dixie," 127
Dodds, Baby, 83
Dodds, Johnny, 53
Domino, Fats, 242, 251
Donaldson, Walter, 44
"Don't Care Blues," 44
"Don't Cross Lay Your Daddy," 182
"Don't Wear it Out," 83
Dorsey, Thos. A., *See* Georgia Tom
"Double Trouble," 227
"Down in the Basement Blues," 170
"Down on My Bended Knee," 200

"Down Where They Play the Blues," 44
"Dream Blues," 54
"Dry Southern Blues," 63
Dukes, West, 100
Dumaine, Louis, 98
Dunn, Blind Willie, *See* Lang, Eddie

"Early Morning Blues," 53, 253
Easton, Amos, 145-146, 192
Eckstein, Billy, 259
"Elevator Woman," 191
Ellington, Duke, 77, 79, 229
Emerson Record Company, 52
"Empty House Blues," 66
Estes, Sleepy John, 93, 125, 193, 194, 217
Evans, "Honey Boy," 40
Ezell, Will, 66

"Falling Rain Blues," 75
"Feather Bed," 123
*Finian's Rainbow*, 231
Fisk Jubilee Singers, 138
"Fixin' to Die Blues," 205
Folkways Record Company, 231
Foster, Stephen, 26
"Fourth and Beale," 124
"Fox Chase," 214
"Frankie," 102
"Frankie and Johnny," 97
Fuller, "Blind Boy," 212, 213-221, 233
Fulson, Lowell, 234

Gaither, "Little Bill," 145, 147, 192
Gennett Record Company, 50, 52, 83, 200
"Georgia Bill," *See* McTell, Blind Willie
"Georgia Tom," 82, 135-136, 184
Gillum, William "Jazz," 175, 183, 190
Gilmore, Otto, 127

Gilmore, Robert, 89, 92
"Globetrotter," 231
"Go Back to The Country," 190
"Goin' to Germany," 124
"Goin' to Kansas City," 103, 132
"Going to Louisiana," 133
"Goin' Up the Country," 154
Gold Star Record Company, 258
"Good Looking Girl Blues," 103
"Got the Blues," 63
"Green Corn," 27
"Grieving Blues," 261
"Gypsy Woman," 249

"Ham Gravy," *See* Washboard Sam
Handy, William Christopher, 34, 36, 37-42, 43, 91, 118
"Happy New Year Blues," 55
Harlem Footwarmers, 79
"Harmonica and Washboard Blues," 218
"Harmonica Stomp," 218
Hart, Hattie, 114
Hauk, O. K., 102
Hayes, Clifford, 109
"He's a Jelly Roll Baker," 84
"He's in the Jailhouse Now," 121
"Hellhound on My Trail," 209
Hicks, Robert, *See* "Barbecue Bob"
"Highway 49," 201
"Highway 51," 204
Hogg, Smokey, 15, 233, 244
Hokum Band, 185
Hokum Boys, 65
"Hometown Skiffle," 65
"Honeycup," 200
"Hoochie Coochie Man," 250
Hooker, John Lee, 197, 233, 244, 251
Hopkins, Sam "Lightnin'," 17, 70, 233, 244, 254-265
Hornsby, Dan, 151
"Hot Potatoes," 53
"House Rent Stomp," 170
House, Son, 55, 197, 247

"How Long How Long Blues," 137, 141, 143, 263
"How You Want It Done?", 171
Howell, Peg Leg, 148-153
"Hungry Man," 193
Hurt, John, 102

"I Be's Troubled," 246
"I Can't Be Satisfied," 249
"I Can't Stand It," 113
"I Feel Like Going Home," 249
"If I Get Lucky," 191
"If I Had My Way," 157
"If It Had Not Been for Jesus," 162
"If They Could See You Back At The Plantation What Would They Think Of You Now," 97
"I Got the Best Jelly Roll in Town," 74, 83
"I Just Can't Stand These Blues," 74
"I Know His Blood Can Make Me Whole," 159
"I'm a Guitar King," 204
"I'm Gonna Move to the Outskirts of Town," 176
"I'm Gonna Run to the City of Refuge," 161
"I'm Not Rough," 78
"I'm Sorry," 240
"It Feels So Good," 74, 82
"It's Right Here for You," 46
"It's Tight Like That," 82, 135
"It Won't Be Long Now," 155
"I've Been Treated Wrong," 189
"I've Got the Sorry I Ain't Got It, You Could Have It If I Had It Blues," 45

Jackson, Al, 116
Jackson, Bud, 117
Jackson, Jim, 101-103, 120, 132-136
Jackson, "Papa Charlie," 49, 52, 65, 136, 170

Jacobs, "Little Walter," 249, 252
"James Alley Blues," 98
Jaxon, Frankie, 136
Jefferson, Alec, 57, 67
Jefferson, Blind Lemon, 52, 54, 55, 56, 57-72, 74, 86, 156-157, 171, 200, 235, 255, 259, 263
Jefferson, Classie, 67, 72
Jefferson, George, *See* Johnson, Lonnie
"Jelly Killed Old Sam," 83
Jenkins, Dub, 116
"Jesus Coming Soon," 161
"Jesus Make Up My Dying Bed," 159
"Jim Jackson's Kansas City Blues," 132
"Jogo Blues," 41
"John Henry," 101, 104
"John the Revelator," 163
"Johnny Boker," 27
Johnson, Angeline, 157
Johnson, Blind Willie, 151, 155-165, 167, 209
Johnson, George, 162
Johnson, James, 74, 75
Johnson, James P., 44
Johnson, Henry, *See* McGhee, Walter "Brownie"
Johnson, Lonnie, 74-85, 86, 136, 171, 183, 212
Johnson, Robert, 197, 206-210, 212, 246, 247
"Johnson's Trio Stomp," 76
Jones, Coley, 149
Jones, Jab, 113, 126
Jones, Maggie, 78
Jones, Richard M., 193
Jones, Sissieretta, 131
Jordon, Charlie, 202
Jordan, Jimmy, *See* Johnson, Lonnie
Jordan, Joe, 44
Jordan, Luke, 92, 95
"Juba," 27
"Just a Dream," 178

"Just Got to Hold You," 188

Kahn, Gus, 44
"Kansas City Blues," 135
"Kassie Jones," 101
"K. C. Moan," 113, 115
"Keep It Clean," 202
"Keep Your Lamp Trimmed and
    Burning," 161
Kelley, Jack, 116
Kemble, Fanny, 20, 22, 24, 25
Keppard, Freddie, 53
Kern, Jerome, 44
"Keys to the Highway," 175, 240
"Kill It Kid," 93
King, B. B., 233
King Oliver, 50
King Oliver and his Dixie Synco-
    pators, 132
King Record Company, 85
"King Solomon Hill," See Wil-
    liams, Joe
King, Totsie, 199
"Kokomo Blues," 144

Laibley, Arthur, 51, 64
Lang, Eddie, 82
"Last Chance Blues," 124
"Last Fair Deal Gone Down," 209
"Lawdy Lawdy Blues," 49
Leadbelly, 117, 228
"Leaving Blues," 230
"Left All Alone Again Blues," 44
"Leroy's Buddy," See Gaither,
    "Little Bill"
Lesters, Robert Lee, 127
"Let Me Roll Your Lemon," 182
"Let Your Light Shine on Me,"
    161
"Levee Camp Blues," 193
"Levee Camp Moan Blues," 77
Lewis, Hambone, 115
Lewis, Noah, 119, 121, 123-125,
    128, 217
Lewis, Walter "Furry," 101-103,
    105-106, 120

Library of Congress Folk Music
    Archives, 246
"Life of Leroy Carr," 147
Lightning Slim, 251
Lincoln, Charlie, 154
Lindberg, Charles A., 113
"Little Anna Mae," 249
Little Johnny, 249
Little Walter, 240
"Little Woman You're So Sweet,"
    217
"Livery Stable Blues," 44
Lomax, Alan, 246
"Lonesome Xmas Blues," 55
Long, J. B., 215
"Long Lonesome Blues," 63
"Looking for My Woman," 215
"Looking Up At Down," 175
"Lord, I Just Can't Keep From
    Crying," 161
"Lost John," 123, 214
"Louis Collins," 102
"Love Me Tender," 239
"Low Down Mojo Blues," 65
"Low Down Rounder Blues," 152
Luandrew, Albert, 193, 249

"M and O Blues," 187
"Ma Rainey's Mystery Record,"
    54
"Madison Street Rag," 121, 122
"Mama, Tain't Long 'Fo Day,"
    94
"Mamie," 216
"Mamma Don' 'Low," 39
"Man Killing Broad," 83
Marsh Laboratories, 50
Marsh, Orlando, 50
"Matchbox Blues," 64
McClennan, Tommy, 198, 202-
    205, 247
McCoy, Charlie, 93
McCoy, Joe, 193
McCoy, Minnie, 192
McGhee, Walter "Brownie," 218-
    231, 233, 245

McTell, Blind Willie, 93
"Me and the Devil Blues," 210
"Mean Mistreater," 240
"Mean Mistreater Mama," 168
"Mean Old Bed Bug Blues," 77
"Mean Old Frisco," 192
"Mecca Flats Blues," 188
Melotone Records, 208
Melrose, Lester, 171, 203
"Memphis Blues," 34, 38, 43, 97
Memphis Jug Band, 108, 111, 114-116, 121-122, 125-127, 173
Memphis Sanctified Singers, 114
"Memphis Scrontch," 106
"Memphis Sheiks," 125
Memphis Slim, 192, 251
Meriweather, Maceo, 192
"Midnight Frolic Rag," 106
"Milk Cow Blues," 215
Miller, Punch, 175
"Minglewood Blues," 121
"Mississippi Heavy Water Blues," 154
"Mississippi River Waltz," 129
"Mister Crump," 38
Morgan, Sam, 155
Morganfield, McKinley, *See* Waters, Muddy
Morton, Jelly Roll, 50
Moss, Buddy, 228
"Motherless Children," 160
"Motherless Chile Blues," 150
"Mr. Davis Blues," 75, 187
"My Buddy Blind Pappa Lemon," 200
"My Fault," 230
"My Love Don't Belong to You," 83
"My Mobile Central Blues," 135
"My Monday Woman Blues," 135
"My Old Pal Blues," 147
"My Woman's a Sender," 193

*Negro Slave Songs of the United States*, 23, 25, 27

"New Oh Red," 216
"New Orleans Slide," 200
"Newport Blues," 110
"Newport News," 108
"Newport News Blues," 113
Nickerson, Charlie "Bozo," 115, 125
"Nile of Genago," 76
Niles Abbe, 91, 95, 133, 150, 159
Noah Lewis and his Jug Band, 125
"Nobody's Fault But Mine," 159
"No More Cane on This Brazos," 260
"Non-Skid Tread," 144
Noone, Jimmy Apex Club Orchestra, 137
"Northern Starvers are Returning Home," 168
Norton, George A., 40
"Number 9 Train," 240

"Oak-Cliff T-Bone," *See* Walker, Aaron
"Oh Red," 216, 227
Okeh Record Company, 45, 47, 64, 67, 73, 75, 77, 83, 89, 126, 167, 205, 219, 227
"Old Dog Blues," 119, 133
"Old John Booker, You Call That Gone," 177
"Old Rounder's Blues," 63
"Ole Dan Tucker," 27
"Ole Grey Goose," 27
"Ole Pee Dee," 27
"One Kind Favor," 263
"Original Kokomo Blues," 215
Oriole Record Company, 208

Pace-Handy Music Company, 41
*Paramount Book of the Blues*, 54
Paramount Record Company, 49, 50-56, 52-57, 92, 120, 131, 168, 200, 205
Patti, Adelina, 131
Patton, Charlie, 55, 197, 205, 247

Peer, Ralph, 45, 47, 89-95, 102, 104, 106, 109, 114-116, 124, 133, 149, 182
"Penitentiary Blues," 265
Perfect Record Company, 208
Perkins, George, 65
"Phantom Black Snake," 188
Phillips, Sam, 237
*Phil Rice's Banjo Instructor*, 26
"Pick Poor Robin Clean," 93
"Pineal Farm Blues," 144
"Piney Woods Money Mama," 65, 70
Pinkard, Maceo, 44
Pittsburgh *Courier*, 47, 167
"Please Don't Go," 201
"Policy Blues," the, 135
Polk, Charlie, 109
"Poor Boy Long Ways From Home," 154
"Pot Roast," the, 142
"Preachin' the Blues," 37
Presley, Elvis, 236-239

Q. R. S. Records, 52
Quinn, Bill, 258

Rabbit's Foot Minstrel Shows, 200
Rachel, Yank, 93
"Ragtime Texas," *See* Thomas, Henry
Rainey, Gertrude, "Ma," 54, 55, 110-111, 136, 166, 184
Ramey, Ben, 109
*Redeemer's Praise for Sunday School, Church and Family*, 164
Regal Record Company, 52
"Rent Party Blues," 229
*Rhythm and Blues Songs*, 242
Rice, Phil, 26
"Roaming Rambler Blues," 77
Robbins, Annabelle, 35
Robie, Milton, 115, 129
Robinson, Alethea, 51, 64
Robinson, Elzadie, 55

*Rock 'N Roll Songs*, 242
Rogers, Jimmy, 92, 249
"Rollin' and Rollin'," *See* "Rolling Blues"
"Rolling Blues," 262
Romeo Record Company, 208
Roosevelt, Franklin Delano, 168
Rose, Billy, 241
"Roundhouse," 108
"Round the Corn, Sally," 25
Rushing, Jimmy, 243

"Sad News from Korea," 260
St. Cyr, Johnny, 78
"St. Louis Blues," 41
"Salty Dog," 52
Sandburg, Carl, 91
"Santa Claus Grave Blues," 55
"Satanic Blues," 44
Satherly, Arthur, 51, 64
"Savoy Blues," 78
Savoy Record Company, 229, 234
"Scandinavian Stomp," 106
Scarborough, Dorothy, 41
Scott, Lonnie, 230
Seals, Baby, 34, 36, 43
Searcy, De Louise, 75, 76
"Section Gang Blues," 77
"See That My Grave Is Kept Clean," 70
Shade, Jennie Mae Clayton, 108, 115
Shade, Will "Son Brimmer," 103, 108-116, 125-129, 173, 207
"Shake That Thing," 53
"Shakey Walter," 110-111
"She Wants to Sell My Monkey," 186, 213
"Shiny Town Blues," 92
"Short Haired Woman," 258
"Shotgun Blues," 262
"Shufflin' Sam," *See* Washboard Sam
Silas Green from New Orleans, 248
Silver Fleece Quartet, 165
*Simply Heavenly*, 231

Sinatra, Frank, 239, 241
Singer, Hal, 230
Sissle, Noble, 44
Smith, Bessie, 37, 148, 166, 241, 242
Smith, Mamie, 45, 46, 89
Smith, "Thunder," 257
"Snag It," 132
"Snaky Blues," 44
Snyder, Ted, 44
"Someday Sweetheart," 132
"Someone's in the Parlor, Honey, Better Come on Downstairs," 97
"Southbound Rag," 53
Southern Music Company, 89, 92, 115
"South Memphis Jug Band," 116
Spand, Charlie, 65
Spann, Otis, 249
"Special Agent," 193-194
"Spider Sam," *See* McGhee, Walter "Brownie"
"Spike Driver Blues," 102
Spirits of Rhythm, 84
"Spirituals to Swing" concert, 177, 218
Spivey, Victoria, 74, 80
"Sporting Life Blues," 229
"Springdale Blues," 121
"Starvation Blues," 171
"Statesboro Blues," 94
Steiner, John, 52, 55
"Step It Up and Go," 221, 227
"Step It Up and Go No. 2," 221
Stevens, Vol, 125
"Stingy Woman Blues," 110
Stokes, Frank, 92, 95
Stone, Jessie, 75
Storyville, 33
"Sugar Blues," 44
"Sun Gonna Shine in My Back Door Some Day," 173
"Sunnyland Slim," *See* Luandrew, Albert
Sun Record Company, 237
Supper, 51

Sykes, Roosevelt, 192

"Take Your Fingers Off It," 126, 173
"Take Your Hands Off Her," 173
Tampa Red, 44, 82, 135-137, 145-146, 175, 184, 233
Tampa Red's Hokum Jug Band, 137
Tarheel Slim, 240
"Tear It Down, Bed Slats and All," 126
Teddell, Saunders, *See* Terry, Sonny
"Tell 'Em About Me," 142
"Tell Me, Baby," 200
"Tennessee Gabriel," the, *See* McGhee, Walter "Brownie"
Terkel, Studs, 181
"Terraplane Blues," 209
Terry, Sonny, 214-221, 228-231
"That's All Right, Mama," 237
"That Thing Called Love," 46
"32-20 Blues," 209
Thomas, Henry, 132
Thomas, John, 170
Thompson, Ashley, 119, 121, 123
"Thousand Woman Blues," 217
"Three Bells Blues," 217
"Three Women Blues," 94
"Throw Your Yas Yas Back in Jail," 216
"Thunder Smith and Lightnin' Hopkins," 257
"Tight Like That," 184
"Time has Done Got Out of Hand," 200
"Times is Tight Like That," 168
"Tim Moore's Farm," 256
"Titanic," 90
"To Do This You Gotta Know How," 76
"Toothache Blues," 74
"Trouble Blues," 144
"Trouble in Mind," 174
"Trouble Will Soon Be Over," 162

Turk, Roy, 44
Turner, Jim, 100
"Two Tight Blues," 150

"Unselfish Love," 83
"Unsuccessful Blues," 261

Victor Record Company, 86, 87, 89, 92-94, 98, 102, 104-105, 109, 114, 118, 123, 125-126, 182, 238
Vocalion Record Company, 103-104, 106, 132, 167, 188, 202, 208, 212
Von Tilzer, Arthur, 44

Walker, Aaron "T-Bone," 155, 235
"Walkin' Blues," 246
"Walk Right In," 124
Walter and Byrd, 66
Wand, Hart, 34, 35-36, 42, 43
"The War Is Over," 261
Washboard Sam, 174, 183, 188-189, 193, 233
Washboard Slim, 228
Washington, George, *See* "Oh Red"
"Wasn't It Sad About Lemon," 66
Waters, Ethel, 148
Waters, Muddy, 197, 207, 233, 240, 244, 245-253, 254
Weaver, Sylvester, 73
Webb, Jordan, 218, 227
Weldon, Casey Bill, 176
Weldon, Will, 109
"West Coast Blues," 53
Wheatstraw, Peetie, 175, 192, 193
"When I Take My Vacation in Harlem," 186
"When You Fall for Someone Not Your Own," 81
White, Bukka, 197, 205
"White Horse Pawin' in the Valley," 69
White, Josh, 178

Whittaker, Hudson, *See* Tampa Red
"Whoa! Mule Get Up in The Alley," 124
"Whoopee Blues," 200
*Who's Who in Rock 'N Roll,* 241
"Why Did You Do That to Me?" 193
Wiley, Jack, 142
Williams, Bert, 45
Williams, Clarence, 44
Williams, George, 53
Williams, J. Mayo, 51, 55, 63, 64, 120, 131, 135, 151, 170, 202
Williams, Joe, 198-202, 205
Williamson, Charlie, 102, 106, 109, 121
Williamson, Sonny Boy, 190-191
Williams, Spencer, 44, 74, 82
Willis, Chuck, 251
"Wipe It Off," 74
Wisconsin Chair Co., 49, 51
Woods, Hosie, 101, 119-120, 123-124, 130
"Workingman's Blues," 222, 227
"Working on the Project," 193
Work, John, 246
"W. P. A. Blues," 193
"W. P. A. Rag," 193
Wyer, Paul, 40

*Yankee Blade,* 34
Yellen, Jack, 44
"Yellow Dog Blues," 197
"Yelpin' Hound Blues," 44
"You Can Have Him, I Don't Want Him, Didn't Love Him Any How Blues," 44
"You Can't Keep A Good Man Down," 46
"You Done Lost Your Good Thing," 74
"You Don't See into These Blues Like Me," 74
"You Gonna Need Somebody on Your Bond," 163
"Yo-Yo Blues," 154